THE REAL
CRACKER

THE REAL CRACKER

Stephen Cook

First published 2001 by Channel 4 Books
an imprint of Macmillan Publishers Ltd
25 Eccleston Place London SW1W 9NF
Basingstoke and Oxford

www.macmillan.com

Associated companies throughout the world

ISBN 0 7522 7260 8

9 8 7 6 5 4 3 2 1

A CIP catalogue record for this book is available from the British Library.

Design and typesetting by Blackjacks
Printed by Mackays of Chatham plc, Chatham, Kent

Picture credits
Page 1: (top) Apex Photo Agency, (bottom) Henrietta Butler; page 2: (top)
Henrietta Butler, (centre left and right) Connors, (bottom left) *Brighton
Evening Argus*, (inset, bottom left) Sussex Police; page 3: (top) Metropolitan
Police, (bottom) Photo News Service; page 4: (top) Photo News Service,
(bottom) *Daily Mail*; page 5: (top) Photo News Service, (bottom) Metropolitan
Police; page 6: (top left and right) Metropolitan Police, (bottom left and
right) Sussex Police; page 7: (top left) Metropolitan Police, (top right)
Hampshire Police, (bottom) Solent News Agency; page 8: Solent News Agency

This book accompanies the television series 'The Real Cracker' made
by Patrick Forbes at ▶ Oxford Films & Television Company for Channel 4.
Director & Producer: Patrick Forbes

READER'S NOTE

In some of the cases in this book, names, times, details of behaviour or location, have been changed or omitted. This is either to protect the identity of victims or suspects later cleared, or to avoid compromising police investigations into unsolved crimes.

THE PSYCHOLOGICAL CAUSE OF DEATH

1

'Profiling has a relationship with science, but is an art in the same way that medicine is an art.'

Richard Badcock

Towards the end of the evening, when most people are turning off the television and heading for bed, a middle-aged man with neatly trimmed grey hair goes into his study on an upstairs floor of a detached Georgian house and closes the door behind him. He sits down at the desk, sighs, puts on his glasses, pulls a buff-coloured folder out of the pile of papers in front of him and flips it open. The folder contains the kind of photographs that are sometimes shown to juries at the start of criminal trials, causing the members to wince and grimace – photographs of somebody who has been raped, murdered, mutilated and then discarded like a sack of refuse at the roadside. The man's face sets into a curious blend of attentiveness and compassion as he picks up a magnifying glass and studies the horrific images one by one, taking his time, making the occasional note on a pad of paper. An hour, two hours later, as the silence of the night takes hold on the West Yorkshire town where he lives, he is still there, studying maps and charts, reading through piles of police statements. Occasionally he takes off his glasses and swings them from two fingers as he stares at the wall, his mind slowly compiling another tragic chronology of human destructiveness.

This is Dr Richard Badcock, a fifty-three-year-old forensic psychiatrist who by day helps to treat some of the country's most violent criminals at

Rampton Special Hospital in Nottinghamshire, and by night is often to be found pursuing his part-time career as one of Britain's foremost offender profilers. He is a mild, reflective man, with a gentle tenor voice finely trained in the art of speaking in the neutral, non-judgemental tones that doctors need when talking to difficult and sensitive patients. When he discusses his work he makes little forays into philosophy and psychoanalysis and cracks obscure jokes accompanied by little bursts of laughter and a surprisingly cherubic smile. He probably knows more about the psychology of destructive behaviour, which has been his special interest throughout his psychiatric career, than anybody else in the country. A grey suit and a bow tie are his working uniform, and he nearly always wears a flower in his buttonhole, as if to counteract the odour of some of the offences he has to contemplate. His office at Rampton – home, like Broadmoor in Berkshire and Ashworth on Merseyside to some of the country's most disturbed offenders – is full of carefully tended potted plants. He has been an offender profiler for eight years and has dealt with hundreds of cases in Britain and abroad: his reputation is firmly established and he is highly respected and much in demand by senior investigating officers from the forty-three police forces in England and Wales.

While Badcock works into the night on his latest case, the chances are that a light will also be burning in the study of a large, detached, eighteenth-century house some seventy miles away in the Leicestershire countryside. The man sitting at the desk is doing the same kind of work as Badcock, studying a similar pile of documents and photographs, trying to penetrate the mind and motivation of a sadistic serial rapist or steeping himself in the detail of a string of perverted sexual assaults on elderly women. But this man is thirteen years younger than Badcock and comes out of a completely different mould: he is taller, with a boyish face, blue eyes, well-kept wavy blond hair, and a personal style that in America would be called 'preppie' – slip-on shoes, chinos and a double-breasted blue blazer with metal buttons. He is Dr Julian Boon, an academic psychologist at Leicester University who specializes in the theory of personality development and teaches a course to his students called 'the psychology of love and attraction' – which seems curiously appropriate for a scion of the Mills & Boon publishing house, purveyor of a thousand bodice-ripping romances.

Boon is a mildly flamboyant character who comes into his own as a performer, whether on the podium of a lecture theatre, holding forth, say, about the unreliability of eyewitness evidence, or sporting a mortar board and a flowing gown in the senate house during his duties as the university's orator, giving a speech about the celebrity who has been awarded an honorary degree that year. His natural sociability has earned him party-animal status and the extra job of admissions tutor, and he contrives a certain louche nonchalance littered with Bertie Wooster-ish phrases such as 'dear boy' and 'old thing'. His friends joke that when he gets into his stride, eyes flashing and hands in motion, he speaks not in sentences but in arias. A casual observer might suspect a certain lack of seriousness, until treated to a disquisition on one of his cases: then the flippancy yields to a tenacious concentration on the task of thinking and feeling his way into the psychopathology of an unknown offender, using the traces of character left behind at the scene of the crime. In mid-explication, Boon can be larger than life, verging on the melodramatic – an arresting and entertaining sight.

Boon and Badcock… or is it Badcock and Boon? Like some old-fashioned comedy duo at the end of the pier, they are completely different, yet curiously alike. Usually they work separately, but they frequently consult each other about their profiling work and in one instance, described in this book, they tackled a case together. In the murder inquiry into the multiple murders of his patients by Harold Shipman, Boon compiled the profile while Badcock assessed the doctor's fitness to stand trial. They have a mutual liking and respect, but cannot resist sniping and poking fun at each other as well, bickering about the treatability of severe psychiatric disturbance or the shortcomings of Britain's adversarial legal system. There is a touch of the master and the talented apprentice in the relationship between the older and the younger man: sometimes Boon will wait for Badcock to take the lead when talking about a case, but will then pick up the baton and run harder and faster. What they undoubtedly share is a firm commitment to their curious part-time activity of profiling, which is partly science and partly art and plays an increasing part in the investigation of serious and difficult crimes in Britain. Their usual task, in Badcock's striking phrase, is to establish 'the psychological cause of death'.

There are only twenty other accredited offender profilers in the country and, like the other members of this elite group, Badcock and Boon find themselves constantly fighting a rearguard action against an image of their work that was planted in the public mind by a television drama series of the mid-1990s. *Cracker* featured the Scottish actor Robbie Coltrane as Dr Eddie Fitzgerald, aka Fitz, the overweight, alcoholic psychologist with a dysfunctional private life who was called in by the police to help them solve their most difficult cases. The screenwriter Jimmy McGovern had found a brilliant way to update and re-brand the concept originated by Sir Arthur Conan Doyle in Sherlock Holmes – that of the instinctive, intuitive investigator whose insights leap far ahead of the ordinary flat-footed mortals around him. The plots of *Cracker* were based on powerful contemporary themes such as Christian cults and the fallout from the disaster at the Hillsborough football stadium in Sheffield in 1989, when ninety-six Liverpool fans were crushed to death. Fitz was a larger-than-life character, routinely depicted haranguing senior police officers, browbeating suspects in face-to-face interviews, and even going into police cells to take personal delivery of tearful confessions from rapists and murderers. It was great television which won several BAFTA awards, and the title of the series entered popular parlance: as late as 1998, two years after the final episode of *Cracker* had been broadcast, the London *Evening Standard* printed a headline about an unpleasant homicide case that read 'Police call in "Cracker" to help find murderer'. The mere use of the word inevitably calls up the suggestion in the minds of most people that some psychological heavyweight is now on the case, picking up the investigation by the scruff of the neck and pulling and pushing it in whatever direction he sees fit.

In the real world, profilers do some of the things that Fitz does, but in general their activities are rather more restrained and low-key: the biggest difference is that Fitz always gets it right, and fast, while his real-life equivalents are painfully fallible and tend to spend much longer mulling over a case. The usual pattern is that they are thoroughly briefed by senior officers – but not necessarily told everything. They are then allowed access to most of the important documents, photographs and videos of the case, and they usually visit the crime scene. The written profiles they eventually produce might suggest the age of the offender, his family background, the formative experiences of his life, his work, his personality, his internal conflicts, his family life and the quality of his relationships with other people. The police might then find the profile helpful in narrowing down their list of suspects or prompting a new line of inquiry, and they might take advice from the profiler on the timing and manner of arresting someone. Profilers offer advice on the best way of interviewing suspects, but they do not conduct interviews with suspects, or even sit in on interviews. Occasionally they might listen in from another room and give advice, but more commonly they would review videotapes of interviews at a later stage and offer their comments. It would be unheard-of for them to go into the cells to talk to prisoners or take part in a police operation to arrest a suspect. But Fitz and his overweight image dog the footsteps of real-life profilers, and they repeatedly find themselves producing lame jokes and complex explanations as they try to distance themselves from him: 'I don't drink as much and I don't gamble and I'm not quite as overweight,' says Badcock. 'He works by intuition, which is really a form of imagination, and in this work, although imagination is useful because it stimulates thought, you can't give it flight and fancy in the way that his intuition works. If what you do is useful then it has to be tied down in some objective way.'

Boon says: 'There is absolutely no connection between me and him, apart from me having too many pounds on me, and I don't mean pounds sterling… All a profiler must do is lay out for the senior investigating officer any information he can provide from the psychological perspective. And it's no good just going in there … and saying, oh well, I feel this, that or the other. You have to say where the information is coming from, why that point of view is being advised, in terms that the officers can understand, not freaked out with jargon. And then having done that you make it crystal clear that it is for them to decide how they utilize the information. The profiler mustn't tell the inquiry how to behave and conduct the investigation, and at no point should a profiler

– and some do, unfortunately, work like this – go barging into a police station and start calling the shots, à la *Cracker*. That should not happen.'

Another difference between *Cracker* and the real thing is that discretion has become one of the iron rules of profiling. Often the police decide not to reveal that a profiler is working on a case, and it has recently become part of the contract between police and profilers that they will talk publicly about their work only in exceptional circumstances and with the agreement of the senior investigating officer. Why, then, did Badcock and Boon and three police forces in southern England – the Metropolitan Police, Sussex and Hampshire – agree to co-operate in the making of a major five-part Channel 4 TV series and the preparation of this book?

The answer is that everybody concerned wanted profiling to emerge from the distorted shadow cast by *Cracker*, shed the negative image caused by a small number of real cases, become better understood and debated by the public, and develop and evolve as an effective aid to criminal investigation. One way to achieve this, they felt, was to allow the cameras to follow Badcock and Boon throughout five different investigations, mixing fly-on-the-wall observation with interviews with the two men and the police officers they were working with. The cases include one of the most gruesome sex murders of the 1990s, the baffling case of an old lady who lay dead for two weeks in her rambling seaside house, and the chilling antics of a highly sophisticated criminal who likes to waylay courting couples, abducting the woman and humiliating the man. These investigations, described in Chapters 3 to 11, took nearly four years and involved the two men in thousands of miles of travelling and hundreds of hours of thought, discussion and writing. The result is a unique insight into the most intriguing modern method of helping police with their inquiries. But before the cases are described, the questions arise: how did Badcock and Boon get into this extraordinary activity in the first place? How do they go about their work? And what are the history and context of it all?

Richard Badcock was born and brought up in the westcountry and went to Cambridge and Oxford Universities. He spent three years training and working as a general practitioner before realizing that his vocation lay in psychiatry and doing further study in Edinburgh and Glasgow. His interest in profiling work began later in his career, when he was asked to lecture at a local detective training school and found that he couldn't fully answer the many questions that officers directed at him about offender profiling. To fill the gaps in his knowledge, in 1993 he enrolled on a course on the subject that was being run annually at Dundee University under the auspices of the Federal Bureau of Investigation, which had pioneered the practice of offender profiling in the United States. What followed was to cause a sea-change in Badcock's career.

'It was what in psychology is described as a cathartic experience,' he says. 'They described a seemingly endless number of cases, which they were able to illustrate through slides showing various horrible things that people do to each other. And I went through the process of sitting through this huge number of cases, and towards the end of the week it suddenly dawned on me that this stuff was for real – that people do things to each other for reasons which aren't clear to them very often, and which are both capable of and in urgent need of being understood. And as a psychiatrist I was in a position to contribute to that understanding.

'All I can remember of the moment of catharsis is that it was a picture of a mangled body, which didn't in itself stand out from all the other mangled bodies but somehow managed to convey that it had happened not because of some purposeless activity on the part of the offender, but quite the opposite. It had happened as a result of an extremely purposeful series of events, which didn't begin and end with the offence and which had had a huge build-up in the offender's mind in the form of a developing fantasy. And that particular one made it obvious that there was something sort of huge and horrible which had to be grappled with, and that without trying to find ways of understanding this stuff, not only is detection harder but life for all of us becomes more difficult.

'It's a bit like the Ancient Mariner, you know – he's compelled to go and tell people about what's happened to him, not because he thinks rationally that he must spread the news, but because it's something he's compelled to do as a result of the experiences he's gone through... It certainly wasn't a sense of excitement on my part – my gosh, here is something I can get into. It was more of a sense of a burden, actually, more of a sense of duty, that here was something we could contribute to as a science and a medical discipline, to try to promote not just the health but the general good of mankind. So I felt it to be a sort of professional duty to try to come to terms with these things, and it coincided with my own interest in trying to understand why people do things: a lot of forensic psychiatry is about trying to understand destructive behaviour.'

In most professions people are required to obtain certain qualifications before they are permitted to practise, but another of the odd things about profiling is that there are no generally accepted qualifications, code of ethics or professional discipline. There are courses such as the one in Dundee and a master's degree course in 'investigative psychology' at Liverpool University, both of which might help with the rather mysterious process of getting into profiling work but do not amount to a licence to be a profiler. The people who do the work are mostly psychologists or psychiatrists, but they come from a variety of backgrounds and display a wide range of approaches; most have evolved their own distinctive methodology. This is especially true of the biggest group of profilers in Britain, which includes Badcock and Boon and employs what is usually known as the clinical approach. In general, they try to pick up and interpret information about the absent offender from the psychological traces left at the crime scene in much the same way as they would piece together a patient's psychopathology from the things he or she reveals on the couch. Badcock says: 'It's easier to solve it when people kill those they know or members of their family, but if they repeatedly kill strangers out of malign personal need, then psychology is one of the few ways of bringing new information into the situation.'

Badcock's first case came soon after the Dundee course. A policeman he had met on the course recommended him to the senior investigating officer on a case of rape and murder in West Yorkshire. Like most cases where profilers are called in, the motive and behaviour of the assailant were something of a mystery. The victim had been found on a piece of waste ground, carefully covered with grass, and the police were given reports that a white van had been seen in the area shortly before the crime and that a group of men had been attempting to abduct a woman. At least half the members of the police investigating team thought this group had something to do with the crime, but Badcock was able to say that the van and the group of men had nothing to do with it because it bore the hallmarks of being a very private affair – the frenzy of a sexualized killing, followed by a different phase of emotional experience where the attacker felt the need to cover his victim, but failed to see that there was a ditch nearby where a body would probably not be discovered for weeks. Badcock was right: the culprit was a man who worked in a late-night takeaway food shop, and had followed the victim and dragged her on to the waste ground where she was killed.

Badcock says the profile he produced was not particularly good, but helped him to start evolving his own approach, discarding some of the things he had learnt on the course and developing others. In particular, it taught him the value of re-enacting the crime as far as possible, something he now does in every case: one of the issues in this instance was whether the victim had agreed to the sexual activity that took place before her death, which seemed quite possible given the inviting grassy spot where the incident took place. Only when the grass had been cut down did it become obvious that the ground beneath was rough and stony – the last place anyone would choose for consensual sex. 'If anyone had gone and lain down there they would have realized that,' says Badcock. 'I always feel a bit daft doing the re-enaction, and some policemen look askance because people shrink from putting themselves in the position of the victim. You can't hit on an exact reconstruction, of course, but you can give it your best shot and you have to keep in mind the appropriate level of interpretation to put on it.'

Another case he talks about to illustrate his particular approach concerns a man who contacted the police in a distraught condition one evening to report that he had returned home with his two sons to find that there had been a break-in and a robbery, and that his wife was slumped in her chair in the living room with severe head injuries, beaten to death. The police thought there was something odd about the case and called in Badcock, who began to notice things even before he stepped inside the house where the murder had taken place: walking up the road towards it, he saw it was the only bungalow where the surrounding plants and shrubs had been allowed to grow up and overshadow the house, giving it a closed-in appearance. Once inside the back door, he saw that the kitchen contained enough pots and pans and utensils to keep several restaurants going, but the fridge was virtually empty and the chest freezer had a large padlock on it. 'This was all about the control of food,' says Badcock. 'And therefore if the woman was controlling in this aspect, it was likely she'd be controlling in other aspects as well. Inquiries about her character led one to believe she was extremely alert, not the sort of woman to let anything past her at all.'

The woman had been killed in the middle of a relaxing evening and had clearly not been startled or surprised by her attacker: she had been in the act of addressing an envelope when the first blow fell. It was therefore clear to Badcock at an early stage that she knew her attacker, but when talking about the case he emphasizes that it would have been wrong to jump to conclusions at this stage, before he had considered the whole scene more fully. 'It's terribly misleading to look only at a single aspect of a case,' he says. 'I find it helpful to illustrate what I mean by thinking about the way we use words and language, and about how we understand from philosophy that each word has two levels of meaning. It has its dictionary definition, as it were, and it has its use in a sentence and its associations with other words in the sentence which give it its exact meaning. "The sky is blue" and "The sky's the limit" – you can only see the difference in meaning when you see the whole sentence. Science, if you like, is about understanding the dictionary definitions of words. Profiling has a relationship with science, but is an art in the same way that medicine is an art, and it focuses on the precise meaning of the word in its exact sentence.

'So coming back to the case, it would have been important at that point not to rush to over-interpret the fact that she knew the person who killed her and look at other aspects of the case as well. She had been killed by someone standing in front of her and the killing had been extremely brutal, blows to the head resulting in massive damage and trauma quite in excess of what was necessary to kill her – in other words, quite a lot of redundant violence. Putting those things together, it was clear not only that the person who killed her was known to her but was also extremely anxious that the killing should succeed.'

Insights of this kind might not have occurred quite so readily to police officers as to someone like Badcock with his wider experience of all brands of human behaviour. He then looked closely around the kitchen, where money had been taken from a jar on a shelf and various objects had been scattered round the room. What he noticed, once again, was the kind of thing the police, with their more factual approach, could easily miss – that the disorder was somehow limited and contrived, with nothing broken and no real sense of violence or chaos: 'This was disorder created by someone whose sense of disorder was inhibited.' He also noticed that the shelf where the jar had stood was so close to the back door that it was difficult for anyone reaching up to it while the door was open to prevent himself from toppling backwards over the threshold. Why then, if the motive was theft as the father and sons maintained, would anybody take the trouble either to scatter things round the kitchen or – more importantly – to go further into the house to find and murder the wife? This was an occasion where re-enacting the alleged movements of the offender provided new information.

Having looked at the whole picture, including the pathological atmosphere which seemed to exist in the family group, Badcock was able to encourage the police to concentrate on one particular line of inquiry – that she had been murdered by someone in her own family. It turned out one of the sons had killed her, but his brother and father were complicit in the crime. The most poignant and revealing aspect of the case for Badcock was that in the week between the murder and their arrest, the husband and sons lived on an excess of pizzas, curries and hamburgers – a binge of junk food which had never been available to them in the over-controlled regime they had endured at home.

Once Badcock started working on cases with the police seven years ago, he found the experience helped him to understand his other patients better. He also felt it helped him with the increasingly important criminological question of risk evaluation – making well-founded predictions about which offenders are likely to reoffend and continue to be a danger to society. But he discovered before long that he needed a break between cases, partly because his profiling work was always crammed into his spare time, moving straight from one case to another would mean getting virtually no leisure. All NHS-based profilers are likely to experience similar problems in finding enough time for profiling. There would be less pressure if they could do some of their profiling work in office hours, but few NHS managers entirely accept their argument that their activities with the police produce benefits for their day-to-day hospital work. But another reason for needing the break was simply the soul-destroying effect of an unremitting diet of murder, rape and mayhem, often studied and dwelt upon late at night. Since Badcock began this kind of work he has become a vegetarian, and he thinks it's not a coincidence – 'Nothing in psychology is entirely coincidental.' Dealing regularly with the evidence of death and destruction left him feeling he didn't want more death and destruction on his plate, although he still manages to eat fish.

'If you make it your business to genuinely try to understand the motives for cruelty, abuse and killing people in the way we do, then it is a little bit like what Nietzsche said about looking into the abyss,' he says. 'It has an effect on you. Not so much depressing as isolating, because if you constantly immerse yourself in it, it somehow separates you from your own humanity, as it were. What impresses itself upon you is the bleakness, the desperate use of destructiveness by offenders as they try to build this false shell of a self which may satisfy them, but also prevents them from becoming a real human being. The exposure to that is enervating, it takes away from optimism about life. You do it because if you can understand a case and you can feel that the knowledge is true and you can explain why you feel it's true, then it does give you a sense of intellectual freedom.' His conclusion is that it's very important that people don't work on profiling as their sole occupation, and are grounded in something different – in his case, his normal psychiatric work and his family. Without that, the constant exposure to horrific cases would colour and distort how he thinks about life. 'Making it a full-time occupation would be to say goodbye to sanity,' he says. 'It would, quite literally, drive you mad.'

At the same time he admits to getting a buzz from a difficult investigation: 'It's not just an intellectual puzzle but a personal challenge, where I pit myself against not the offender but the offence – a sense of pleasurable anticipation that I'm about to do something difficult where I might fail, but I might also succeed. But in terms of the profile, that buzz is a seduction and a snare. It's no use to me because it distorts my judgement and gets in the way of my assessment of the case. I need to acknowledge it, see what it means, and lay it aside, otherwise it will encourage me to jump to conclusions, be sloppy in my reasoning and misuse the subjective feelings created by the case. The correct interpretation of your subjective experience can be an important part of the analysis, but you can't do anything with it if your mind is clouded by a buzz. However, there have been times when I've been frustrated in my ordinary work when I think: why doesn't somebody ring me about a murder? I need a case to work on.'

Julian Boon, with his libertarian political instincts and a liking for classic cars and expensive wine, is cheese to Badcock's chalk; he also comes from a different branch of the profession. While Badcock is medically trained – a psychiatrist – Boon is a psychologist; while Badcock's main job is the treatment of patients, confronting and wrestling with their traumas and disturbance from day to day, Boon is a teacher and an academic and he does not have the same kind of hands-on experience; and while Badcock believes that even severely disturbed patients can be helped and even cured, Boon is highly sceptical about the effectiveness of treatment in such cases. The more unpleasant criminals are commonly referred to by him as 'reptiles', a description unlikely to pass the more compassionate lips of Badcock.

Boon had a suburban upbringing in West Wickham, on the borders between London and Kent, and went to the City of London School and the University of Aberdeen before becoming a lecturer. He likes to tell the story of being asked about his outside interests during the interview for his present job at Leicester University. 'Claret and blondes and Aston Martins,' was his reply, which apparently went down poorly – especially since he's married to a brunette – but didn't prevent him being offered the post. The interest in high performance cars is a genuine and long-standing one, and he dabbled in motor racing when he was younger:

now he drives a Rover 75 family saloon. When he was recently offered the chance to drive an Aston Martin DB4 round the circuit at Goodwood Motor Circuit, famous in the 1930s heyday of big, brutal racing cars, he slid down into the driving seat and murmured: 'The name's Boon – Julian Boon.' Driving round the circuit at speeds of about 100 miles per hour, jousting with Ferraris and Porsches, he delivered one of his arias about the decline in fast and skilful driving: 'It's simply because with this perishing nanny state mentality we've got, everything is designed with safety uppermost. No matter what you do, you're going to be safe. Now that sounds on the surface a very nice way of doing things. But in reality it erodes into personal responsibility, erodes into free will, erodes into decision making, erodes into creativity and all the things which are biophilous in life… Now I'm not suggesting anybody should do anything dangerous, drive dangerously, behave dangerously. But I do think that people should be allowed to do what they want so long as it doesn't hurt other people. Now, let's have a little burst of speed here.' On the subject of wine, he can be equally opinionated, and has been known to refer to his favourite Pouilly Fumé or St Emilion as 'super duper nectar' or, more demotically, 'the horse's knob'.

Boon specializes in teaching about personality development and forensic psychology, and his department runs a master's degree course in forensic psychology which is one of the best-regarded in the country. He has published research work on suggestibility – how easy it can be to get people to believe and say things they don't necessarily subscribe to – and he likes to tease his students by telling them, rather melodramatically, that he could make any of them do anything he chooses – 'I know the means by which it would be done.' He also claims to know how to commit the perfect murder, but declines to reveal the knowledge in public. The course he most enjoys teaching is one that attempts to explain why people make particular choices in life. 'It's about why we become attracted to good and bad paths,' he says. 'Why we choose the people we do to spend our life with – everything from mates to spouses to children to why we love stamp collections and train spotting, and why it is that some people develop into serial killers and others spend their lives doing more altruistic things.

'The reality is that psychology is a very broad discipline: some of it is highly statistical, some of it is highly clinical, some of it relates to computers, there is sports psychology, health psychology, the whole raft. But there's a particular section of psychology which happens to be my thing, and that is understanding personality. I'm always surprised when people say, why are you interested in psychology – it seems the very stuff of our existence. So while other people want to become medical doctors and study how to mend broken bones, that's very useful and congratulations, that's your life. But for me I want something just a bit more than nuts and bolts. I want an understanding of why some people turn out to be old ma Theresa and others turn out to be old ma Hindley... If you were a psychologist you'd find people coming up and saying, oh, are you analysing me, ha ha ha. And most psychologists are at pains to say, no, I'm not that sort of psychologist, I'm the sort that tests people's memory or looks at bits of the brain to see what underpins left-handedness. But I'm the sort of psychologist who says, yes, I am analysing you – unless of course the person is unbelievably boring, in which case I can be quite honest and say, no, I'm having a day off. I don't flatter myself, but I am good at anticipating other people's reactions and responses.'

Boon's interest in profiling intensified after he took part in the same course as Badcock in Dundee and realized for the first time that wrongdoing and extreme, deviant behaviour were in fact explicable and could illuminate his central interest in personality development. Like Badcock, he soon made his own modifications to the methods he'd heard about on the course, and has developed an approach where he regards nothing as irrelevant and tries to draw up a list of what he calls the salient case details – a process described in detail in Chapter 8. He quotes a case where he considered that the shape of house roofs was an issue because the offender had a peculiar vendetta against people with houses with a particular profile – not the kind of detail that would automatically be noted by the police, perhaps. 'You try to articulate which details among the potentially infinite variety are going to be useful in understanding the case,' he says. 'That may seem to lay members of the public to be a very easy thing – you've got a dead body, it must be murder. But there's murder, murder and murder again, and trying to decide exactly what

kind of murder we're talking about – whether it's preconceived or acci-
dental or outraged murder – is a very much more specialized business.'

As an example of an incident where he was able to give the police
some useful advice, Boon talks of a case in southern England where a
woman was found dead with some unusual marks on her body. The man
who lived with her was arrested, but denied absolutely that he had killed
her: all he would admit, rather bizarrely, was that he had cut her wrists
after finding her body in order to discover whether her blood was circu-
lating and she was still alive. The police found themselves getting
nowhere and running up fast against the deadline when they had to
either charge or release their suspect. As a final throw they contacted
Boon, staying up all night to describe the case to him and ask him about
it. He quickly told them that he thought the pair had almost certainly
been involved in a sado-masochistic relationship with overtones of
necrophilia, and recalls that he could almost hear the officers thinking,
'That's rubbish.' But the police overcame their scepticism and, when
they put it to the suspect that he was a sexual deviant and they knew all
about him, he was thrown off his guard and eventually confessed to the
crime. Boon's detailed understanding of the origins and nature of sado-
masochism had enabled the police, quite dramatically, to make progress
they might otherwise not have made.

Boon also talks about a rape case where he formed the view that the
offender would have raped several women in the past who would not
have come forward because they had been drunk at the time and would
have been concerned that no one would believe they had not
consented. The police were planning to publicize the case on the BBC
TV programme *Crimewatch UK*, and Boon encouraged them to slant
their presentation towards appealing to any previous victims to come
forward, reassuring them that they would be dealt with sympathetically.
Several women did indeed come forward and the rapist was soon identified, prosecuted and jailed.

So far Boon has looked at more than 400 cases of rape and murder.
Like Badcock, he finds that repeated exposure to crimes of this nature
takes a severe personal toll: 'I mean, it takes up evenings when you could
be doing other things, sitting beside a fire and relaxing, for example. It

takes up a huge amount of time. And it's very seldom that someone says, there's absolutely no hurry on this. Usually the pressure's on because there could be serial angles to the crime, it may be that the offender's likely to get away, that interview strategies need to be considered. But if you feel genuinely that personality psychology, in my case, can be used to good effect, then without being sanctimonious about it, you do feel inclined to assist. It's as simple as that. I mean, if it were just playing games that would be a hugely different matter but there is an element of responsibility involved – a big element.'

As with Badcock, Boon's work and his family life keep him insulated from the negative effects of repeated exposure to the effects of depravity and violence. But there have been times, especially in cases involving the murder of children, when he has been unable to keep it all at arm's length. In particular, he remembers tackling one case late at night, with his family asleep in the rooms above his study, looking at the unbearable images on the desk in front of him and thinking of his own children with tears rolling down his face.

'INFORMED GUESSWORK'

2

> *'The conclusion was that it was time*
> *to set up a list of accredited profilers.'*

Don Dovaston, former Assistant Chief Constable of Derbyshire

When the clinical psychologist Paul Britton was told that he would have to appear before the disciplinary committee of the British Psychological Society at the beginning of the year 2001, an important episode was drawing to a close in the short but vivid history in Britain of the fledgeling science of offender profiling. Britton had offered the police advice about the kind of person who might have killed Rachel Nickell in front of her two-year-old son on Wimbledon Common in July 1992, and had ended up playing a central role in an elaborate undercover operation targeting Colin Stagg, who was strongly suspected by the police of being the murderer. When the case came to court in September 1994 the judge threw it out in short order, calling the undercover operation 'deceptive conduct of the grossest kind', and leaving in tatters the reputation of offender profiling in general and Paul Britton in particular.

In the six years since the trial, profilers and police officers who use their services have been struggling to escape the negative publicity of the Nickell case and set up checks and balances that would prevent any repetition. The disciplinary hearing, the result of a complaint by Colin Stagg's solicitor, was convened to decide whether Britton had contravened clauses one and five of the BPS code of conduct: bringing the profession of psychology into disrepute, and undermining public confidence in the professional ability of psychologists. He faced being reprimanded, expelled from BPS membership and removed from the Register of

Chartered Psychologists – sanctions that would have serious professional consequences for him, but would not legally prevent him from practising as a psychologist or pursuing a lucrative career as a consultant.

While *Cracker* was the fictional bugbear of profiling, the Nickell case was the real-life equivalent. When people in the small world of profiling refer in conversation or at conferences to the adverse effects of 'a few high-profile cases', they are invariably referring to this particular case. Profilers working on fresh incidents say privately that they think that Britton went on a 'power trip' in the Nickell case, and talk of their fear of 'entering Paul Britton territory'. Julian Boon thinks that the case was a prime example of what he calls 'the psychological tail wagging the investigative dog' – giving unwarranted weight to the inevitably speculative views of the profiler and involving him in the decision-making role that should always be retained by the senior investigating officer. Richard Badcock considers, in typically paradoxical fashion, that the Nickell case has actually helped the process of profiling: 'It stopped in its tracks a trend which was extremely dangerous, and it showed that profiling has to be extremely careful about how it defines the limits of its own value.'

One useful way of understanding what went wrong in the Nickell case is to see it as the culmination of a period when profiling was insufficiently regulated and individual practitioners were tempted to push back the frontiers of what they were doing. From the mid-1980s, well before Badcock and Boon came on the scene, it had become increasingly common in Britain for police officers running difficult and problematic cases to ask for the help of psychologists or psychiatrists with expert knowledge of criminal behaviour. It has always been an article of faith among responsible profilers and police officers that a profile can never in itself be evidence: the fact that a suspect fits the profile does not necessarily prove anything, for there may be hundreds of other people who would fit the profile just as well. Real evidence is also required.

Paul Britton was one of the pioneers of modern offender profiling in the UK. He is a clinical and forensic psychologist who has spent most of his career running the NHS regional secure unit at Arnold Lodge in Leicester, a centre for the detention and treatment of the most intractable arsonists, paedophiles, rapists and murderers. Britton had a problematic family background, failed his 11-plus examination, completed his higher education later in life, and gradually established himself as a respected adviser to police forces, first in the Midlands and then round the country. He was involved in several of the most notorious cases in the UK of the last fifteen years, including those of Colin Pitchfork, the first person in the UK to be convicted of murder as a result of a mass DNA swabbing exercise in 1987, and Rodney Whitchelo, who contaminated tins of dog food and baby food, and was eventually jailed for seventeen years in 1990. Another case he worked on was that of Michael Sams, a one-legged misfit with a grudge against society who murdered the part-time prostitute Julie Dart and kidnapped the Midlands estate agent Stephanie Slater, traumatizing her by chaining her up and imprisoning her in a tight, coffin-like container in his garage until a ransom was paid. Britton also advised on the investigation of the shocking murder of the toddler James Bulger on Merseyside in February 1993, and the sensational case of the multiple killer Fred West and his wife Rosemary.

In most of these cases Britton's contribution, described in detail in his autobiographical book *The Jigsaw Man*, followed the fairly standard procedures of police briefings, studying statements and photographs, visiting the crime scene, drawing up a written profile and offering periodic advice. In the Whitchelo inquiry he was invited to go somewhat further, advising the food manufacturers and police on the general strategy of negotiating with the offender as his latest blackmail demands arrived. In the Sams case he coached a young undercover policewoman to deal effectively with the criminal as she followed his complex instructions by note and phone when the ransom of Stephanie Slater was being negotiated. In the Nickell case, however, there was a quantum leap in the level of Britton's involvement. Initially, he drew up a normal profile in which he suggested that the culprit was a sexual deviant whose violent and sadistic fantasies would be extremely rare; but as the investigation progressed, things became much more elaborate.

The murder on Wimbledon Common on a sunny July morning had horrified the country with its violation of Rachel's beauty and her son's innocence, and the police were under enormous public pressure to find the culprit and bring him to justice. It was not long before they became convinced that Colin Stagg, a lonely twenty-nine-year-old man from a nearby estate, who had never had sexual intercourse and was interested in occult religion, was the culprit. Then they discovered by chance that Stagg had once answered a lonely hearts advert placed in *Loot* magazine by a young woman called Julie Pines, who soon terminated the correspondence because Stagg's letters began detailing fantasies of outdoor masturbation and sex with strangers. In the light of Britton's profile, police interest in Stagg increased at this point – but they had no real evidence against him. Eventually, as they struggled to kick-start a stalled inquiry, they asked Britton to devise an undercover strategy which would be based on the profile and designed to establish the guilt or innocence of their main suspect. Britton agreed; it was a fateful decision.

He and the police drew up a bizarre plan for an undercover policewoman to contact Stagg, pretending to have been given his address by Julie Pines, and build up a relationship with him. The idea was that she would gain his confidence by pretending to be interested in fantasies similar to his, and eventually admit that she had been a member of an occult group and had witnessed the ritual murder of a woman when she was seventeen years old. As Britton puts it in *The Jigsaw Man*: '...she believes she could only enter fully into an intimate sexual relationship with a man who had had actual experiences that were very similar to her own and could consequently understand and share the extraordinary psychosexual sensations that followed'.

Leaving aside any arguments about the social and psychological plausibility of this scenario, the intention was that it would present Stagg with an opportunity to reveal any involvement by him in the Nickell case, or say nothing and effectively rule himself out. Senior Metropolitan Police officers and the Crown Prosecution Service apparently gave their approval to this high-risk strategy, and a young undercover police officer codenamed Lizzie James was selected from SO10, the secretive Scotland Yard department that does work such as infiltrating drug gangs and posing as criminals. Britton coached her in the detailed history of her 'character' and the best way to communicate with Stagg and draw him out: he was already deeply involved with the conduct of the case in a way that would make most other experienced profilers very uncomfortable.

When Lizzie was ready she wrote to Stagg, and before long she was involved in steamy correspondence with him. 'You ask me to explain about how I feel when you write your special letters to me,' wrote Lizzie. 'Well, firstly they excite me greatly but I can't help but think you are showing great restraint, you are showing control when you feel like bursting. I want you to burst, I want to feel you all-powerful and overwhelming so that I am completely in your power, defenceless and humiliated. These thoughts are sending me into paradise already...' Stagg wasn't slow in responding: 'You need a damn good fucking by a real man and I'm the one to do it. I am the only man in the world who is going to give it to you. I am going to make sure you are screaming in agony when I abuse you. I am going to destroy your self-esteem, you will never look anybody in the eyes again...'

This repellent and risible correspondence continued, monitored by Britton and the senior officers on the case, and Stagg's fantasies became increasingly obscene. Then the pair graduated to telephone calls, and before long Stagg told Lizzie that people in his area had been spreading rumours that he might have been responsible for the murder of Rachel Nickell. She took her chance and responded: 'Quite frankly, Colin, it wouldn't have mattered to me if you had murdered her. In fact, in certain ways it would make it easier for me because I've got something to tell you. I'll tell you on Thursday that, you know, it just makes me realize that it's fate has brought us together.' Soon after this the pair had their first face-to-face meeting at the Dell Cafe in Hyde Park in central London, a mile or two from the headquarters of New Scotland Yard, with Lizzie James wearing a concealed tape recorder. She told him about her involvement with the 'ritual murder' at the age of seventeen, and how she could be intimate only with a man with a similar history, but his response was to restate apologetically that he had nothing to do with the murder of Rachel Nickell.

He did, however, send her a written fantasy which was set in a woodland scene similar to the murder location on Wimbledon Common and involved him, Lizzie and a strange man in three-way sexual activity where a knife was produced, drawn across Lizzie's body without cutting her, then used to draw blood from the stranger's arm and drip it on to her nipples. The fantasy contained many of the elements Britton had suggested in his profile to be the hallmarks of the offender's deviancy, and the mention of the knife in particular now made the police feel that Stagg was beginning to incriminate himself. Stagg then told Lizzie in a phone call that he had murdered a young girl and hidden her body in the New Forest, but when the police checked this out they concluded that it was an invention, presumably intended by Stagg to speed the day when Lizzie would agree to sex with him.

She began providing him with more lurid written fantasies, and at their next meeting she started asking him what he knew about the Nickell case. He told her that when the police had interviewed him they'd shown him a photograph of Rachel's dead body, and he described the state of her private parts and the position of her hands. When this was reported to Lizzie's superiors, they felt they finally had a real breakthrough. This was because they considered that the particular photograph shown to Stagg was not the kind of close-up that would have allowed him to see anything about the condition of her private parts or the position of her hands: here, at last, the police considered, was guilty knowledge. After one more meeting in which Stagg admitted to feeling sexual excitement at the thought of what happened to Rachel Nickell, the covert operation was called off and he was arrested.

At the end of February 1994 there was a committal hearing at which the stipendiary magistrate, Mr Terry English, decided that there was sufficient evidence for Colin Stagg to go for trial by jury. But just before the case came up, Mr Justice Waterhouse ruled at Leeds Crown Court that evidence derived from an undercover operation similar to the one conducted in the Nickell case was not admissible. Alarm bells began to ring, and when Stagg's trial began at the Old Bailey on 5 September it went straight into detailed legal argument that couldn't be reported. Nine days later Mr Justice Ognall produced a judgement that lasted eighty minutes and condemned the undercover operation in the most scathing terms, saying that it amounted to entrapment: 'I would be the first to acknowledge the very great pressures on the police in their pursuit of this grave inquiry, but I am afraid this behaviour betrays not merely an excessive zeal but a substantial attempt to incriminate a suspect by positive and deceptive conduct of the grossest kind,' he said. 'The prosecution sought to persuade me that the object of the exercise was to afford the accused an opportunity either to eliminate himself from the inquiry or implicate himself in the murder... I am bound to say that I regard that description of the operation as highly disingenuous.' He excluded the evidence under Section 78 of the Police and Criminal Evidence Act on the grounds that it would have 'an adverse effect on the fairness of proceedings'. It was quite clear from the judge's decision that it was the aspect of entrapment which had been fatal to the prosecution case, rather than the other main element within it – Stagg's alleged guilty knowledge about the condition of the body. But the judge also said that he regarded the alleged guilty knowledge as a very small piece of evidence that would not amount to incriminating material or a confession.

The question also arises of what would have happened if the case had gone ahead and the prosecution had sought to argue that the similarity of Stagg's sexual fantasies to those described in Britton's profile amounted to evidence against him. The likelihood is that the court would have concluded that this was a form of 'evidence of propensity', which is usually ruled inadmissible in British courts – evidence, for example, that a man accused of a stabbing usually carried a knife, or had previous convictions for offences involving knives, also falls under the heading of evidence of propensity. Britton himself had emphasized before the case began, however, that the similarity between Stagg's fantasies and the profile could not by itself amount to evidence against the accused – there would have to be more substantial evidence as well. To that extent, he was sticking to the accepted notion of what a profile can or cannot be. At the end of the day, therefore, he was sunk not by the profile as such, but by his willingness to take part in what the judge considered to be little better than a 'sting'.

If the judge had decided otherwise and the trial had proceeded to a guilty verdict, Britton would have been perceived by many as a public-spirited genius and the story would have provided a ready-made plot for a movie or a special two-part episode of *Cracker*. But the plodding, principled ways of the real world rarely match the heightened, rule-free world of fiction, and the outcome of the case was a catastrophic blow for Paul Britton. Overnight he was pilloried in the media as a manipulative Svengali who had set out to frame an innocent man. 'Fantasy justice', read the headlines, and 'Who's in the dock now?' It was implied that he had persuaded the police to launch the operation and overcome objections from the Crown Prosecution Service. Those unsympathetic to Britton, including rivals in the world of offender profiling and the why-oh-why merchants of newspaper comment columns, did not bother to conceal their scorn. It was also noticeable to Britton and some psychologist colleagues how those who had approved and supported the undercover operation confined themselves to a brief written statement about the case and were otherwise unavailable for comment as the critics flocked to Britton's front door. Eventually he was removed ignominiously from the list of profilers accredited by the Association of Chief Police Officers, and the comments of the judge were compounded by the BPS disciplinary committee hearings and the fresh surge of media interest they inevitably aroused.

Britton denies emphatically that the undercover operation was his proposal or that he sought to persuade reluctant police and lawyers to put it into effect. He did say that there were similarities between his profile of a rare sexual deviant and the sexual fantasies of Colin Stagg, and that it was highly unlikely that more than one person with such a rare deviancy would be present on Wimbledon Common on the morning of the murder, as Stagg was. But he also made it clear that similarities between his profile and the sexual fantasies of Colin Stagg did not amount to evidence against him: there would have to be real evidence before he could be convicted – forensic evidence, perhaps, or conclusive evidence of guilty knowledge. The defence Britton prepared for his BPS disciplinary hearing, therefore, was that he had stood by the main tenets of profiling and done nothing wrong.

What some considered to be the all-time low in the story of profiling in the UK had been preceded only seven years earlier by one of its high points. This, ironically, involved one of Britton's rivals in the world of profiling, Dr David Canter. He was an academic psychologist at the University of Surrey in Guildford, with a special interest in the statistical approach to criminology. He had been given a Home Office grant to set up an Offender Profiling Research Unit, which was to construct a database on the sort of people who committed serious crimes, especially murders and rapes, and offer an operational service to police forces around the country.

The unit's first notable success was the advice it gave to the Metropolitan Police which helped them catch and convict John Francis Duffy, a cruel psychopath who murdered three women and raped at least twenty others. Canter's deductions about Duffy, known as 'the railway rapist' because most of his crimes were near stations in and around London, included the place he was likely to live and the nature of his earlier criminal history. The profile helped police to narrow down their list of suspects, put Duffy under surveillance and eventually arrest him: he was jailed for life. The case provoked a surge of media and public interest in profiling: fortunately Canter's aquiline features were a gift to newspaper photographers eager for the kind of bony profile popularly associated with Sherlock Holmes.

Canter's use of statistics and computers was a far cry from the 1950s and 1960s, when it was not unusual for senior detectives to listen to mediums and fortune tellers in the hope of getting a new lead in difficult cases of murder or rape. There were cases when police forces expended huge resources trying to locate cars with registration numbers revealed by witnesses put under hypnosis by the kind of practitioners who presented shows in seaside theatres. In those days it was also considered legitimate for senior investigating officers (SIOs) to keep all the information about a case in their own head and to make decisions according to what they called their 'gut feeling'. By the 1970s, however, the steady growth in serious crime and the advances in forensic science and information technology began to lead to a more managed and professional approach to detection. The two factors that probably played the largest part in bringing offender profiling into the modern era were developments in the United States and the Yorkshire Ripper murders of the late 1970s. The first showed the kind of thing which could be done; the second was a watershed in the modernization and professionalization of criminal investigation in Britain.

The first dramatic coup for psychological profiling is commonly held to be the case in 1956 of the 'mad bomber' of New York City, George Metsky. From a study of the criminal's letters and examination of the scenes of the bombings, a psychiatrist called Dr James A. Brussel predicted that the person responsible was an unmarried, heavily built middle-aged Roman Catholic immigrant from eastern Europe, who hated his father, lived with his brother or sister and would be wearing a neatly buttoned double-breasted suit when he was finally arrested. The culprit was eventually found as a result of steady detective work rather than Brussel's intervention, but the profile turned out to be uncannily accurate: the only wrong detail was that Metsky lived with two sisters. It was partly because of feats such as this that the Federal Bureau of Investigation began in the late 1970s to explore the possibilities of using psychological profiling as a standard part of serious criminal investigations.

This innovative work was carried out by the Behavioral Science Unit (now called the Investigative Support Unit) at the FBI Academy at Quantico, Virginia, where researchers set about extending developments in forensic science into the psychological sphere. Forensic science had been making significant strides in such matters as blood grouping and detection, and would eventually lead to the huge breakthrough of DNA testing, but in general it could come into play only once a suspect had been arrested and comparisons could be made between him or her and the traces left at the scene of the crime. Only rarely could physical forensic science tell detectives about the *kind* of person they were looking for – for example, when a hair found at the crime scene indicated the racial group of the offender. The new task was to develop a way of describing the probable personal characteristics of the perpetrator so that the field of potential suspects could be narrowed down.

The unit approached the task by interviewing thirty-six convicted sexually orientated serial murderers, supplementing the information they gave them with known details from the crime scenes and collating information about similar crimes from a large number of highly experienced detectives. The idea was that if a new crime was similar in various ways to one of the known crimes, the new offender was likely to share some characteristics with the known offender, and an entire predictive system could be computerized. The result was a framework based on a basic division of sexually motivated murders into 'organized' and 'disorganized' crimes – the former where the criminal targets a stranger, plans carefully, displays control at the scene, and leaves few clues, and the latter where there is no planning and the behaviour at the scene is disorderly and haphazard. Soon afterwards a series of interviews with forty-one convicted serial rapists led to four types of rape classification, known as power assurance, power assertive, anger retaliatory and anger excitation. Developments and refinements of these early classifications led to the publication in 1992 of *The Crime Classification Manual*, which puts forward a systematic approach for the production of psychological profiles.

Such profiles follow a standard format that puts up a series of hypotheses about the offender, starting with information about age range, race, occupation and marital status. It adds intelligence and education, offending history, military background, family relationships, social habits, age and type of vehicle, personality (including possible forms of mental illness or deviancy), and suggested interview techniques in the event of an arrest. This profiling system has been widely used in the US, where experience has shown that it is more useful in working on crimes where the offender's behaviour has been particularly extreme, involving torture, ritualistic behaviour and the acting out of fantasy. This US model of profiling has been widely criticized, especially for relying too much on broad classifications and paying too little attention to the individuality of each criminal; but the practice of profiling in other countries, including Canada, Holland and the UK, is based largely on the FBI's pioneering approach. Many UK detectives and psychologists have visited the Quantico academy and taken note of its methods.

Both Richard Badcock and Julian Boon acknowledge the usefulness of many FBI profiling concepts, but have developed what they regard as a more flexible approach, which in Boon's case is derived from theoretical frameworks, and in Badcock's from clinical psychiatric experience.

'The Americans built up a body of profiles and tried to do profiles of new cases from bits of complete ones,' says Badcock. 'This was not so much making use of past experience as taking past experience as the whole thing. That's dodgy because it reduces your ability to judge the current case and distorts things to fit previous cases.'

While developments in the US provided one impetus for offender profiling in Britain, the second came from the Byford Report of 1982, which was commissioned to identify shortcomings in the handling of the case of Peter Sutcliffe, Britain's longest-ever criminal investigation. Sutcliffe murdered thirteen women between 1975 and 1980 in and around Bradford, and became known as the Yorkshire Ripper because of his habit of mutilating his victims. The report showed that he would have emerged as a prime suspect much sooner if a more effective system had been available to handle the mountains of paperwork produced by the inquiry, which relied on old-fashioned card indexes. What followed was, in effect, a revolution in Britain's approach to detective work: over the following years systems were put in place to check whether serious crimes were part of a series, to train senior investigating officers, to establish rules for inquiries that involve more than one police force, to set up specialist detective and forensic support teams, and to make the best use of computer technology. One of the most significant advances was the introduction in 1987 of HOLMES (Home Office Large Major Enquiry System), a computer system capable of handling and cross-referencing huge amounts of information fed in by the staff of an incident room: if it is asked, for example, to find all references in hundreds of statements to a brown-haired man driving a red car, it does so instantly.

Part of the enhancement of detective skills required by the Byford Report was the official consignment to history of the 'gut feeling' school of criminal investigation and a more discriminating approach to the use of outside advisers, including the increasing numbers of people who offered police the kind of help that was increasingly referred to as profiling. This more rigorous approach was led by Don Dovaston, then Assistant Chief Constable of Derbyshire and a member of the profiling sub-committee set up by the Association of Chief Police Officers (ACPO) after the case of John Duffy first brought profiling into prominence.

'There had been some less successful exploits than the Duffy case,' Dovaston said in a recent interview. 'Millions had been spent on the advice of people who thought they were doing the police a favour, when they weren't. We had psychologists saying the offender was a 6-foot 4-inch mentally disturbed black man who had recently arrived in the country, when the culprit turned out to be a 5-foot 8-inch white man who was perfectly stable and had lived here all his life. We began to delve into people's credentials, and found they often didn't have the level of expertise which was required, and the conclusion was that it was time to set up a list of accredited profilers.'

It is not an easy process to set up an accredited list when there are no recognized qualifications specific to offender profiling and no governing body or code of practice: an unusual emphasis falls on the personality and experience of the practitioner, and the abilities of the accrediting body to judge his or her character. Nevertheless, ACPO succeeded in setting up such a list in 1992 and police forces were urged to refer to it before using the services of a profiler. This coincided with a report for the Home Office by Paul Britton, who had not yet run into the controversy caused by the Rachel Nickell case, which concluded that there was positive potential for developing offender profiling as an investigative tool and recommended that it should be firmly under the control of the police in the future. The Home Office began a research programme into the subject which is still under way. In 1995, the stewardship of the accredited list was transferred to the National Crime Faculty (NCF), a new central resource of information and expertise set up within the Police Staff College at Bramshill in Hampshire to help police forces with their most serious and difficult cases. Individual police forces and SIOs continued to go directly to profilers they knew and liked, but two years ago ACPO agreed a policy requiring every SIO who wants to use a profiler to approach the NCF and be allocated an appropriate expert from the accredited list. The twenty-two people on the current list are mostly psychologists or psychiatrists with forensic, clinical or academic experience of the more extreme forms of criminal behaviour.

Offender profiling is an idiosyncratic occupation, and there are almost as many approaches to it as there are practitioners. The basic difference, however, is between those who adopt a clinical approach and those who adopt a statistical approach. The most highly developed version of the statistical approach is a database whose acronym appears to have been even more tortuously crafted than HOLMES: CATCHEM (Centralized Analytical Team Collating Homicide Expertise and Management) was set up by Derbyshire Police and contains details of 8,800 homicides of women under twenty-one and boys under sixteen committed since 1960. The decision to establish such a database had been made in 1986; as with HOLMES, the hope was to prevent a repeat of a shocking serial crime – in this case the abduction and murder by Robert Black of three young girls from different parts of the country: Susan Maxwell, Caroline Hogg and Sarah Harper. CATCHEM is now consulted on average once every ten days by police forces in this and other countries who are asked to describe the salient features of the crime. These are fed into the computer, which will point to similar murders that may have been committed by the same offender and suggest the likely characteristics of a person who would commit such a crime. It is also able to offer statistical information that is likely to help an SIO devise his or her investigative strategy. For example, if a child has been murdered and there is no evidence of sexual abuse, there is an 86 per cent probability that the killer is a parent or guardian; if there is evidence of sexual abuse, however, that probability falls to 6 per cent.

Another important statistical method is geographical profiling, developed by Dr Kim Rossmo, a detective inspector in Vancouver, British Columbia, who has devised a computer programme that predicts where an offender is likely to live on the basis of where his crimes have been committed. One of the staff at the National Crime Faculty in the UK, Neil Trainor, is a geographical profiler who has worked with Dr Rossmo and was one of the experts consulted in two of the cases described in this book. A third statistical method, which also relies strongly on clinical concepts, is that developed by Professor Canter, the profiler who helped to catch the 'railway rapist', John Duffy, in 1987. This approach is known as 'multi-variate statistical analysis' and is especially useful in multiple crimes. The types of behaviour shown in each crime are computerized so that new crimes can be compared with previous crimes, both solved and unsolved, to assess whether they might have been committed by the same person and what the characteristics of that person might be.

But the most widely used approach to profiling is the clinical approach adopted by Badcock and Boon, so called because it uses the techniques of the psychiatrist's or psychologist's consulting room. The fundamental article of faith is similar to that of the forensic scientist – that every contact leaves a trace. But instead of a trace of physical contact, the profiler looks for traces of behaviour that might provide an indication of identity or character. The degree of anger indicated by the nature of the wounds inflicted on a victim might indicate how the criminal presents himself in everyday life; the way he treats and talks to a victim might indicate the nature and quality of his own family relationships; the length of time he spends at the scene and the things he does there might indicate his deeper desires and preoccupations. Clinical profiling is a process that is hard to define because it treats each case as unique and draws on a mixture of reasoning, experience and intuition. Badcock describes it as 'starting from informed guesswork', and 'a little bit like intelligence – everybody knows what you mean, but if you try and define it, it's actually quite difficult'.

It is fortunate for society, in a sense, that most serious crimes are committed by intimates or associates of the victim and are therefore solved with comparative ease. Fewer than 10 per cent of serious crimes fall into the category of what some detectives describe as 'stickers', defying the most determined, long-term investigative efforts. Such crimes tend to be committed by people who, for complex reasons determined by background and experience, suffer from a compulsion to kill or rape selected strangers, and to do it repeatedly. To the world at large such crime often seems a horrific mystery, involving something more hidden and complex than the standard mainsprings of love and hate, greed and envy. It is in cases of this kind, however, that offender profiling is most at home, and in the last ten years offender profiles have been called for in many hundreds of them in the UK.

There is still a widespread scepticism about profiling among many police officers in Britain, some of whom regard it as little better than palmistry or gazing into a crystal ball. But most SIOs nowadays will call in an offender profiler if there is no definite prospect of a solution to a serious crime within forty-eight hours of its discovery: the recent murder of ten-year-old Damilola Taylor in Peckham in south London is a case in point. Don Dovaston, who as a young detective in Liverpool saw clairvoyants consulting tea leaves about the whereabouts of a murderer on the run, says: 'I think offender profiling is here to stay.' The cases detailed in the following chapters indicate the kind of contributions profilers can make, and whether Dovaston is right in his prediction.

THE MYSTERY OF
TENNYSON ROAD ³

*'We knew we had a real whodunnit
and we decided to get the profiler in.'*
Detective Chief Inspector Steve Scott

Leaning against a breakwater at Worthing, watching the sun go down across the pebbly beach, Julian Boon was reminiscing in typical style about childhood seaside holidays and weekly visits to his dear old granny in Brighton. He wasn't a great one for swimming, he confessed: 'I'm afraid I've grown rather old and soft and tired and I might freeze to bits if I went in – but in my day I've done my paddling, dear boy.' Now he was winding down after a day of intensive personality analysis – the extremely difficult kind, where the subject could be almost anywhere in the country, is not available for interview, and is determined to remain so. He had been helping the local police force to make sense of the latest case that was puzzling them.

Fourteen weeks earlier, there had been a phone call to the town's police station from one of the many elderly ladies who live in this quiet Sussex town. She was concerned about a friend of hers who lived alone in a house nearby and had been failing to answer the telephone for two days: the women had a standing arrangement to contact each other regularly so each could check that the other was all right.

Two female officers were dispatched into the hot July evening to check the report. When they reached Tennyson Road there was a single light on in the first storey of number 9, a large and run-down semi-detached house with a pillared portico surrounded by overgrown trees and bushes. They banged on the door and shone their torches in the windows, illuminating rooms piled full of newspapers, old boxes and dilapidated household appliances. But there was no sign of life, and eventually they went down the side of the building under a tunnel of greenery and smashed a pane of glass so they could open one of the windows. The WPC who climbed in had a quick look round the ground floor. Lying on the carpet of a spare bedroom, covered with a blood-stained blanket with the feet sticking out at one end, was the decom-posing body of an elderly woman. The victim's pink dressing gown had been pulled over her head, and her skull had been smashed in by a series of blows. One slipper was still on her foot, the other was resting against her calf. A spray of bloodstains covered the nearby wall and curtain to a height of eighteen inches.

The officer went to the front door and let her colleague in, first moving a chair that had been placed in front of the letterbox, appar-ently so that the householder wouldn't have to bend over to pick up mail and newspapers. The two women then called their sergeant and had a quick look around the large and rambling house, picking their way care-fully among the teetering piles of hoarded possessions. Soon the CID and scene-of-crime officers arrived and examined the setting more care-fully, drilling open the locked doors of some of the rooms. The house and garden were cordoned off, and by the end of the evening of Monday 26 July 1999 the body had been moved to the local mortuary and a full-scale murder investigation was under way with Detective Chief Inspector Steve Scott as the senior investigating officer. Scott – aged forty-one, with twenty-three years in the Sussex police – is a persistent and determined detective with a strong commitment to a modern, managerial approach to running important investigations.

The body turned out to be that of Jean Barnes, aged eighty-seven, a reclusive spinster who had lived an unusual life. The daughter of an East Anglian clergyman, she had been one of the first women graduates of Cambridge University and could speak six languages, including Italian and Russian. The man she'd hoped to marry had been killed in the Second World War, and she had spent most of her life working as a translator in the Foreign Office and other government departments. She'd never married or had children, her only sister had died earlier, and a poignant picture came to light of the way she had lived for more than forty years – alone in the oversized and neglected house she'd inherited from her family, seeing her nephew rarely, keeping in contact with a few local friends, declining support from the social services department. She took *The Times* every day, did the crossword, then added it to the great piles, dating back more than twenty years, which cluttered the stairs and the rooms. She also listened a lot to the radio and her large collection of taped classical music. One of her friends did the bulk of her shopping for her, and she went to the shops herself from time to time, always wearing the same clothes, summer and winter: a woollen bobble hat and a tweed coat tightly belted round the waist. She also visited regularly a partially sighted neighbour in order to read the newspaper to her – this was the woman who had raised the alarm after their usual telephone code had misfired. So Miss Barnes, although reclusive, was not entirely isolated.

At the same time it was not unusual for nobody to see her for two to three weeks at a time, and one of the first questions facing the investigators was how long she might have been dead. Dr Vesna Djurovic, the Home Office pathologist who conducted the post-mortem, found that nine heavy blows to the head with a blunt instrument – it was not clear exactly what – had killed Miss Barnes. The pathologist thought the victim might have been dead for between two and five days, but admitted that it was hard to be sure because the warm summer conditions and the covering blanket might have produced an unusual rate of decomposition. The body had been invaded by rare scuttle flies, and the police decided to call in two expert entomologists, Dr Henry Disney of the Department of Zoology at Cambridge University and Dr Zakaria Erzinçlioglu, a retired Cambridge academic, to study them and work out how long they might have been there. Other clues were that her last phone call had been made on 10 July and the *Radio Times* was open at the page for 12 July, and one local resident thought she'd seen Miss Barnes mowing her front lawn on 15 July. When the entomologists' report arrived, their opinion was that she may have been killed at least ten days, and possibly as long as two weeks, before she was found – which would have meant 12 July. So the time of death, variously estimated from two to fourteen days before the discovery, was one of many factors that made the investigation particularly difficult.

Another was that there was no sign of forced entry, raising the possibility that Miss Barnes had known her attacker or been persuaded to admit someone she didn't know. Yet another was the huge accumulation of possessions in the three-storey house, any one of which might hold some clue as to what had happened to the victim. Four scene-of-crime officers were to remain at the house for two entire months, longer than in any previous criminal investigation by the Sussex police force, trawling for clues through every room and logging some 2,300 exhibits. There was some valuable furniture in the house, and there was evidence that some of it had been recently removed: in one upstairs room, for example, there were two miniatures on the wall and a lighter patch on the wallpaper where the third one had been. There were two rooms – Miss Barnes's bedroom on the first floor and a spare bedroom on the second – which had been ransacked, with drawers turned out over the beds; but other rooms, some containing valuable objects, were virtually untouched. At the back of a cupboard, wrapped in newspaper in a box, was silverware worth about £20,000 – surely the kind of thing the attacker would have found and taken had he simply been a burglar in search of loot. Documents showed that she had various investments and savings, including £87,000 worth of National Savings for which the certificates were missing. Before long it was clear to the investigators that Miss Barnes, who had lived in semi-squalid conditions and appeared to survive on tins of corned beef, soup, eggs and lentils, was worth about half a million pounds.

In the early days of the inquiry there were about 200 officers involved, many of them making detailed house-to-house inquiries in the neighbourhood. These yielded several leads, one of which led police to arrest a local drug addict and question him until it became clear that he had been in prison at a crucial time in the story. Another prompted them to go on the BBC TV programme *Crimewatch UK* to issue the description of a man who had been seen in the area of Tennyson Road telling people that his car had broken down and begging them to lend him £15 to get home to Rye. The man, Raymond Price, quickly came forward and confessed to having used this ruse successfully on many occasions in the past, but denied having anything to do with Miss Barnes. In the end police believed his denial of the murder and prosecuted him instead on multiple counts of deception. There were also reports of a stocky elderly woman with iron-grey hair, in the company of a man, knocking unsuccessfully on Miss Barnes's door in March, telling people who spoke to her that Miss Barnes was a difficult old woman and wouldn't come to the door. A white girl with dreadlocks had also been seen in the road. Finally, two men had been seen near the house on the day before the body was found – one in his twenties, and one in his fifties, carrying a box.

The most promising development came when the local milkman came forward on the day after the murder was discovered and handed police a note that he said Miss Barnes had left for him six days earlier. The note asked him to cease delivering milk because she was going into hospital for an operation and would be living in a nursing home afterwards. This immediately aroused police suspicions because nobody else who had talked to them about Miss Barnes knew anything of such a plan, and inquiries in local hospitals and nursing homes showed the information to be completely untrue. By this time the police had realized that some of Miss Barnes's keys were missing and that newspapers delivered after the likely time of her death had been added to the piles marching up the stairs. All this added up to the probability that the note, along with a second one that the milkman had received and retrieved for the police from a rubbish bin, had been forged, and that whoever had forged them had been coming in and out of the house since the murder. Indeed, a man from British Gas who knocked on the door five days before the body was found, when Miss Barnes was probably dead already, heard the TV or radio playing inside the house.

So several samples of handwriting that was definitely that of Miss Barnes were gathered together and sent with the suspect note to be examined by two handwriting experts, Kim Hughes of the Forensic Science Service in Birmingham and Janet Hill of the FSS in London. Meanwhile, the milkman was also asked for a handwritten note about where he left Miss Barnes's bread and milk and where he collected the bottles from, and the suspicions of the police were aroused when he replied that he would type the information on his computer and print it out. When he then failed to keep an appointment with police and later said the information he'd been asked for had been deleted from the computer by his three-year-old son, the police became even more suspicious: the milkman and his father, also a milkman, were arrested and the computer seized so his account of the deletion could be checked. Nothing conclusive was found against the two, but they remained suspects for a considerable time, partly because of the sightings by witnesses of the pair of men in Tennyson Road on the day before Miss Barnes's body was discovered. It was the start of a long and unfortunate saga that eventually resulted in a claim for wrongful arrest against the Sussex police.

While the results of the handwriting tests were awaited, the police checked their own records to find out if Miss Barnes had ever been in touch with them. Sure enough, they found out that she had reported two burglaries in January 1999, when she had lost a barometer and some paintings from the walls of her house. She had been cautious about her safety, and immediately had the locks changed. Then, in February, she had been attacked on her front doorstep at 3.45 a.m. when – keeping late hours as usual – she was putting out her milk bottles: she hadn't been badly hurt, but her glasses had been broken. (This event contributed to police suspicions about the involvement of the milkman.) On 23 April she had also contacted the police to report that somebody purporting to be from her bank had telephoned her and asked her to give details about herself. She had complied, but obviously felt uneasy at doing so; and, being so security-conscious, she had had the locks changed again at this point.

On 10 May a new Barclaycard and Alliance and Leicester bank account had been sent to her, and she cut up the card – the pieces were later found in the house – and closed the account without using it. Now, when the police contacted the bank, they found that two application forms had been received in the name of Miss Barnes, but turned out to contain mistakes such as the incorrect spelling of her second name, Helena, and a wrong maiden name, Jenkins, for her mother. These forms were promptly sent off to the handwriting experts, along with two suspicious cheques – one written to Co-Op Dairy, and one to Seeboard in settlement of a final electricity demand. Both, recovered from the bank, were dated 19 July, which could easily have been after her death.

Just over a month after the murder, the first results came back from Birmingham: all six documents sent to the experts were demonstrably not in Miss Barnes's real handwriting. The experts were unsure of the forger's sex, but they said he or she was likely to be in their fifties or sixties, and was not making a strong attempt to disguise their own writing. What now looked certain was that somebody had coldly plotted to use this elderly lady's personal details to get access to her money, and had eventually killed her. Then the killer had tried to conceal her death, and apparently had been trying to take away her assets bit by bit.

This was a major turning point that prompted the police to seek further expert help from outside the force. 'As soon as we realized the notes were being forged, we knew we had a real whodunnit and we decided to get the profiler in,' DCI Scott said later. 'I had used one in previous cases, and he'd been helpful but never provided what you'd call earth-shattering support. In the Jean Barnes case, I wanted to know what type of person could do this kind of thing – age, sex, manner, lifestyle, attitudes. This was the kind of information that would help us to prioritize our actions, because we'd had hundreds of calls and taken dozens of statements, and we needed help in deciding which ones to deal with first.'

Scott had sent Detective Inspector Sally Simmonds on a preliminary visit in September to Julian Boon at Leicester University, where they outlined the case to him. He listened carefully and gave them some preliminary observations, focusing principally on the calm, methodical and well-planned aspects of the crime. But the pressure of Boon's day job at this busy time at the start of the academic year meant, as so often with profiling work, that it was several weeks before he could find time for the next stage of the process. So it was not until early November that he was driving smartly down to Worthing in a borrowed 1967 Rover 3.5 litre P5 with leather seats. The purpose of the trip was a more detailed briefing and a visit to the scene of the crime. Inevitably, perhaps, the local paper headline read: 'Cracker called in'. Scott's response was: 'I don't care what newspapers say as long as they say it on the front page and as long as we get exposure of our murder.'

Boon was introduced to the investigation team and immediately took a modest, self-deprecating line, keen to emphasize that he was not coming in to take over 'like Emperor Nero'. The police remained very much in the driving seat, he said: 'There is no coming in and making out like *Cracker* does that he knows all the answers. It simply isn't like that and it's not my job to tell anybody anything, in the talking-down sense. Where I think I might be useful is to come from a forensic psychology perspective, which may be different from investigative experience. I stress, not better but different: it's a bit like looking for an illegal radio station broadcasting somewhere on the moors – if one person has a fix from one angle, and one person from another, and we both come to similar conclusions but for different reasons, that strengthens the value of those conclusions. If for some reason we come to different conclusions, then it stimulates discussion and new ideas are generated, on the one hand from investigative experience, for which I have the greatest respect, and on the other from what we know of the psychology of offenders and offending behaviour.'

This delicate courtship by Boon of the foot soldiers of the investigating team speaks volumes about the nature of the developing relationship between police officers and profilers. This new race of experts has received the imprimatur of approval from the Association of Chief Police Officers and most senior detectives have now been on courses that have convinced most of them that profilers, while never a panacea, can be extraordinarily useful: a case in point is the senior investigating officer in the next case examined by this book, an old-style, down-to-earth, sceptical copper who quickly appreciated that here was something that could help him – a new tool in the toolbox. At street level, however, the resistance is stronger. Police officers as a breed are not easily impressed, whether by the stories they hear from people caught doing something wrong or by the highfalutin pretensions of experts and intellectuals. As will be seen in other cases, the constables and sergeants who do the legwork will often curl a lip and talk about palmistry and entrail-reading when the word 'profiler' is mentioned. Boon had been taken on by Scott and knew he had the support of the top brass on this investigation; but he also knew he would not be universally welcomed and needed to strike a modest and unpretentious note.

This state of affairs was acknowledged by Scott when he was asked on another occasion what his impressions were of the occasionally eccentric Julian Boon: he admitted that a lot of officers were suspicious of profilers, as they were of anything new: 'I think he's a really lovely man. He's obviously extremely intelligent, although he can go off at tangents and follow things through on different lines than perhaps I or my colleagues would do as police officers. But he's very approachable and he seems quite easy to do business with, and I'm sure that as the months go by our relationship will become a bit closer.'

As the management meeting went on, the dominant impression was that the investigating team was drowning in detail, and feeling – in Scott's words – 'down in the dumps'. In the fourteen weeks since the murder, they had accumulated a huge amount of confusing information, including copious detail about earlier parts of Miss Barnes's life, but no really good evidence had yet been found and none of the four suspects so far looked likely to be charged. Even a reward of £20,000 put up by the police and the executors of Miss Barnes's estate had failed to bring in the vital witness or tip-off. The milkman remained the chief candidate, even though it seemed unlikely that he would have handed in the crucial forged note if he had been the attacker and had written it himself. His clothing was still being screened for blood by forensic scientists. 'And we mustn't lose sight of all the other people we're interested in, we must progress our various lines of inquiry,' said Scott. But there seemed to be little real progress and it was clear that the police were looking to Boon to introduce a sense of focus into the case.

He listened carefully as the officers ranged from one aspect of the inquiry to another, but at the end of the meeting confined himself to two preliminary remarks: that there might be more than one person involved in the plot, and that whoever had killed Miss Barnes had done it without anger, enjoyment or personal malice: it had been done quickly and efficiently, he said, as part of a carefully worked-out strategy.

Now the team took Boon down to Tennyson Road to look round the house. The road is not far from the town centre and contains a number of large houses turned into flats and nursing homes. The green tunnel of foliage leading to number 9, which had once been so thick the Post Office had threatened to suspend deliveries, had been cut down to allow for police searches, and the main hazard now was the carpet of rotting apples covering parts of the garden. The local papers were invited to take a photograph of 'Cracker' Boon, and reminded repeatedly by Scott of the large reward still on offer and the determination by Sussex police to solve the case. Then Boon was taken inside to study the remnants of Miss Barnes's reclusive lifestyle and the clues and riddles left behind by her killer.

Downstairs, there was the question of how – if he had a key and had come and gone through the front door – he might have managed to manoeuvre the chair back into place under the letterbox, presumably to make things look normal to whoever delivered the papers. The *Times* for the day of the discovery of Miss Barnes's body was still on the chair, but earlier copies had been added to the pile on the stairs – the principal indication that someone had been coming in and moving the papers for many days after the death. Boon asked whether they were in precise sequence by date, and was told they were rather mixed up. He pointed out that this indicated the intruder may have returned every few days rather than daily. He was also told there had been a letter on the floor, a leaflet urging 'Say No to Karaoke', a loaf of bread, and opened tins of corned beef in the room used for storage. The search team had also found a tissue bearing a few specks of an unknown substance on it in a downstairs room next to the spare bedroom where Jean Barnes had been found dead.

The procession continued upstairs, past some boxes containing antiquated toy trains made of tin, past the precarious piles of newspapers, to the kitchen, living room and bedroom where Miss Barnes spent most of her time. There was a dresser in the kitchen where she had kept a lot of papers, and in the bathroom beyond the kitchen the sink had yielded traces of her blood – had her killer washed his hands there, or was it merely the place where she applied plasters to her deteriorating feet? In the bedroom, where her financial papers had been tipped out on the bed, a note to the milkman asking for wheatmeal rather than wholemeal bread was found, bizarrely, behind one leg of the dressing table. This note was genuine. In her sitting room the books included volumes on Italian poetry – she had routinely spoken Italian to the man who occasionally gardened for her, helping with the roses she cultivated in isolated patches among the overgrown greenery. Several ornaments had been moved from the top of a cabinet to a table, but valuable pictures, furniture, a mirror and a clock had not been moved. 'A normal burglar would have come in and taken a lot more stuff,' commented Boon. 'And would have got out without doing many of the things he has done. Two possible reasons for that, I suppose: one being that they knew they could come back and filch it at any time, and the second being that they were principally interested in money.'

Back at the police station, fortified by lunch, Boon had an opportunity to study the forged documents, including the application for a bank account that had said Miss Barnes planned to deposit the £87,000 worth of National Savings. (The certificates for these savings were still missing and might, the police thought, have been taken in the earlier burglary in January.) Then the officers in the inquiry team began to ask Boon for his further impressions about the crime. He agreed immediately with Scott that the culprit was unlikely to be a drug addict, but for different reasons: Scott's argument was that the drug-taking community was so desperate for money that the £20,000 reward would have prompted someone to 'shop' the offender; Boon's reason was that the crime was simply too orderly to have been done by a drug addict, whose behaviour he thought would have been more disorganized and chaotic. This was an example, he added, of what he meant by his earlier analogy of getting fixes from different directions on an illegal radio station broadcasting on the moors.

Could Miss Barnes have been held hostage? asked one officer. No, said Boon, because there was no evidence of torture, gagging or the paraphernalia of restraint. Would the offender have known her? He definitely knew *of* her, was the reply, and was likely to have visited the house for some reason, although she might not have known him in any way. Would he have done something similar before and be likely to do it again? The offender was 'a reptile', replied Boon, but was clearly imaginative and resourceful and this was unlikely to be a one-off attempt to fleece old ladies. Might the offence relate to the offender's experience with his mother? asked one Freudian-minded officer. 'No, I don't think so.' And would he be a professional, educated person? Intelligent, literate, able to understand money matters, capable of delayed gratification, said Boon – 'but that doesn't mean he's a director of the Bank of England'. Male or female offender? – 'Such levels of naked aggression would, I think, have stacked it heavily towards a male offender. If however it turns out to be a female and they have a psychotic background and so on, I promise never to come back to Sussex again.' Crucially, he also considered it likely that the culprit lived close to the victim and knew her situation extremely well.

After the meeting, as Boon left the breakwater and strolled along the beach in the fading sunshine, he reflected on the day and summarized his views. It was not a quick, vicious crime, he said, committed by somebody taking advantage of a sudden opportunity, such as a drug addict or a casual burglar 'who stumbled on a house, burgled it, grabbed what they could, ran off to the nearest fence to get shot of it, and clouted the old lady in the face because she said she was going to tell'. Nor did it have sexual overtones. He was struck most strongly by the ordered aspects of the crime, and by the evidence that the criminal intended an 'extended intervention': this made it much more likely to have been committed by someone who was mature, experienced, capable of understanding finance, working out a complicated plan and seeing it through in phases. 'The conception of the plan is decidedly clever, done by someone who is able to delay gratification,' he said. 'Indeed, I would go so far as to say they were unlucky it was terminated as soon as it was. If it had not been for the presence of this friend, that lady could still be lying there to this present day, having had everything of value filched and fenced from the house.'

A person capable of such a plan would be likely to have a criminal history of theft, forgery, deception or burglary, he said, perhaps carrying a weapon on his burglary expeditions. The violence didn't play a strong part in the case, because it was not dwelt upon, enjoyed or extended in any way. But the efficient, ruthless and calculated nature of the violence indicated that the criminal was a psychopath – 'in its correct sense, as in someone who has no conscience or compunction but to follow and pursue their own aims and to manipulate others... It's not as the popular image would have it – some bloke walking along, baying at the moon, dragging his knuckles along the ground. It's not that sort of thing, it's someone who has no capacity for conscience, who is not going to worry at all about manipulating others for his own ends, who is completely cold and looks on people out there as things to be had.'

It was an impressive summary after a comparatively brief acquaintance with a very complex case. But the question was, would the police find it useful?

After Boon had departed for Leicester in his blue Rover, DCI Scott was full of enthusiasm and compliments: 'A lot of what he was saying makes sense, and a lot of it is what has come out of our briefings,' he said. 'But it's interesting to hear it from a non-policeman because it gives us reassurance. Here's a professional person coming in and looking at it from a different angle, and much of what we're doing is confirmed by what he said. It helps us to link in with the handwriting expert and some of the other scientists, and so overall it helps us to progress the inquiry... As I've always said, we use the profiler as just one tool in the senior investigating officer's toolbox. We're talking to the forensic scientists as well as the handwriting expert, and I think it's our job now as a management to start to put things together and prioritize. We do have a number of people who are arrested and on bail at the moment, and some of them do actually fit what the profiler said today. Julian said the offender would be likely to have visited the house and would feel comfortable going there at a certain time. Well, of course, the milkman has been arrested and he would visit the house and he would feel comfortable going there in the early hours of the morning, and that would fit with February when she was attacked on the doorstep. So there are some common threads between what Julian's telling us and what we already know.'

The unfortunate milkman, then, was still the main focus of police attention. But even before Boon's contribution to the case, Scott had already decided to do something that would change the course of the inquiry completely and put the milkman and the other suspects out of the frame for good: the power of television was about the enter the case of Miss Jean Barnes for the second time.

'A CUNNING AND RUTHLESS MAN' 4

*'If you ain't got a conscience,
you can't go to the shops and buy one.'*
Julian Boon

Crimewatch UK, the popular BBC TV programme presented by Nick Ross and Fiona Bruce, has become one of the fixtures of British television. It has a catchy, upbeat theme tune and specializes in reconstructions of sensational incidents, live interviews with senior officers, and heartfelt appeals and homilies by its resident stars. Opinions are divided about whether or not its appeal lies in idle curiosity and titillation, but the fact remains that it has played a part in solving a large number of serious crimes since it first went on the air in 1984. There have been 701 arrests as a direct consequence of the publicity it has given to more than 2,000 cases, and in the last four years alone the programme claims there have been eighteen convictions on the strength of evidence gained as a result of the programme. It is hardly surprising, therefore, that there is strong competition among senior investigating officers to get their cases on the programme and in front of the seven million people who watch it every month.

DCI Scott had already succeeded in getting a spot for the Jean Barnes case in the middle of September when he was anxious to trace Raymond Price, the man seen in the street saying his car had broken down and asking for money to get back home. Price had come forward, been eliminated from this inquiry, and prosecuted on other matters. It was now November, the forged documents had become one of the most promising lines of inquiry, and Scott was negotiating for a second appearance on the programme. He wanted to publicize the handwriting on the forgeries in the hope that someone would recognize it or recall how another elderly person had been targeted in a similar way to Miss Barnes. He had decided to do this independently of any advice from Julian Boon, and it turned out to be an inspired and effective move.

The new appearance on the show was scheduled for 16 November, and Scott travelled up to BBC Television Centre in west London with two senior members of his team, Detective Inspector Sally Simmonds and Detective Inspector Martyn Underhill, known as Tosh. On the way there, Scott explained what he hoped the TV appearance would achieve: 'Make Miss Barnes a person. Tell a bit about her. Get people interested in her and in solving the crime that was committed against her. Show the handwriting, the targeting, the bogus applications, the telephone call.' At the same time, he was aware of the risks of showing the handwriting on national television: the criminal, if he was as cunning as he appeared to be, would be alerted to its significance and might take steps to cover his tracks. It was a prescient fear on the part of Scott, but he felt the potential benefits far outweighed the possible disadvantages.

Boon had not been requested to advise the police on what to put into the *Crimewatch* programme, but an interviewer asked him to put his views on record anyway as he prepared to watch the programme at home in Leicester. He saw no purpose in appealing to the better nature of the offender, he said: 'You might just as well ask a shark not to bite, it's simply not possible.' A more fruitful approach, he thought, might be to try to play on the conscience of any associates the criminal might have. He also gave his psychologist's point of view about the programme's fascination for the public: 'First of all, I don't want to denigrate *Crimewatch* or the people who watch it, but the principal reason for watching it is not so they can say, oh gosh, I saw someone like that walking down the High Street and had my memory jogged and can help. They watch it because it's a series of little titillating vignettes of so-and-so being held hostage or held up and beaten brutally round the head. It's outwith their normal ken, it has novelty value, it has thrill – just like

Hannibal Lecter, it's fascinating because it's extreme, it's sensational, and above all it's real-life crime.'

When the police team arrived at BBC Television Centre, they were taken to the *Crimewatch* studio and introduced to Nick Ross. Soon they were caught up in the organized chaos of TV production: researchers tripping over cables, anxious floor managers, visits to make-up, fiddling with microphones, spats of temper, quick glances at the clock. For the Jean Barnes case, *Crimewatch* had decided to produce one of the mini-reconstructions that are part of its stock-in-trade. This was ideal for Scott's purpose of trying to present the victim as a real person. The officers had the opportunity to watch the filming of an actor playing the part of Miss Barnes receiving the phone call asking for details of her bank account, then telephoning the police to report the incident ('Why do you want all this, you've got it all... oh, very well... Now I want to report a very peculiar phone call to my house, a man...') During the rehearsals Ross, who has presented the programme from its inception, studied the samples of the bogus handwriting with interest, but expressed the opinion that viewers were more likely to remember other cases of targeting elderly people than they were to recognize the handwriting. Time would tell whether he was right.

The programme began with another distressing case, the murder of the research assistant Elizabeth Stacey by a colleague in the psychology department at University College, London, and continued with the story of the headmaster and a houseparent at a school in Hereford, who had been convicted of sexually assaulting some of their pupils. Then it moved to Miss Barnes, saying there were new clues and a new appeal. Soon the screen was filled with blown-up copies of the handwriting on the forged documents, and Ross carefully pointed out the salient characteristics. 'Look at the G there, which doesn't have a tail on it, whereas the Y does, and that's typical,' he emphasized. There was also the unusual habit of putting a colon between numbers on the cheques, the mixture of upper and lower case letters, the use of an ampersand that looked like a lower case E. If anyone else had suffered a burglary followed by a bogus telephone call and the unexpected opening of new bank accounts, he said, they should get in touch. Scott was interviewed and emphasized that the reward had now been increased to £30,000, half of it put up by the police and half by the relatives of Miss Barnes. Then the programme moved on to an appeal to put a name to 'the sunglasses gunman, a Jasper Carrot look-alike', and a burst of Bangla music introducing an item about an attack in east London. 'With your help we'll make life even safer,' concluded Ross. 'So don't have night-mares, do sleep well, goodnight...'

As Scott and his team set off back to Sussex from the BBC studios, he declared himself satisfied: the handwriting, the reward, the *modus operandi* – his three main concerns – had been successfully put over to a mass audience. Uppermost in his mind, however, was not the *Crimewatch* programme itself, but some interviews that had been done earlier in the day. In a businesslike piece of media exploitation, the Sussex team had realized that taking a case on to *Crimewatch* would be a story in its own right for local TV stations, especially since the reward had just been increased by £10,000. They had been interviewed at Burgess Hill police station in Sussex earlier in the day, before travelling up to the BBC, and an item trailing the *Crimewatch* programme had been broadcast locally in the early evening. Even before the programme went on air, people had been phoning the incident room of Operation School – the name given to the Barnes inquiry – in response to these local news bulletins. One man had telephoned to say that an elderly woman who had died six years earlier in Worthing had been the victim of forged notes, and more calls had come in as the evening went on. Scott was torn between excitement and the caution born of the slow progress in the investigation – a caution that meant his conversation was peppered with repeated references to 'peaks and troughs', which became something of a running joke. But he was already planning to go and consult Julian Boon about how the suspect should be interviewed – if any of the calls did indeed lead to a suspect.

One of the people who contacted the police was another elderly resident of Worthing, Mrs Audrey Ridpath. She remembered how, in the summer of 1996, she had been walking her dog Poppy along the beach and had got into conversation with another dog-walker, a small middle-aged woman with straight dark hair in what she called a pageboy cut.

Mrs Ridpath had happened to mention that she needed some work done on her house, and her new acquaintance had offered to ask her husband to come round and do it. Mrs Ridpath had agreed, and in due course one David Munley, a man in his fifties, had appeared at her house in St George's Road and been engaged to put up some shelves for her, do some painting on the back of the house, and repair the balcony. Next door lived Winifred Smith, a woman of ninety-three, and soon Munley had been doing some work for her as well. It hadn't been long, however, before Mrs Ridpath, who did book-keeping for Mrs Smith, had realized that someone had taken cheques from different parts of Mrs Smith's chequebook, written out sums totalling more than £4,000, and cashed them. When Mrs Smith had gone to the bank to query it, they had produced a letter purporting to come from her, saying she was going into a home and was authorizing her nephew, someone called 'David Armstrong', to run her affairs for her. The account had been closed, but there was no proper inquiry and no one was prosecuted.

Mrs Ridpath also thought that the handwriting she'd seen on the news bulletin, with its distinctive Gs and Ys, was the same as on the invoice for £80 that David Munley had presented to her three years earlier. The police quickly went round to interview and take a statement from her, taking away the invoice and her diary that contained notes of the dates of the events she described to them. ('You won't be able to read it,' she warned. 'I scribble it in bed.') Other leads, meanwhile, produced another suspicious case – that of Gerald Black of Flat 2, 12 Byron Road, who had died in November 1998. Someone had applied for a cash point card in his name and used it after his death, and had apparently also filled Mr Black's bin with rubbish in order to create the impression that he was still alive. For a while the police focused on the fact that the milkman, who was still a suspect and on bail over minor matters, had delivered milk there. Then they realized, after checks on the electoral register, that one of the occupants of Flat 3 in the same house was David Munley.

Scott was to say later that before the *Crimewatch* programme his inquiry had had a potentially huge suspect list of 30,000 people with a history of crimes of burglary and assault against elderly people. The phone call from Mrs Ridpath – one of nearly 200 calls prompted by the broadcast – had been the first mention of the name of David Munley, but they had rapidly put him first in the top six calls to be followed up after the programme because of a combination of factors, including the instinct and experience of the police officers on the inquiry and the similarity between the Barnes case and Munley's earlier attempt at forged handwriting. But a third and crucial factor was that a check through the criminal records system had shown that Munley's only previous conviction had been for fraud in 1983, and Boon had told them that the culprit's previous 'form' might involve fraud rather than the more obvious burglary and assault. He had also told them the criminal would be a mature man and would probably have targeted elderly people before. 'When we put all that together, Munley became the priority,' said Scott. 'Her phone call was a very exciting development.'

Spirits were now rising rapidly in the incident room of the inquiry as Scott and his officers looked at the 'Armstrong' letter and the invoice given to Mrs Ridpath and prepared to send them off to Birmingham to be compared with the handwriting in the case of Miss Barnes. 'It's so bloody uncanny,' said Scott. 'I mean, Nick Ross made such a big play on the Gs and they're there, aren't they? And the upper case and the lower case, yeah, the upper case Armstrong, and the "th" on "them"… I mean, it really is, as they say, sexy stuff. Even to the naked eye, let alone to an expert, there are some classic similarities. So, yes, we are on a high. But we have to keep our options open. We're going through a peak at the moment so let's hope there isn't a trough around the corner. It's interesting that the handwriting expert is saying it's somebody in their fifties – this man is in his fifties. It's interesting that the profiler says that it is somebody that would live in the area and would not be regarded as unusual walking up Tennyson Road. Putting it all together, he does fit both of the experts' suggestions. So it's only right and proper that we put him up on the priority list.'

The preliminary verdict came through quickly from the Birmingham handwriting expert, Kim Hughes. There were a number of similarities between the new samples and the Barnes documents that could not be there by chance, he said: the probability was that they had all been written by the same person. This allowed Scott to be quite definite in his view that David Munley was now the main suspect, and that the next thing to do was establish his identity and plan for an eventual arrest. Further inquiries showed that Munley had been separated from his wife since 1985, was living with a woman believed to be his mother, and was suffering from financial problems that included twelve county court orders for debt registered against him. It also turned out that Munley's flat in Byron Road – part of a poet's corner of Worthing streets – was only 250 yards away from Miss Barnes's house in Tennyson Road. The police felt that another of Boon's observations – the likely proximity of the offender to the victim – had proved correct. There was no reliable indication of how Munley might have come into contact with Jean Barnes or of the nature of their relationship, if any. But it emerged that he had a Jack Russell called J.R., which he and the woman took out for walks, and it was known that Miss Barnes had been in the habit of talking to dog walkers when she went out.

But some harder scientific evidence was beginning to emerge: Munley's fingerprints were in the criminal records system from his conviction in 1983, and they proved to match the prints found on the letter to Mrs Smith's bank from 'David Armstrong'. As for the bank card obtained in the name of the late Mr Black, the police had an image from a cash point camera where the card had been used, which they thought was Munley, but it was distorted by the camera angle: eventually they asked an expert in facial mapping to look at the image and a photograph of Munley, and he concluded there was a definite match. More pieces of the jigsaw began to fall into place – for example, the grey ponytail of the elderly woman he lived with, believed to be his mother, matched the description of the woman seen near Miss Barnes's house in March. The police became increasingly confident that they had the right man, and that they knew enough about him to begin planning his arrest.

Ten days after the *Crimewatch* programme, while the extra information about Munley was being gathered, Scott was anxious to organize a consultative meeting with Julian Boon to ask his advice about their plans for the arrest of Munley and the best way to interview him once he was in custody. They also decided to kill two birds with one stone and invite Kim Hughes, the handwriting expert from the forensic science laboratory in Birmingham, to the meeting. The earliest the two men could manage was three days later on Monday 29 November, when Scott and his team drove up to Leicester University and Hughes came across from Birmingham. Boon was in a jokey mood while waiting for the others: 'Well, if the suspect turned out to be someone who is a model character, who was highly wealthy, who had never so much as dropped a piece of litter in the street and was a committed member of the Salvation Army, that would cause modest shock, yes. But if someone has been identified and there are very good reasons and the case looks very strong, there would be an element of gratification that they had apprehended a very ruthless, dangerous individual... happy might not be the right word, but it's certainly good news.'

The officers brought Boon up to date on the discovery of Munley, whose description did not include membership of the Salvation Army, and were quick to acknowledge the role of the two experts. 'What's interesting for me,' said Scott, 'is that in the early days Kim is telling us that we should be looking for people in their fifties because of the style of the handwriting and you, Julian, are telling us we should look at people who have targeted elderly people in the past, and now we have a suspect who fits both profiles and we are quite excited about this.' They gave more documents for examination to Hughes, who asked them to collect as many samples as possible of Munley's handwriting from his flat on the day of the arrest, especially things like cheques that could be compared exactly with the forgeries already in his possession. He also asked them to get Munley to fill out a variety of application forms once he was in custody, again for direct comparison with the forgeries: then he left in a hurry for the laboratories in Birmingham.

The officers had discovered that Munley's birthday was imminent and asked Boon if this would be a bad day to arrest him. Boon thought that arresting him on his birthday wouldn't present particular problems because family events of this kind wouldn't be important to someone with his type of uncaring personality: 'Blowing candles off the cake ain't going to be his style.' As for interviewing him, Boon's view was that the best way to get him to talk and prevent him clamming up would be to take a low-key approach, without drama or flashing lights or raised voices. He also repeated that, since the suspect was, in his view, a manipulative psychopath, there was no point in using one of the traditional weapons in the policeman's arsenal – the appeal to conscience and an invitation for the suspect to do himself a favour by 'getting it off his chest'.

On the other hand, if the woman believed to be his mother was playing a part in the crimes, Boon thought it might be productive to appeal to a sense of common decency in her. It also occurred to him that the absence of violence in Munley's previous history might mean that he saw himself as a sophisticated fraudster or con-man, rather than a brute: 'I think he would feel resentful if it were put to him, did he get a thing out of beating up old ladies? I don't think he would be comfortable at all with having the focus on the violence… what most of us have agreed on is that this offender will undoubtedly do it again, particularly if he gets away with it this time and he begins to consider he's invincible.' He speculated that when Munley was arrested, there might be some pseudo-anger, but there would be a cold and callous response underneath and no capacity for genuine remorse. And he reflected again on psychopaths and the difficulty of getting them to change: 'All the research on psychopathy shows that it is remarkably difficult to alter this kind of personality. Therapeutic intervention is completely useless, ineffective. While they can pretend that they have changed very successfully, the research literature shows that it is remarkably difficult to intervene. It is an enduring personality. If you ain't got a conscience, you can't go to the shops and buy one.'

The police team thanked him and departed southwards to continue their exhaustive preparation and planning for taking their psychopath out of society. They declared Boon had again been helpful, but declined to elaborate on what their interview strategy would be: they would simply be asking the suspect some 'open questions' about what he had been doing and giving him a chance to explain himself. Three days later, after extensive planning, they raided Munley's flat: it was at 7 a.m. on 2 December 1999 – his fifty-sixth birthday.

It was a large operation involving two team of officers: one to arrest the suspect and the woman they thought was his mother and whisk them off to different police stations, and one to seal off the flat and its surroundings and start an intensive search for evidence. The idea was to get the suspect off the scene without allowing him to see the search team waiting to go into the flat. But the operation was also as low-key and undramatic as possible, following Boon's suggestion, with the minimum of drama and disturbance. Within ten minutes Munley, a short man with unkempt grey hair and beetling eyebrows, was on his way to Crawley in a van, stunned and silent. His 'mother', to everyone's surprise, turned out to be his ex-wife Judith, who was eighteen years older than him and had allowed him, some time after their separation, to return and sleep on the sofa in her flat. She was taken to the local police station in Worthing to be questioned separately.

As Scott waited anxiously for Munley to arrive in Crawley, he was more forthcoming about the interview strategy. The plan was to hold very little back – 'We want to tell him the evidence we've got and invite him to comment on it and explain it... we want him to know that we mean business. He is obviously a very cunning and ruthless man and we'll have to deal with that in the interview, but we can just put the questions to him in an order that is logical and hope that when he starts to see the links that we've made, he will talk to us.' When the van finally arrived, blue lights flashing, Munley was escorted into the custody suite, his clothes were taken from him, and he was given a white paper zip-fronted suit to wear – normal procedure in serious cases where any item of the suspect's clothing could yield vital evidence when examined carefully in the forensic laboratory. But when the police doctor saw Munley, he said he had a headache and hadn't slept: he was given some Coproximol tablets and told he could sleep for three hours before the interviews began. The officers paced around the station, champing at the bit, suspecting that Munley's headache was merely a ruse to gain time to think. A press release about the arrest was issued.

Back at Worthing, DI Sally Simmonds and the officers interviewing Judith Munley found, to their surprise and pleasure, that she was co-operative from the start and prepared to talk freely: Munley, it seemed, may have been defrauding her as well as his various alleged victims. She said that he had persuaded her to let him take over her finances, and after she agreed to this, her chequebook had gone missing, and she had received a letter from the bank saying she was overdrawn. The officers also discovered that Munley had been lying to her about his employment and his whereabouts in recent days. As the interviews with her continued, the search team were going through the flat with a fine-toothed comb. Some bank statements and pawn tickets had already been found, but no documents with the all-important samples of Munley's handwriting on them: perhaps Munley had indeed seen the *Crimewatch* programme, realized how important handwriting would be if the police were to catch up with him, and made sure there was nothing lying about the flat that had been written by him. Out in the garden the search team found a key, but it was quickly established that it did not fit the lock at 9 Tennyson Road. Two more keys were found concealed in the bathroom, and they also proved negative. Progress was slow and frustrating.

Ten hours after the arrest, the two specialist police interviewers at Crawley finally got down to work with David Munley. He denied knowing Miss Barnes, denied having been in her house, and denied any involvement in the murder: it was clear this was going to be a long haul. The two police interviewers had been told about Boon's recommendations on the most fruitful way to approach a character like Munley, but there was no direct consultation with him on the telephone in the breaks between the interview sessions: the two officers were specialists who probably felt no need of such continuing advice, and it would have been unlikely that Boon would have been available on demand during a normal working day. During one of the breaks, Scott was in the kitchen of Crawley police station wearily describing the stalemate in the interviews when his second-in-command, DI Underhill, bustled into the room with the latest update from Worthing. His expression and body language were unmistakably upbeat, and here, at last came the golden moments of the investigation.

'When they searched the flat,' said Underhill, 'they went into communal areas of the house, because the warrant covers the whole house. There's a communal cupboard at the bottom of the stairs which everybody can use – it's a meter cupboard, it's huge, and there's a lot of stuff in there. First thing they find is a suitcase, and in the suitcase is his birth certificate and his diaries. So we've got his handwriting. Then in the suitcase there's lots of clothing, and we're not sure if that's women's clothing. Then they find a tent spike, and bear in mind that could be the murder weapon. Then they lift the suitcase out and there's a loose floorboard, and then it gets better. Under the floorboard is a civil service membership card...'

'Whose?' interrupted Scott.

'Jean Barnes.'

'Great.'

'And a broken green and mauve candlestick which we think came from her house...'

'So we've got Jean Barnes's civil service card in his house under the floorboards. That's what you're telling me?'

'Yes,' replied Underhill.

'It's coming together, Martyn, isn't it? Which is good, we've just got to press on. We've got to get back to Sally, thank her very much indeed and make sure the team presses on, because it's been ten or twelve bloomin' hours already. Oh, I think I need a cup of tea. Tosh, that was worth waiting for.'

There was more to come. The search team had obtained Munley's phone bill which indicated that on 15.24 p.m. on 23 April 1999 he – or someone in his flat – had made a telephone call to Miss Barnes's number: almost certainly the call in which she had been asked for details about herself which were then used for the fraudulent applications for a bank account and cheque card. Underhill was unable to stop himself grinning as he related the news. 'It's coming together,' said Scott. 'We've got the property, we've got the phone call, and we've got the handwriting. It's a good start.'

Meanwhile, in the interview suite, David Munley, in the presence of his solicitor, was slowly but surely beginning to incriminate himself. He was denying involvement in the false letters and applications involving both Miss Barnes and Winifred Smith, but was refusing to give fresh samples of his handwriting. He was admitting that he knew Mrs Ridpath, but said he had always been paid in cash – he was unaware that the police had by now recovered from the bank the cheque that Mrs Ridpath had made out to him. He was saying that items he'd sold to local antique shops, which the police knew had belonged to Miss Barnes, had been the property of an aunt of his who had died. As for Mr Black, he admitted to helping him when he collapsed and was taken to hospital, but he'd never used his card or PIN number: again, Munley was unaware that the police were establishing his connection with the card by facial mapping. And when he was shown a letter to the county court about his debts, he agreed it was his handwriting – not knowing that the writing had already been linked by the experts to the writing seen in the forged Smith and Barnes documents. 'We've now got him,' said Scott. 'We probably want to put one more interview in tonight before we put him to bed.'

Before closing down for the day, Scott visited the superintendent in charge of Crawley police station to warn him that he would be applying for an extension of the twenty-four-hour time limit within which suspects must normally be released or charged: this was so that the interviews could continue and more challenging questions about such things as the civil service card, the candlestick and the phone call could be put to him. The team at Worthing also needed to resume their search in the morning, using metal detectors to check the garden for buried objects. The superintendent indicated that he would be ready to sanction the extension early the next morning.

So now they seemed to have their man, how valuable was Boon's profile? As Scott wound down at the end of a hectic day, he was asked how the interviews had matched what Boon had anticipated. He replied: 'Okay, what's interesting is that Julian said that he might not talk to us, but he has. Other than that, much of what Julian said is actually what we're finding with him… his anticipation of the kind of character we're going to be talking to has proved correct. He's not concerned about his birthday at all, it hasn't been an issue with him. He is lying, and he is thinking about his answers. He's very calm, as Julian said, very calculating, he's trying to make a bit of a joke with the officers and trying to say, this is not me, it's a big mistake, I'm a painter and decorator and I don't know what you're talking about. He doesn't seem worried at all – I'll probably give Julian a ring as well and let him know how things are going.'

The next morning Munley's approach began to change as the more challenging points were put to him: he stopped making jokes, put on an impassive expression, and repeated the same stonewalling answer, like a minister at question time in Parliament: 'I refer you to the answer I made earlier.' After a total of five and a half hours of interviews, on 4 December 1999 David Munley was charged with the murder of Jean Barnes and remanded in custody by Crawley magistrates to await his trial. A few weeks later, another two important pieces of evidence fell into place: the specks on the piece of tissue found in one of the downstairs rooms of 9 Tennyson Road were, in fact, tiny droplets of blood. The DNA from these droplets was found to match the DNA taken from the blood sample given by David Munley after he was charged with the killing; and a shoeprint found on linoleum in the initial examination of the house turned out to match one of Munley's shoes.

Early in the year 2000, as the police prepared the papers on the case for the Crown Prosecution Service, they invited Boon down to Sussex to look at some of the tape recordings of Munley being interviewed. This was not something they were required to do – there are few rigid procedures in police–profiler relations. But it was clear that relations were so good that they wanted to go out of their way to thank him for his help and make it clear that they looked forward to working with him again (since the Jean Barnes case Boon has in fact been back to help Sussex police on a series of rapes). Scott began by repeating that the profile, combined with the input from the handwriting experts, had allowed the team to give priority to half a dozen of the scores of calls that had been received after the second *Crimewatch* programme. Fortunately events had shown they were the right calls to prioritize, and the process of focusing on them had speeded up the inquiry and produced the arrest of Munley. The process of selection had also saved the police many thousands of pounds that they might otherwise have spent sending officers round to interview callers who had nothing of real relevance to tell them.

Thanks weren't the only motive for the meeting, however: Scott also wanted to offer Boon the opportunity to match his profile of the offender – drawn up without any specific knowledge of the man – with the personality and performance of the real person they had arrested and interrogated. The feedback might help Boon to hone his skills, as it were, and give him further thoughts useful to the police. Boon was also told about something he didn't yet know: the important discovery following the arrest and charging of Munley that antique furniture and paintings – some marked on the back with 'Ricketts', which was Miss Barnes's mother's maiden name – had been sold to five dealers in Worthing in September 1998. This was the most decisive evidence that Munley had been successfully targeting his victim and stealing from her house for at least ten months before the murder, either on the few occasions when she went out or while she was asleep in her upstairs bedroom. They had also found two stolen passports in his ex-wife's flat, in one of which the photograph had been replaced with his own, as if he had been preparing a possible escape route abroad.

The tapes that Boon watched confirmed how Munley's attitude had changed as the questions became harder. They also confirmed a pattern predicted by Boon when interviewed a few days earlier in Leicester about what he expected the tapes to show. He had said that Munley, providing he was encouraged to tell all he knew in a relaxed atmosphere, would talk freely until he was presented with incontrovertible evidence and the pressure increased; he would then most likely switch to 'no comment' and feigned incomprehension, which would indicate his probable guilt. In the first tape, Munley was indeed relaxed, making expansive gestures and trying to share a joke with the police. But he began to tense up when the police asked him how the tip of the blade of a carving knife, the rest of which was found in his jacket, came to be found in the space underneath the floorboards of the meter cupboard where Miss Barnes's identity card had also been found. At first Munley insisted that he had never been in the cupboard, but then admitted that he had gone in there a few times and the blade must have fallen out of his pocket. As if realizing that he had compromised himself, he then stopped smiling altogether and retreated into saying nothing or referring the interviewers to his previous answers. The police challenged him on twenty-six points in all, using the mantra-like question: 'How can that be?' Munley was unable to give a satisfactory response to any of the questions, including those about the handwriting evidence, the fingerprints, the telephone calls, and the fact that the print of his shoe matched the one found in Miss Barnes's house.

Boon was visibly fascinated and often amused as he watched the interviews progress.

He noted how Munley started out as 'a very cool customer', elaborating and embellishing his answers, holding his palms open as if eager to co-operate. There was then a 'sea-change' as he was asked about his fingerprints on the letter that opened the bogus 'Armstrong' account. The police comparison between Munley's stonewalling answers and the behaviour of ministers draw an enthusiastic and politically revealing response from Boon: 'Yeah, actually that's a very good analogy, because if you look at Tony Blair's face at Question Time, what we call the non-verbal communication is very uncomfortable indeed. And if there's a question which comes up which shafts him, the look in his eyes is one of terror, almost. It's more like someone being hunted than the confident image he tries to portray.' He noted Munley's head dropping down, his defensive gestures, as he was pinned down about the sales of the antiques and his earlier lies about selling them on behalf of a deceased aunt. 'He's not a happy bunny, is he?' said Boon. And when Munley was asked to spell Mrs Ridpath's name, and spelt it Redpath as in the receipt he'd given her, Boon described him as 'adopting the so-called IRA tactics – gazing at the wall straight opposite, giving absolutely no trace of emotion whatsoever, quite the different boy from the one flicking his hands around and cheesily grinning'.

Halfway through his viewing of the tapes, the police asked Boon what he expected Munley's defence to be and were surprised to hear him say that he expected him to change his plea to guilty, possibly just before his trial. Boon's argument was that in all things, Munley was likely to make a hard-headed calculation of his own self-interest and take 'the line of least resistance'. If he began to feel that the evidence was stacked so high against him that he had no chance of being found not guilty, and that he would get five years more in jail if he'd been shown to be lying in court throughout a long and expensive trial, then he would abandon a not guilty plea and possibly even 'turn on the waterworks' and affect great remorse. Some people, Boon went on, would stick to a not-guilty plea, even in the face of overwhelming evidence, because a confession would not square with their self-image or might alienate their relatives –

paedophiles, for example, often spend years in jail trying to argue that the whole case against them was a mistake: 'But in this instance, this man does not have a self-image where he cares a tinker's what people think of him… I think his self-image is one of a professional criminal.'

Interviewed after viewing the tapes, Boon awarded himself a reasonably high mark out of ten: 'It was entirely commensurate with the sort of person profiled earlier on. And his reactions fit very clearly with someone who does not have anything by way of a conscience. He does not have anyone's interests but his own in mind, and truth is not something which is of any importance to him. I am confident he will follow the line of least resistance, as I suggested. In my view, he is a psychopath – I don't see that one could come to any other conclusion whatsoever. But the good news – and I put that in heavy inverted commas – is that he's not a sadistic psychopath. That is a very dangerous combination. I mean, you could have people who are out of touch with reality, maybe paranoid schizophrenics, who can enact some pretty violent crimes. They don't come under the category of psychopathy. But this was a very systematic, planned, cold-blooded attack, and to do it to a defenceless old lady, you have to have a very special absence of a human quality, of empathy, of conscience.

'One thing I would say about him, though, is that there aren't delusions of excess or grandeur. On that tape he seemed to me to be relatively in touch with the scale of what was against him, and can see the potency of the evidence which seems to be stacked against him… He's on a one-way ticket off and he ain't going to come back.' It was a typical Boon remark, and he capped it with a mock-recantation of his earlier strictures about *Crimewatch*: 'I think *Crimewatch* is a wonderful programme! And everybody watches it for just the right reasons, and we all see what good value it is!'

David Munley's trial began at Lewes Crown Court on 14 November 2000 with a plea of not guilty to murder, eight counts of burglary and six of forgery. The case had cost £600,000 to bring to court, and 900 statements had been taken by the police. DCI Scott had earlier offered a hostage to fortune with the remark: 'I share Julian's view that there will be a guilty plea at the end of the day.' Shortly after the start of the trial Boon was told about the not guilty plea and called it 'disappointing intelligence'. But he emphasized that it wasn't his role to say whether Munley was guilty or not – 'merely that if he's guilty, the reason he won't be saying so isn't because he's forgotten he's done it, isn't because he's prancing around in some fugue state. It's quite simply because he's wanting to save his own skin and he thinks he'll get away with it. In some ways this is commensurate with the sort of brass-necked character that would be willing to undertake such a crime for mercenary gain. And it may be that he has underestimated the might of the evidence against him.'

The prosecution case was painstakingly presented through nearly eighty witnesses, including several antique dealers who had come forward after seeing press and TV coverage of the arrest of David Munley. They told how, before and after the death of Jean Barnes, he had sold them various valuable items that were demonstrably hers, some bearing a label from 1931 showing her mother's maiden name of Ricketts. The objects, eventually recovered from places as near as Leicester and as far away as mainland Europe, included paintings, a superb bracket clock, and a Davenport desk with a secret compartment.

But the trial lasted a shorter time than expected because the defence, by contrast, called only one witness: David Munley himself, dressed smartly in a grey suit with his thinning grey hair neatly brushed. He described how he had been born in 1943 in Bedlington, Northumberland, been a promising footballer until he sustained a severe knee injury, and was still obsessively interested in football. Between 1984 and 1991 he had had a job fireproofing buildings, and when his employers went into receivership he had bought the fire protection division and operated it himself. But the business had failed with debts of £18,000, and he had sold his house to pay them and started doing occasional building or gardening work supplemented by dealing in antiques. He denied ever going into Miss Barnes's house, saying the DNA evidence must have been planted by the police and that many thousands of shoes like his own had been manufactured. He also denied having lifted the floorboard in the meter cupboard of the house where he had lived in his wife's flat, and said that cigarette ends found under the floorboards with traces of DNA from his saliva on them must have been swept in there by the cleaner. His sales of Miss Barnes's former property were explained by elaborate and implausible stories, three of which the police had to hurriedly check out and discredit over the weekend.

Apart from this, none of the denials came as a surprise to Scott and his team as they sat in court after giving their own evidence, worrying that the jury might fasten on the fact that there was no single incontrovertible piece of evidence that Munley had killed Miss Barnes – a murder weapon with her blood on one end of it, for example, and his fingerprints on the other. What did come as a surprise, however, was an admission by Munley that he had forged the letter to Mrs Smith's bank and three of her cheques. It was unclear what his strategy was in doing this: possibly he was just hoping that an admission to lesser charges might soften the jury towards him on the main charge of murder. The admission cheered the police, however, because the handwriting experts had drawn a link between the handwriting on the Smith documents and that on the Barnes forgeries. For the court, the admission was a mild inconvenience, because it had been decided at the start of the trial to exclude the Smith forgery charges, among various others that did not directly relate to Jean Barnes, from an indictment that already had fifteen counts on it. Munley was, in effect, admitting to charges for which he was not being tried.

On 6 December, the seventeenth day of the trial, Mr Justice Alliott sent the jury out at 10.15 a.m. and the various observers of the trial entered that curious limbo of waiting that might end in three minutes' or three days' time. Twice the jury of nine women and three men came back with queries and requests, but at 3.15 they reassembled and the forewoman was asked for the verdict on the murder charge. 'Guilty,' came the reply. Munley, who had looked grey but calm in the closing stages of the trial, closed his eyes, put his face in his hands for a few seconds, then stared at the floor as the same verdict came for seven of the eight burglary charges and all six forgery charges. Possibly the most emotional person in the courtroom at this point was DCI Scott, who wiped away a few tears as eighteen months of his life reached the desired conclusion.

The charges about Mrs Smith were then put to Munley, who pleaded guilty; the remaining charges were left on the file. The defence counsel,

Christopher Kinch, asked the court to take into account Munley's age and 'relatively creditable background'. The judge said he was prepared to accept that the killing had not been premeditated, but called it callous in the extreme: 'To let her lie where she fell while you continued your depredations was beyond belief. You have showed not a flicker of acceptance of guilt or remorse.' The sentence was mandatory life imprisonment for the murder, five years to run concurrently for each burglary, and four years to run concurrently for each forgery. The judge paid special tribute to Mrs Ridpath for responding to the TV bulletin about the *Crimewatch* programme: at the time of writing the police were proposing that she should receive £25,000 of the reward, with the remaining £5,000 split between two public-spirited antique dealers.

In front of the pale stone colonnades of the court, Jeremy Winn, Miss Barnes's sixty-year-old nephew, paid tribute to his aunt in a tremulous voice, calling Munley a 'swine' and hoping he would come to regret what he'd done during his long years in prison. Scott, dry-eyed once more, thanked everyone who had contributed to solving the case: 'David Munley tried one lie too far – he tried to fool all the people all of the time and the court did not accept that.' And as he and his team swept along the pavement towards the nearest pub, he paid a final compliment to the contribution of Julian Boon. 'We took what Julian told us,' he said, 'and at the end of the day we knocked on the door of the right man.'

FRIDAY THE 13TH

5

'The facts I have to build up are psychological facts,
which are real enough but very hard to demonstrate.'
Richard Badcock

When Joseph Scudder returned home from an evening shift as a packer at a local factory, he was perplexed to find that he couldn't get his key into the mortise lock of the ground-floor flat he shared with his fiancée. The flat was in Cricketers Close in Erith, an unlovely riverside town in northern Kent flanked by the marshes of the Thames estuary. For some reason another key had already been inserted into the lock from the inside and left there, immovable. After scrabbling around without success for a while, he began to feel alarmed and decided to go outside to look in the window of their flat.

Six hours earlier, he'd said goodbye to Yvonne Killian, the pretty, dark-haired law clerk with whom he'd bought the flat two years earlier. They were an established couple who'd known each other for five years and were intending to get married as soon as they could afford it. She'd returned from her working day at the magistrates' court in Bromley, a London suburb a few miles to the south, and they'd chatted and drunk tea together before he'd left for work at about 7 o'clock. Yvonne had a second job, doing occasional night shifts as a data clerk at the Lynx Express depot in nearby Dartford. She was intending to go to bed and get a few hours' sleep before going to work there at 1 a.m. Joseph was planning to come home and give her a lift to the depot. It was all a normal evening routine for them, and nothing had seemed out of the ordinary when Joseph left.

Joseph went back out through the main doorway of the block of flats, which was controlled by an intercom and a numerical pad where residents could key in their security code. It was about one o'clock in the morning, the dank March darkness lit by the flat yellow light of the sodium street lamps, and he made his way over the slippery grass to the front of the flat. Several lights were burning inside, and to his alarm he found that the glass of one of the living room windows had been smashed and the window was hanging open. And when he reached in to pull the curtain aside he was confronted with a scene of the utmost depravity and violence which was to blight his life for ever.

Directly in front of him was the dead body of Yvonne, propped up on the sofa as if put on display for deliberate and macabre effect. Her top and skirt were pulled up, her legs were spread apart and a pair of tights was wrapped tightly around her neck. Whoever had raped and strangled her had also made a crude attempt to set fire to the scene, using vodka from a bottle left by the body, but had succeeded only in charring part of the sofa near Yvonne's head, scorching some of her hair and burning her face badly. Joseph, deeply shocked, managed to climb through the window and find a towel to cover the violated body of the woman he loved. Then he phoned for the police. He had just discovered one of the most brutal and twisted sex crimes of the decade, committed on Friday, 13 March 1998.

The area of Cricketers Close was quickly sealed off and the routines of a big murder inquiry set in motion: detailed forensic examination of the scene, door-to-door inquiries, interviews with friends of the couple, members of their families and work colleagues. The man in charge of the hunt was Detective Chief Inspector Chris Horne of the Metropolitan Police, a forty-eight-year-old veteran of the crimes and misdemeanours of south-east London, based at Shooter's Hill police station on the old road to Dover. He was a highly experienced and thoughtful officer, bespectacled, of medium build, trying hard to give up smoking. His track record included solving twenty-one murders in his eleven years as a detective inspector, and colleagues thought highly of him as an old-style, hands-on policeman. In interviews he described the crime as 'particularly nasty' and asked for anyone who knew Yvonne to come forward so police could build up a picture of her lifestyle, and work out who might have killed her. He speculated that she might have been killed by a disgruntled client – perhaps somebody who had taken against her in a divorce case.

One of the first steps by the police, however, was to arrest Joseph Scudder within twelve hours of the murder. He had been the last person to see Yvonne alive, and there was always a possibility of the kind of tensions and jealousies that can lead to domestic murders. He voluntarily gave a blood sample so his DNA could be checked against any traces of bodily fluids left behind by the attacker, and he was released on bail while the results were awaited. It was an extra trauma for a young man already suffering shock and bereavement, but the police felt they had no choice and Joseph later acknowledged that they had to do it.

Local inquiries failed to produce much useful information. There were no reports of screaming or other disturbances, but one of the neighbours in the block of flats had heard three loud thumps at about 7.30 p.m. He'd gone outside to investigate and seen nothing suspicious. Reports from other local people led the police to appeal for information about an unshaven young man aged between twenty-five and thirty, six foot tall and wearing a khaki jacket and mushroom-coloured jeans. He'd been seen at the end of Cricketers Close at 6.30 on the evening of the 13th, but it was a line of inquiry that was to lead nowhere.

The picture built up by police of Yvonne's character and habits was also quite unhelpful. She had been born in Ireland, one of three children, and seemed to be a hard-working and conscientious young woman, intelligent and perhaps a little naive. She was studying part-time at Westminster Law College, working for a legal agency the rest of the time, and hoping to become a solicitor's clerk. She appeared to be living a settled life with Joseph, with no reports of any affairs, although Yvonne's mother was later to say that the couple had rows and arguments and that he had a hot temper. It seemed Yvonne was the driving force in the relationship with Joseph, who had less education and could read and write only with difficulty. Perhaps the most notable aspect of the young woman's life was an earlier family tragedy: her father Daniel had been killed in 1981 when she was only five years old. A man who was later convicted of manslaughter had pushed Daniel down a flight of stairs in a pub in Rotherhithe where the Killian family was living at the time. Horne rapidly ruled out any connection between that incident and Yvonne's murder.

The post-mortem was conducted by Dr Dick Shepherd of St George's Hospital Medical School in Tooting, who found that Yvonne had first been partly strangled from behind by someone's right hand before the tights were wrapped around her neck from the front to kill her. He discovered that she had been brutally raped, and subjected to oral sex, before or around the time of her death. He also thought it was probable that she had been killed in the bedroom of the flat before being moved to the living room and propped up on the sofa. The fact that there were no wounds of the kind that Yvonne might have suffered in the course of defending herself raised the question of whether at least some of the sexual activity may have been consensual. But perhaps the most encouraging thing for the investigators was that the fire started on the sofa had failed to destroy the semen found on Yvonne's breast and in her mouth. This meant there were strong hopes of recovering samples of the attacker's DNA, using modern techniques to express its virtually unique pattern as a string of figures. The sample could be compared with those on the national database of DNA from convicted criminals, or with those requested from any list of suspects the police might compile.

Like the results of the post-mortem, the examination of the scene failed to produce information that would indicate a clear sequence of events. It was intriguing, but confusing. Outside the window of the flat were two piles of human faeces that were likely to have come from the attacker in the throes of excitement or nervousness, and these were another potential source of DNA. There was a sleeping bag lying empty on the grass. Scene-of-crime officers dusting the windows for finger-prints found instead something very unusual: what looked like an earprint on one of the intact panes of glass. And there was a fence post that had apparently been used to break the window and matched another lying in the bushes nearby, suggesting the criminal might have known the location or checked it out in advance.

Inside the flat there were signs of a struggle in the bedroom, with a footprint and smears of faeces on the bed and living room floor that investigators thought might have resulted from the spontaneous evacuation of the bowels that strangulation can produce. In the living room Yvonne's bra lay neatly folded on the sofa, and various other items of women's clothing and underwear were spread about, including several pairs of tights. One of the most significant discoveries was that a Sony Playstation belonging to Joseph had been stolen, along with several games, and one immediate theory was that these might have been carried at first in the sleeping bag that had been found discarded outside the flat. These items were discovered later the same evening by a group of Boy Scouts, placed neatly under a tree in the churchyard of Christ Church, Erith, about a quarter of a mile away. It looked as if they might have been put there to be collected later, although the confusing thing was that there was no apparent attempt to hide them.

In the early days of the investigation, Joseph remained the main suspect and there was some debate about whether he should be charged, not least because the pathologist considered it possible Yvonne had been killed as late as 1 a.m., when Joseph would have been back from work. But Horne held back, waiting for the results of the DNA test on his blood sample. Another possibility was that the killer could be someone else in her circle of friends and acquaintances. Failing that, the crime might be an attack by a stranger – either a stalker, a sex attacker or a burglar who had lost control of the situation. It emerged that Yvonne's bag had been turned out and her mobile phone and £40 taken, as well as the Playstation: the phone was later found by a member of the public, opening yet another line of inquiry that proved frustrating. But other valuable items in the flat, including more money, had not been taken, which suggested that the principal motive was something other than stealing things. It was all a mystery, a jumble of confusing and contradictory elements, and the officers on the case were having trouble working out a coherent version of what had happened in the little ground-floor flat in Cricketers Close. Ten days after the discovery of Yvonne's body, Horne decided it was time to seek some outside advice.

He hadn't used a profiler on any previous investigation, but two years before he had attended a course at the police staff college at Bramshill in Hampshire on the management of scenes of serious crimes. The course had impressed upon him that crimes where there was an element of uncertainty about the criminal's motives and actions were precisely those where a profiler might be able to help. Horne now phoned the National Crime Faculty, the unit at Bramshill that advises police forces on major investigations; they conducted a rapid review of the situation and recommended the profiler they considered best suited to the job. It was Dr Richard Badcock, who at the time was still employed at the regional secure unit in Wakefield and had, over the years, become one of the country's foremost offender profilers, with a special knowledge of sex murderers.

When he received the call summoning him to the Yvonne Killian case, Badcock adjusted his diary to make a trip at short notice to south-east London. DCI Horne met him at Shooter's Hill police station to give him a general description of the crime and show him statements, maps and photographs. It was at this first meeting that Badcock made the first of several references to the unrealistic expectations that some people have about profilers: 'What both I and the police are desperate for is an understanding of the case. What I try to provide is information about it from the psychological perspective. It's not to play some sort of second-rate detective and say whodunnit. And our biggest problem is *Cracker*, because that is what he does and he does it effortlessly, and he manages to combine flawed but engaging humanity with reassuringly infallible professional judgements. He turns up for fifteen seconds on the screen, has a casual look around, gets drunk and is able to work out exactly what happened.'

At this first meeting, Horne pointed out the possibility that Scudder might be the culprit and said they might require advice from Badcock on how he should be questioned if he was interviewed again. But right from the start Badcock was sceptical and encouraged them to hold back from charging Scudder. Instead he wanted to hear more information about the couple and their lifestyle, and said on the way home from the meeting that he was intrigued by the case, especially the 'sense of development' in the crime, the unusual method of strangulation and the comparative tidiness of the way things had been done. Particularly puzzling was that fact that Yvonne appeared to have taken off the clothes she had worn during the day, and then got partially re-dressed: she may have done this in order to answer the door, and one implication of this might have been that the sexual activity had at first been consensual. It was therefore vital to establish if there had been any pre-existing relationship between the victim and the attacker. Badcock again used one of his favourite images, comparing the crime to a sentence in which the sense of the various elements only becomes clear when the other elements have been put in place and the context is complete.

This initial meeting was a long one and there was no time to take Badcock to visit the crime scene. But soon afterwards he made a second visit to south London, and he and Horne were driven with other members of the investigating team to Cricketers Close in Erith. At first they looked at the flat where the murder had taken place from the outside, following the path down the side of the building that had been taken by Joseph Scudder when he made his gruesome discovery. Here were the broken window, the places where the sleeping bag and fence post had been found, the patches of excrement left behind after samples had been taken for DNA analysis. Then they followed a short cut from the block of flats to the nearby main road, and across it to the churchyard where the Sony Playstation and games were found, speculating that the offender must have had a detailed knowledge of the locality; then they returned for a close look at the interior of the flat.

Every room had been exhaustively examined by forensic teams, and the walls were damaged and discoloured by the use of powerful and dangerous chemicals that can reveal the slightest fingerprint or mark that might be of evidential value. Otherwise the flat was still in substantially the same condition as it was when Yvonne's body had been removed nearly two weeks previously. The bed was still stained and dishevelled, the sitting room strewn randomly with clothes and shoes; her legal file from her last day at work was sitting on top of the fridge, and lying around was the vodka bottle that Badcock thought might have been used to inflict some of the injuries to the victim's private parts. The pathologist, Dr Dick Shepherd, joined the group, and they moved through the flat, talking quietly about the position of various objects and pieces of clothing, trying to imagine a sequence of events that would make sense of what they saw. They looked at Yvonne's underwear and the several pairs of tights, which were quite widely scattered round the flat, a Valentine's card in the living room and some soft porn magazines.

Badcock raised a number of questions the police had not mentioned as he tried to understand more of Yvonne's personality and the nature of her relationships: his interest in the magazines, for example, and in the style of Yvonne's underwear and the frequency with which she changed it, were directed at understanding how she related to Scudder and whether she might have been having an affair with anyone else. They discussed the faecal staining in the flat as a guide to where she had been killed; Dr Shepherd repeated his view that most of the sexual activity had taken place before or around the time of death, and that Yvonne had been killed in the bedroom and moved to the living room. It was a melancholy and slightly voyeuristic scene: a group of men dispassionately fingering and discussing the intimate wreckage of two people's lives, with the occasional joke in dubious taste to release their nervousness and self-consciousness.

Before the visit to the scene of the crime, Badcock had already formed the opinion from discussions with police and written statements that Scudder – still the main suspect – had not been involved in the crime. Now he was even more definite about it, not least because there was no plausible reason why Scudder would have removed his own Playstation from the flat and placed it in the churchyard. 'He doesn't have the need or the right psychological attitude or the right degree of subtlety to create a false position in this way,' said Badcock. Another of his early conclusions had been that there was something very deliberate and calculated about the placing of the body, and now he felt even more strongly that it had been put on display to express a sense of triumph over both Yvonne and Joseph, and that therefore the offender knew one or both of them in some way. This seemed to be reinforced by the fact that the Playstation had been very precious to Joseph, and it had been taken while other valuable objects had been left behind – apparently another calculated act of spite. 'The essence of it is to take things away from Yvonne and from Joe,' said Badcock. 'The motivating force, if you like, is likely to be envy.'

Once he had returned to Wakefield and reflected for a few days, he gave a more considered view of the sequence of events: 'At the moment it seems likely Yvonne was inside the flat, was undressed, somebody rang the door or used the intercom, maybe she got dressed hurriedly and opened the door. We know that dried flowers in the hallway were knocked over, so quite possibly there was a scuffle when her assailant came in. Thereafter there was an exchange in the bedroom, and that involved both conversation and sexual activity, and it looks as if there was physical violence on the bed.

'It looks as though the violence was confined to the bed area, and as far as we can tell the disturbance is confined to the bed and bedding. It seems likely that Yvonne was attacked in there and strangled. After her death she was carried through to the lounge area, put on the floor initially, and then the body was placed carefully on the settee, and it was placed in a specific way. Her upper body was exposed, her T-shirt was lifted up, her legs were left spread apart – which very much looks like a gesture of contempt or triumph. I'm thinking at the moment that the next step would have been to remove the Playstation, dispassionately as it were, and the Playstation discs at the same time. The next thing was either setting fire to the body by getting the vodka bottle, or it was going back to the bedroom to see what was going on, the curtains being left in a slightly askew position. Setting the fire was one of the last things he did before he left the flat.

'The rape could be based on anger, or on power, and in either case I think the person who did it could be somebody who's already in a relationship that is conflicting or difficult in some way. Perhaps someone who has affairs or loses arguments with his wife when he's at home could be tempted by the rape of Yvonne and her murder as the expression of anger or retaliation. As for the tights, they aren't such an unusual way of strangling someone, but they seem to have been used in a complicated way – they've been spread, wrapped around twice and then pulled without a knot from the front. That suggests the person is methodical, or it could mean he wanted to experience the full physical sense of the strangulation. Sometimes they want to prolong the actual physical sensation and they do that by making a process of it all. We've got somebody here who is paying quite a lot of attention to what he does and to Yvonne after she is dead, and is paying a certain amount of attention to the way the death is created.'

Badcock was keen to emphasize that his observations were not just a matter of inspiration or intuition on his part: psychiatrists and psychologists simply do not work in that way, despite the impression created by *Cracker* and the cult in crime fiction of the brilliant investigator with a nose for the guilty man: 'It comes from a mixture of having talked to people who've done this kind of thing and from knowledge of the theory of destructive and aggressive behaviour. But above all it's a matter of trying to think as carefully and simply as possible about what it is we've actually got at the scene. A lot of people feel it is just common sense. The test is, would an ordinary person going to a crime scene look at it the same way, come to the same conclusion? And the answer usually is that they don't – so the scientific part of it is focusing on observation, rather than simple emotional reaction. The main impression in the flat was how terribly claustrophobic it was, and how much time and care the person had spent on putting the body on the settee, so I find myself thinking about why they did that, and the excited behaviours such as going outside and defecating. The ferocity of the attack is obvious, and it looks like something that developed because sex didn't happen properly, which stimulated further developments in the form of anger and increasing power and dominance – seeking for power and control which in the end he could only get from her body after she was dead.'

Some of Badcock's remarks, especially about the attacker's other relationships and his use of the tights for the murder, were to prove remarkably prescient. He was also right about Scudder, whose DNA sample proved negative soon afterwards, along with four other men close to the family who had given blood samples. The DNA mismatch didn't absolutely rule him out, because he could have killed Yvonne in a jealous rage after she'd had sex with someone else, but by now other developments had convinced police he was not the culprit. The question that simmered in the background, however, was whether the police were finding Badcock's observations of any use. DCI Horne continued to send him statements and information about the case, then took a day away from the incident room to travel to Wakefield to see him. Horne was still facing a choice of theories: was the murder committed by someone who knew Yvonne and Joseph in some way, or by a stranger, who might either be a burglar or a sex attacker? The first theory made the pool of suspects relatively small and manageable; the second made it potentially huge, raising the prospect of long and costly investigative work. His personal view was that it wasn't a burglar, simply because so much valuable property – jewellery, watches, cash – had been left behind. 'So what I'm looking for from Dr Badcock,' he said, 'is some clues as to the behaviour of the person who killed Yvonne… I will be looking for a bit of a steer as to which of the two theories we should be looking at.'

The meeting was long and complicated, trying once again to build snippets of evidence into a plausible and coherent sequence of events. Why was Yvonne's pyjama bottom missing? Why were her bra and an extra pair of tights in the lounge? The pyjama top had a fragment of glass on it – had it been used as a glove after the window was broken? Why had Yvonne told her friend Tracey that she would be late for work that night? Had the offender taken Yvonne's mobile phone because it had his number on it? At the end of an often bewildering session, Badcock felt they were dealing with a man given to 'tidiness and destructive controlling behaviour, which do form part of an obsessional personality structure'. He confirmed and developed his theory about the sexual events – that the attacker had failed to ejaculate during normal sex, and in his anger and frustration had turned violent and attempted anal and oral sex as well, before or just after murdering Yvonne. Badcock and Horne also felt they'd arrived at a sequence that made sense: the attacker had been let in the front door, killed Yvonne in the bedroom and moved her to the sitting room, left the flat by closing the front door on the latch, decided he needed to get back in to destroy forensic evidence, had broken the window to do so, then turned the key in the front door mortise lock as a precaution and attempted to set fire to the body. They also agreed that the killer knew his victim in some way.

'I shall be extremely disappointed if this turns out to be a burglar,' remarked Badcock.

'So will I,' responded Horne. 'Because the cost and resources of going down that road would be enormous.'

On his way back to London, Horne said he was pleased that the meeting had confirmed his own view that they should be looking for someone who knew Yvonne and Joseph. He also revealed that a programme to seek DNA samples from all their known associates had actually been set in motion that very morning: such samples can easily be taken by a police officer running a swab inside a person's mouth, gathering a few cells from the inside of the cheek. 'What the meeting has done for me,' Horne said afterwards, 'is given me the opportunity to have advice from outside the police service from an expert in his field who can say yes, this is probably the right direction we're following. Now my priority is to pursue inquiries in relation to the first theory, and if we are unsuccessful we will know in due course and will still have the second option to go down. What I will say is that the second option is not completely abandoned because in this case we have forensic evidence that will no doubt convict the perpetrator in due course. So if we do end up looking at theory number two – that is, a stranger attack – then I am convinced we will get the offender eventually.'

What he did not reveal at this point was that he was in fact pressing ahead already with the second option – the theory that the crime had been committed by a stranger, or by someone whose relationship with Yvonne was unknown to anyone else. This was not because of any lack of faith in the advice he was getting from Badcock – he simply felt that his best chance of a quick arrest lay in advancing on several fronts at once, unless and until he could restrict the field of inquiry with greater certainty. So the DNA swabbing programme that had begun that day included people who were not known to be friends or acquaintances of the couple, but who lived in the area and had come to police attention in the past for minor crimes of a sexual nature or involving violence –

people, in other words, who had stepped on to the lower rungs of a ladder that might eventually lead to rape and murder. Badcock had earlier remarked that someone like this might be responsible, but police officers had evidently come to the same conclusion independently, and the choice of the names to be put on the list had essentially been guided by information contained in criminal records or put forward by intelligence officers who specialized in keeping tabs on local criminals. So this third meeting with Badcock had, it seemed, not played a crucial part either in the decision to go ahead with the DNA swabbing programme or in the selection of names to put on it.

In early June, nearly three months after the crime, the scientific investigations and the 600 statements taken from the couple's associates and members of the public had still not thrown up any really useful leads, and Horne decided it was time to hold a press conference. He wanted to appeal for anyone who knew the couple to come forward so that his list of the couple's friends and associates was as complete as possible; he wanted to release an 'e-fit' picture of the man seen by neighbours in Cricketers Close on the evening of the murder; he wanted to announce a reward of £5,000 from the Crimestoppers Trust for information leading to a conviction; and he wanted to give the media their first chance to interview Yvonne's mother, along with her fiancé and one-time suspect, Joseph Scudder.

It was a harrowing and tearful occasion for the family as they were asked to relive their trauma and talk about their feelings for Yvonne. 'Joe,' asked one reporter, 'you must have gone through it over and over in your mind – do you remember the last time you spoke to Yvonne?' Joe wept as he replied: 'I remember that... I remember that very clearly...' Yvonne's mother Audrey was also asked to talk about the killing of her husband seventeen years before, and clearly found the memories very difficult to deal with emotionally. Horne issued his appeal for anyone who knew the couple to come forward, and afterwards declared himself delighted with the reaction of the media and confident that the material they would publish would help the investigation.

Although Horne did not say so at the press conference, the national DNA database in Birmingham had now told him that samples from the scene did not match any of those within the system: the offender, in other words, was not a convicted criminal or one awaiting trial who had been swabbed before. The list of those from whom they were seeking fresh swabs had now, therefore, become the main focus of attention. Horne discussed this in an interview after the press conference and said that – after many delays caused by the pressure of other work – Badcock had now sent him a preliminary ten-page report that contained the likely sequence of events and many of the views that had emerged at earlier meetings. In particular, it repeated that the offender was likely to have known Yvonne and Joe in some way, and said that he might have convictions for minor offences. The report was a useful investigative tool, Horne remarked cautiously, and had to be looked at in conjunction with all the other evidence. And he raised the tantalizing question: 'Supposing Yvonne had met somebody and knew their name and nobody else in the world apart from those two knew about their meeting or knew his name? Yvonne's dead now and we don't know that name, so we would have to treat the situation as if that person were a stranger.'

Horne's views on the report and its usefulness touched again on the ever-delicate question of what police officers thought of profilers and vice-versa – a question that was to come into the foreground when Badcock delivered his final report soon afterwards and then travelled down to south-east London to discuss it with the police investigating team. Earlier in the case Badcock had described the differences between his role and that of the police: 'I suppose the most important difference is that it is the police officers' job to gather evidence. My job is to gain information – the facts I have to build up are psychological facts, which are real enough but very hard to demonstrate.' He had also spoken highly of the 'psychological-mindedness' of some police officers and their receptiveness to his approach to investigations. Now, before the meeting began, he confessed to feeling a certain amount of trepidation and excitement: 'Police officers are usually very sensible, so they don't want bullshit… I imagine some of them will be pretty sceptical about the whole process. But our job is not to produce a consensus view. The officers' job is to detect and gather evidence, while mine's different – to focus on the reasons for the killing and to try to work out what that tells us about the person. What we do is not very different from what the pathologist does in post-mortem. He aims to work out the physical cause of death. I aim to establish the psychological cause of death. And because physical facts and psychological facts aren't quite the same thing, the process of evaluating them is different, and it's important for me to have a discussion and dialogue as a means of getting to the truth.'

Horne said quite frankly before the meeting that some police officers were sceptical about the work of psychiatrists and psychologists, and it was no secret that difficulties existed between the two professions. When the meeting got under way, it was a nervy and slightly tense affair, with Badcock deferring to the officers as Julian Boon had done in the Jean Barnes case, telling him their expertise was far and away the most important factor in the investigation while his role was quite minor. He talked about the bad publicity his kind of work had attracted in 'a number of high profile cases' – code in the trade for the Rachel Nickell case – and again mentioned how in real life people like him never achieved the skilful and speedy expertise seen in *Cracker*. 'I think the official view of profiling is that it's somewhere above witchcraft and somewhere below a reliable science,' he said. 'In doing the analyses I rely on my clinical experience and my powers of reasoning, but I don't want you to think what I'm offering you is more than a form of educated guesswork. The best I can do is to tell you what I think and describe why I think it, because then you're in a position to take it or leave it. Any picture I give you is going to be two- rather than three-dimensional… you need *Cracker*, I'm just crackers.'

This rather lame joke failed, however, to defuse all the tension. Initially there was some discussion about the mobile phone that probably belonged to Yvonne, which had just been traced, following the public appeal at the press conference: someone had found it abandoned on a garden wall about a mile away, next to an empty can of lager and a McDonald's Chicken McNuggets box. But when the meeting moved to discussion of Badcock's report, it wasn't long before one of the officers, Detective Constable Callum Sutherland, took issue with one of its main strands – the contention that Yvonne's body had been positioned deliberately to convey a sense of triumph. It was the aspect of the report which perhaps contained more psychological interpretation than any other, and there was a sense in which Sutherland seemed to find it just too fancy. It quickly became clear that he was sceptical about the kind of complex motivation and sequence of events posited by Badcock and preferred a more simple, down-to-earth account. Like another member of the investigation team, he wasn't happy with the idea that the offender was let in at first, and then broke the window to get back in afterwards: he thought it more plausible that he'd broken the window in the hope of grabbing the Playstation and getting out in forty seconds, and then become involved in a physical confrontation with Yvonne when she unexpectedly appeared on the scene.

'I tend to think there's a possibility it was a burglary,' said Sutherland. 'Those Sony Playstations are very saleable, everybody wants them. If he disturbs her, if he's woken her up, he's got to restrain her, but in restraining her the power takes over, and he's now got to control her, and the urges come on then, he does whatever else he wants to do… If he's made her perform oral sex or whatever, she's sat on the edge of the settee, he would have to lie right over, but on the edge, he pulls too hard, she falls back, her leg is up…' Sutherland mimed the actions he was describing. Badcock suggested, as he had before, that an opportunistic burglar who was disturbed would be more likely to leave the premises quickly than get involved in a complex sexual assault, but Sutherland countered: 'I feel the sexual assault happened because it happened, he didn't know she was in there and he has to restrain her. It started off just trying to grab her, but then something else takes over, it gets worse and goes beyond what his original intention was.'

At the end of the exchange Badcock said: 'I'm still sticking with what I said.' Sutherland responded: 'I'm going with what a lot of people in the office have said, that's all.' It was a moment that seemed to crystallize the potential conflict between no-nonsense, street-wise, seen-it-all-before coppering on the one hand, and complex, airy-fairy theorizing on the other. As if to illustrate this, Badcock said to the officers at one point: 'One of the things I do assume, forgive the philosophy, is a principle called Occam's Razor – if you are trying to analyse an unclear situ-

ation, the simplest situation which fits all the facts is the one to go for.'
It was a fair bet that not many of those present were familiar with
William of Occam, a fourteenth-century Franciscan friar and Nominalist
philosopher from Surrey, who wrote a political tract that upset the Pope
and enunciated the principle *Entia non sunt multiplicanda praeter necessi-
tas* – usually translated as 'Ontological entities are not to be multiplied
beyond necessity.' Even in translation, this is not a phrase much bandied
about in police station canteens.

At the end of the meeting Badcock asked the team to write down
their theories and send them to him, and declared himself quite pleased
with the session: it had helped to point out the strong and the weak
areas in the analysis and made him feel he still needed to know more
about Yvonne and her lifestyle. Once he was back in Wakefield, he
talked again about police attitudes to his work, and how police officers
tended to understand violence: 'They want to understand the violence
in terms of things they're familiar with themselves. It's quite tempting to
think of a killing in terms of a robbery that goes wrong or an attempted
rape that goes wrong, whereas if you look at the details of the case you
can see pretty clearly that the attacker was always focused on the death
or destruction of the person. The superintendents, the senior policemen, they're not only very intelligent, they're also very well versed in
human behaviour, they know the rich variety of ordinary life, as it were.
So they're not against a psychological understanding of life at all. It's just
that if you don't have the kind of professional background or experience that lets you look at these things in detail, they're not ideas which
present themselves naturally to you. They only come from a background
of looking at things with a psychological perspective.'

It was now three months into the investigation, and the twenty-odd
officers still working on the case were inevitably beginning to feel stale
and frustrated. Their initial suspect had been ruled out, several promising avenues had turned out to be dead-ends, and the profiler had made
interesting and potentially fruitful contributions to solving the riddle of
the evidence without offering them the magical insight which most
detectives secretly long for. What they were left with was plodding
through the solid routine work that such investigations usually involve –

including the painstaking, time-consuming work of requesting and taking DNA samples from a list of 500 men which might not include the culprit at all. As senior investigating officer, Horne was feeling the pressure of an unhappy situation more intensely than anyone.

But five days after his team's meeting with Badcock, while Horne was in a meeting to brief his senior officers on the progress of the investigation, his pager suddenly went off. The discussion halted and all eyes switched to him as he smiled apologetically, stood up and left the room. It was Monday 23 June, nearly fourteen weeks after the murder of Yvonne Killian. Was this going to be just another routine message, the everyday stuff of the investigation? Or could this just be the moment they had all been waiting for?

'WE'VE GOT A HIT'

6

*'He was caught as a direct result
of intelligence-led policing.'*
Detective Chief Inspector Chris Horne

When Horne checked his pager in the corridor outside the meeting room, he found an urgent message asking him to ring the Birmingham forensic laboratory that was dealing with the DNA tests. The senior scientist there, his voice full of excitement, told him that a match had just been found between the sample from the scene and a swab that had been given by a local Erith man called Karl David Stirk. Horne, equally delighted, restrained himself from punching the air and jigging down the corridor to celebrate this long-awaited breakthrough.

The only shadow on the triumph was that Stirk had been only the second man to give a DNA swab, some two months earlier on 24 April. If his swab had been processed more quickly, the police would have secured a faster arrest and thousands of pounds would have been saved in police working hours and the cost of many of the DNA tests done subsequently. The explanation of the delay, Horne was to discover, was the way in which the laboratory carries out the tests. The swabs arrive in boxes and aren't necessarily tested in the order in which they were taken from people on the suspect list, and some swabs fail to produce an immediate result and are put further down the queue for a second attempt to be carried out later. Fortunately, the police say they have no evidence that Stirk had carried out any further crimes in the two months between the taking of the swab and the discovery of the match.

Horne returned calmly to the meeting room and handled the development in a typically understated way. 'I resumed my seat and carried on with the business of the meeting for a few moments,' he recalled later. 'I was aware that a few colleagues were looking at me curiously, and after a little while I turned round in a polite way and said, "Don't let's waste any more time talking about it, chaps, because we've got a hit."'

In the mid-1980s a maladjusted teenager from a broken home was caught committing a burglary and several acts of arson and was convicted at juvenile courts in Sussex, Suffolk and Bexleyheath in south-east London. Then, in November 1989, there was a particularly disturbing crime when two women in their twenties were approached on the same day in isolated parts of Bexleyheath by a young man who, without warning and without saying a word to them, took out a pocket knife and slashed their throats. The attacker ran away, but the injured women were able to give police a description that helped them to arrest a sixteen-year-old. He was Karl David Stirk, the child of a local burglar and a woman who had worked as a prostitute. Officers found the knife used for the attacks on the women in the lining of his coat, and also established that he had committed the earlier burglaries and arson. Stirk – later to be described vividly by Dr Richard Badcock as a young man with 'a seriously disturbed boiler' – was convicted at Croydon Crown Court in 1991 of unlawful wounding and sentenced to eight years in custody. Although the women's wounds were serious, they were fortunately not life-threatening or likely to cause permanent scarring.

Four years later, however, Stirk was released. He was now a strongly built and good-looking young man, and not long afterwards he began a relationship with a young woman called Karen, who was twenty-five years old. He moved into a flat with her in Erith, worked in a local factory and as a window cleaner, and in spite of tensions and difficulties the relationship lasted until early 1998. But in February that year Karen decided the relationship was going nowhere and Stirk moved out, deeply upset by the break-up. He went back to live with his family in Maximfeld Road – which backed onto Cricketers Close and the flat shared by Yvonne Killian and Joseph Scudder. It was hardly surprising, then, that when the police began to trawl through criminal records and intelligence reports to compile their list of local people who might be responsible for Yvonne's murder, Karl David Stirk was fairly high on the agenda. When he was seen by the police and asked for a mouth swab for DNA screening on 24 April, it was his right under the law to decline. But he apparently expressed no surprise that he was being asked for the sample, and complied quite happily: he probably knew that there had been no facility at the time of his conviction in 1989 for his DNA to be put on the national database, which was not announced by the Home Office until 1991. He might also have thought that he had been successful in destroying DNA traces by starting the fire in the flat. Here perhaps was vindication of the early police decision not to publicize the fact that DNA evidence had in fact survived – a decision designed precisely to avoid alerting the culprit.

'If I did dance on the table,' Chris Horne recalled, 'it wasn't until later, after we'd had a bit of a drink. From the moment I told the meeting, it was sheer delight: the staff officer raided the fridge for beer, and then I came back to Shooter's Hill police station to get the team together, tell them the news, and change tactics: the priority now was to trace Karl Stirk.'

When the police went to Stirk's home to try to arrest him, however, they found that he had given up his job on the night shift at a local glass factory and was no longer living in the area: he had moved to Dundee on 9 June, apparently intending to start a new life. Horne and colleagues flew to Scotland the following day, and found Stirk living in a small down-at-heel hotel run by his stepfather's brother. The operation nearly misfired when they used a master key to let themselves into what they thought was Stirk's room, and found it empty. They checked the register, realized it should have been the room opposite, found Stirk in bed, and arrested and handcuffed him without a struggle. He was brought back to London by plane, interviewed in the presence of a solicitor over a period of two days, charged with murder and remanded in custody.

The police were now in a position to test one of the questions that had haunted the inquiry from an early stage: did Stirk know either

Yvonne or Joseph? Badcock had said in his report that he believed the offender did know one or both of them in some way, and Horne and some of his team were inclined to agree. But urgent inquiries by the police in the Erith area failed to bring to light any known relationship that might in turn have produced evidence to supplement the vital DNA breakthrough – the police were always conscious that courts can be hesitant to convict people on DNA evidence alone. However, friends of Stirk did remember him talking about seeing a Playstation in the local churchyard on the weekend of 14 and 15 March: he had apparently said that he had found it lying there and had gone back later to pick it up, only to find that it had disappeared. The police considered this to be a vital extra piece of evidence: at the time Stirk talked about the Playstation, they believed, there had been no public announcement about it and only the murderer could have known its whereabouts. Another potential source of corroborating evidence was the earprint found on the window of the flat, which forensic scientists in Lancashire were soon to compare with a print taken from Stirk. It was later to be examined by experts from Holland as well, and eventually a perfect match was established.

Soon after the arrest Badcock travelled down from Wakefield again to talk to Horne, and one of his first questions was how Stirk came to be in the pool of people selected for DNA testing. Horne replied that it was because of police intelligence, and Badcock remarked: 'Well, that's a big mark for police intelligence, isn't it?' Horne replied: 'Very much so, yes.' There was perhaps a rueful element in the exchange, because it was beginning to become clear that the investigation was virtually over as far as gathering evidence was concerned, that it was another triumph for forensic science, and that there was no direct link between the profiling work done by Badcock and the arrest of Stirk. Nevertheless, Horne was still interested in feeding information to Badcock and knowing more about the questions that still baffled him, such as why Stirk had chosen Yvonne as his victim and the real sequence of events in the flat. Likewise, Badcock was still interested in receiving the information and processing it – in fact, now that there was a real person to get his psychological teeth into, he seemed more interested than ever. And the more he heard about Stirk – where he lived and worked, his relationship with his former girlfriend – the more he was undeterred by the lack of hard evidence that he and Yvonne knew each other.

'I'm still inclined to think from the evidence about the killing itself that the person who did it knew her,' he said. 'I appreciate there's no linked trace between them, other than the residential link, which isn't an immediate one because he couldn't actually see the flat from where he lived. But it seems to me that he would have to know something about her lifestyle. The killing's just too coherent, really, it's too focused for something that develops on the hoof. Knowing her doesn't have to be part of a social relationship, but it does have to be real knowledge of her as a person, it has to be real information about what she looks like, what she does, where she is at particular times and so on; prior recognition of her existence, perhaps as discreet as targeting her in advance... I suppose what I'm saying in terms of the investigation is that I shouldn't be too deterred by the absence of an obvious link.'

Badcock was also given the opportunity of reading through police interviews with Stirk's former girlfriend Karen, and shown a photograph of her that revealed how similar she was in appearance to Yvonne Killian. Karen's statements to the police showed that she was the more dominant and successful of the two and had become the driving force in the relationship, which started to deteriorate when Stirk gave up his job at one point. She described in the statements how, fairly early on in the relationship, she had found a carrier bag containing damp women's underwear that she thought he had taken from a washing line. Then she had found a kitchen knife under their bed, and when she had asked him about it he had denied he had put it there. ('I know if I found a knife my wife had put under the bed,' said Badcock, 'I would be very careful.')

Although these incidents alone would have prompted many women to end the relationship, Karen's concerns were apparently assuaged by Stirk's denials. But the incidents continued. There was an occasion when Karen was travelling home by car and saw Stirk walking along a pathway following a woman; concerned for the woman's safety, Karen had got out of the car and called to Stirk, but he had ignored her, even though the woman had heard her and turned round. Karen's statement to the police read: 'I caught up with him but he did not want to speak to me – I think he was shocked that I was there.' Then Karen had found a pair of her black tights in Stirk's pocket, and when she asked him about them he had said he had taken them so he could feel closer to her. Badcock commented at this point: 'Now that's bullshit, but it's a sort of romanticized bullshit. It suggests that what he's trying to do with her is keep a romanticized aura about her, keep her on a pedestal, and therefore treat her in a false way.' Karen's statements also revealed that Stirk had liked her to keep her tights on while they had sex together and had enjoyed ripping them – something that connected very obviously with the manner of Yvonne's murder.

Karen's statements went on to say that things had reached the point where she was concerned that Stirk might be attacking women, and her suspicions had prompted her to go through his clothes. On one occasion she had found a pair of gloves with lipstick marks on them as if they had been pressed over a woman's mouth, but when she confronted him he had again denied it. 'That's how Karl deals with things, isn't it?' commented Badcock. 'He doesn't have an explanation for it, doesn't try to dissemble, he simply blanks it out and presumably carries on as normal.' Eventually, however, Stirk's denials of his perverted behaviour had failed to satisfy Karen and she had ended the relationship. Stirk, angry and frustrated, had gone back to live with his parents for a while. Not long afterwards, someone had damaged her car and fixed a wedge on her door buzzer to make it sound continuously: she had assumed it was Stirk, and was so frightened that she had changed the locks on her door. Asked later why he thought Karen had continued for so long to live with somebody about whom she had the gravest suspicions, Badcock replied: 'Women tend to be very loyal, don't they? As long as they perceive things to be all right inside a relationship, they tend to put more emphasis on that than on what their partner might be doing in the outside world.'

Although Karen was not able to provide direct evidence that would help to convict Stirk, the police thought her testimony important enough to ask her to appear as a witness at his trial. Badcock, meanwhile, was like a child presented with a box of new toys as he continued to read through the documents: 'Dark clothing, black jeans, black boots, green and brown suede jacket, a black jumper that he wears in warm weather, his Arsenal black hat. Well, the guy's a prowler, isn't he? If he's a burglar, I bet you a modest wager that he's a burglar in the overall interests of being a prowler. In other words, what he wants is to approach people in a particular way. He wants experiences that he can control, that give that sort of frisson of excitement and tension, just that little edge of uncertainty. But basically, things that he can control.

'I also think that we're likely to find that this behaviour is very actively going on during the relationship with Karen and has a part to play, if you like, in keeping the relationship with Karen going. I suspect he's tried his hand at being normal, it's not working for him, Karen's gaining the upper hand, as it were, in the relationship. He's trying to compensate by building up his own image of himself, and at the same time is trying to deal with the more negative feelings in the relationship by divorcing them from that relationship and acting them out in relationships with strangers. Part of the pay-off for him in going prowling, doing these things while he's got a relationship with Karen, is that in his eyes it helps him keep his relationship with Karen going for longer. Well, it makes him terribly interesting, although it doesn't actually prove that he killed Yvonne. But what it does show is that Karen is able to spontaneously describe a whole background of development that leads up to the kind of mental state for more destructive things later on.'

Badcock also watched the tapes of police interviews with Stirk, in which the suspect ignored questions, avoided eye contact, stared at the desk, and retreated into himself when asked difficult questions about such things as the tights Karen had found in his pocket and the DNA match to the scene of Yvonne's murder. The videos confirmed Badcock's view that Stirk was not good at explaining or exploring situations verbally, and his only defence – in the interviews as in his relationship with Karen – was denial: 'Not only does he withdraw from talking to the officers, he actually withdraws from confronting himself about anything.' It was becoming clear that Badcock, in a professional sense, was now extremely interested in Karl Stirk: he talked about the anxiety that would have prompted him to choose to be a prowler rather than sorting out fundamental problems about himself, and expressed the hope that a good forensic psychiatrist with knowledge of abnormal sexuality would be appointed to assess him before his trial.

As Badcock talked, however, it was noticeable that a tone of impatience seemed to be creeping into the responses of Horne and his officers: they listened politely and kept offering Badcock more statements, interview videos and maps of the crime area to take away with him, but an impression was developing that their interest in Stirk was waning now they felt they had enough evidence for a conviction. As the session drew to a close, Horne and Badcock agreed that it might be useful to have one more meeting when the defence statement was issued in advance of the trial, in case it contained information about the planned defence that might relate to the contents of the profile or indicate how Stirk's mind might be working. Then there were mutual congratulations, cheery goodbyes in the car park, and the gates of the police station closed behind Badcock's car.

Afterwards Horne was asked in an interview about the contribution made by the profile to an investigation that was now all but wrapped up. 'As Richard mentioned when he did the briefing in June to the investigation team, he was a small cog in a big wheel,' Horne replied. 'We didn't deny having his expert evidence available to us. I'm not going to say that he was 100 per cent wrong or right, because there are still a number of uncertain scenarios, unanswered questions, and I don't even think that the outcome of a criminal trial is going to answer those questions. We've still found no evidence yet to say that Yvonne didn't know Stirk or Stirk didn't know Yvonne. And Richard could be 100 per cent accurate in his findings and his conclusions. I think we're going to have to wait and see. But I also want to know what actually happened – it's still intriguing, it's still a mystery. We don't know whether he genuinely just broke in out of the blue, found her inside the premises, or whether she actually invited him in, or he conned his way in. These are unanswered questions, which he may answer much later on, after his trial.'

On the way home from the meeting with Horne, Badcock turned the latest developments over in his mind, reflecting on 'the goodness of fit' between Stirk's psychological attributes and the crime. He conceded

that the Playstation had a different significance to the one he had orig-
inally given it: it had been taken, he now thought, not as a specific act
of spite against Joseph, but merely because the intruder had a similar
interest to Joseph in computer games. There was also the continuing
uncertainty about whether and how Stirk and Yvonne knew each other,
but otherwise Badcock felt that the psychological portrait that emerged
from Stirk's history and behaviour matched what had been found at the
scene of the crime. In particular, the presence of several pairs of tights
in the living room of the flat – one pair was believed to belong to Karen
rather than Yvonne and would therefore have been brought in by Stirk
– was now explicable as part of the personal rituals developed by him in
his career as a sexual pervert.

Badcock's view was that Stirk was a severely damaged and psycho-
logically limited person, although he was capable of maintaining at least
a pretence of a normal life, including holding down a job most of the
time and keeping his relationship with Karen going for a number of
years. He was someone who had always had to struggle with a sense of
anxiety and despair, had never quite worked out what the rules of life
were, and had never quite convinced himself that he fitted in with
society and could cope with and adapt to normal relationships. His
sexual misbehaviour was partly a way of building up a different kind of
self-reward, and things had developed to the stage where it was easier for
him to continue with the deviant behaviour than to be a normal person:
'He gets an easier ride, a better sense of self fulfilment from the abnormal things because they subject him to less anxiety. Now for most of us
it would be the other way round, we would be much more anxious about
going out and doing some of the things he's done, than we would about
pursuing a normal relationship. But for him it may be the other way
round – that he's hung on to the abnormal behaviours, not simply
because they're satisfying in themselves, but because they get round
specific difficulties that he has in relationships. But also because they
challenge him less, they make him confront himself less, and therefore
he has to change less if he does these abnormal things.'

Badcock considered that Stirk's relationship with his former girlfriend
was crucial in understanding what had happened to Yvonne. While he was

trying to have a normal relationship with Karen, he was unable to prevent himself from doing things like stealing knickers and following women about, and when the relationship was broken off by Karen he may have fixed on Yvonne because she looked a bit like her and was the same kind of independent, hard-working woman. He had a history of going out at night for the stealthy pursuit of women, and for some time his natural route to work had taken him past the flat shared by Yvonne and Joseph. On the night of Friday 13 March his original intention had been to rape Yvonne, Badcock thought, but it went beyond that and he had ended up killing her and displaying her body in a ritual way. After he'd left the flat he'd needed to go back in, partly to remove evidence and partly to do other things: 'I don't think he was trying to destroy all the evidence of what he'd done in the flat, because I strongly suspect that what he'd done represented his finest achievement to date. In other words, if not pleased with what he'd done or proud of it, I think he was satisfied with what he'd done, not necessarily that he liked it or that he gained pleasure from it, but that he felt fulfilled by having done it.'

Badcock's therapeutic interest was clearly in full flood, and his concluding remark was that he hoped he would have the chance to go and see Stirk once the trial was over, in order to build up an understanding of him as a person. It was surprising, he said, how many serious offenders were prepared to talk to psychiatrists in prison: they suffered from a sense of shame or puzzlement about what had happened and felt a need to try to make sense of it.

Karl Stirk's trial started at the Central Criminal Court on 11 January 1999, with the accused pleading not guilty. Before the hearing got under way, Yvonne's mother, Audrey Killian, sat in a cafe opposite the Old Bailey and expressed some of her feelings about the defendant. Unlike Dr Badcock, who looked forward to interviewing him, she wanted to see him dead: 'What I would want to come out of it at the end if he's found guilty is the death penalty, because without it justice would never be done, as far as I'm concerned. You might think it's a bit barbaric, but there are far too many of these murderers of children or innocent people, and the majority of them are let out after a while. He's a nasty person, a psychopath I would say, because of the things he did to her. No normal person could do to her what he did, because normal people value life. He is evil, definitely evil – I wouldn't say he is sick or something, he's just evil. Because it's a life for a life I would burn him alive and it would never be enough. I know it sounds cruel, but it's justifiable because of what he did to her. I lost their dad, you know, and it was very hard, it was terrible. When you lose your other half, half of you is gone, but with a child the whole of you is gone. It's very difficult, very hard to pick up the pieces...'

DCI Horne arrived at court feeling confident about the evidence against Stirk – there were the DNA samples and the matching earprint on the flat window that was to feature strongly in novelty-hungry press reports, and there was Stirk's failure to tell the police when he was arrested about his statements to other people that he had found the Playstation in the churchyard. In the run-up to the trial, new elements had also emerged: on the garden post used to break the window, fibres had been found that matched gloves and a hat found at the house of Stirk's parents; and Stirk, who had denied any knowledge of Yvonne in police interviews, had now come up with a defence case in which he said that he was having an affair with Yvonne and she must have been killed by someone else after he left her. Horne seemed a little nervous about this defence, wondering if it might have been built to some extent around Badcock's profile of the attacker, which speculated about such an affair. The profile had been released to the defence lawyers as part of normal procedure, and the possibility that it might have put ideas into Stirk's mind and was now being manipulated to thwart the prosecution case was a source of some anxiety. Horne was circumspect and police-manly about the prospects of success, saying you could never predict how a trial would go and hoping that the jury would reach the right decision.

There were no unexpected developments as the evidence from family, police officers, pathologist and forensic scientists was laid before the jury of seven men and five women by David Walters QC, the prosecuting counsel. Then Stirk went into the witness box and gave his account of events, the only real support for which was somewhat tenuous – the fact that there were no signs on Yvonne's body, such as skin under her fingernails, that she had fought to defend herself. He had met Yvonne early in 1998, just after Christmas, he said: he had fancied her and begun an affair with her. He'd been round to her flat on at least ten occasions, he said, usually on Tuesdays and Wednesdays and sometimes on Fridays as well, and she had referred to him as her 'treat of the week'. On the night of the murder he'd had consenting sex with her at the flat, and they had together hatched a plot to get back at Joseph and claim some insurance money: Stirk would break the window with a fence post to make it look like a burglary, then take the Playstation and leave it in the churchyard to be collected later. He'd left Yvonne alive and well, and gone home to change for work. This inherently unlikely story again pointed the finger at Joseph Scudder, who had earlier been directly accused by the defending counsel of murdering Yvonne when he came back to the flat later in the evening. This had reduced Scudder to tears as he denied the allegation vehemently and pointed out that the police had investigated him and rapidly ruled him out.

The trauma of this allegation appeared when Scudder was asked about it a short while before the jury was sent out to consider its verdict. He complained about the way the barrister had revealed that he was unable to read, dragged up incidents from his past and tried to make Yvonne sound like someone she wasn't. 'The final question he asked – if I murdered her – well, I just couldn't believe it,' he said. 'I answered it a bit louder than the other questions, because I never did it and I couldn't see the point of being asked it. People I spoke to afterwards were shocked, people in the gallery who were watching couldn't believe that they actually asked me that. I just want it to come to an end and get some answers – for the last couple of weeks I've had sleepless nights, been agitated. It's not always easy because it's always there, in the papers, people come up and ask you about it. I don't particularly hate anyone, but in this case I hate the person who's done this, destroyed a young girl's life and in the process destroyed a load of other people related to her and her friends. I still miss her, remember the good times and the bad, certain dates...'

Scudder did not have to wait much longer for the final confirmation of his innocence. The jury was not impressed by Stirk's defence, and after less than four hours of deliberation on 28 January they came back with a verdict of guilty. Stirk stayed impassive in the dock as Judge Geoffrey Grigson sentenced him to life imprisonment, telling him he had committed a truly terrible offence and would always be a danger to women. As he was taken down to the cells, the rest of the people involved in the case spilled into the street outside the Old Bailey for the rituals of relief: the congratulatory remarks, the tears, the impromptu press conferences. Horne told the cameras how pleased he was with the outcome and hoped it would ease the pain for Joseph Scudder and Yvonne's family. 'Karl Stirk was caught as a direct result of intelligence-led policing, which is a policy that goes on throughout the Metropolitan Police today,' he said. 'I agree wholeheartedly with the judge's comments that he is an extremely dangerous man and a threat to women, and I'm delighted we've been able to take him off the streets of London.'

Yvonne's mother Audrey said she was delighted with the verdict and it had given her some relief from the terrible strain of the last nine months. 'Yvonne would have been proud because the law was her career,' she said. 'She'll always be in our memory. I'll never forgive that man for the way he tried to slur her character, it was unforgivable what he tried to do in court – that scum deserves to be where he is now.' Yvonne's sister Mandy burst out: 'Even right up to the end he was smirking.'

It was notable that Horne, in his remarks outside the Old Bailey, did not mention or thank Badcock, and when asked about the profile he replied: 'I don't want to go into great detail about the offender profile because it's arguable. Suffice to say we are delighted by today's result given by the jury.' Since the case, however, he has used a profiler on another investigation, and has declared himself a strong supporter of using people like Badcock in important cases. Major inquiries nowadays, said Horne, are increasingly a matter of teamwork between police and other experts, especially forensic scientists and pathologists. 'Profilers are needed more than ever before as part of that team,' he said. 'They are another investigative tool, and an important one.'

So where did the outcome of the case leave Richard Badcock and offender profiling? Had his contribution been helpful and, if so, to what extent? He had been right in saying from the start that the boyfriend was not the culprit, and this had perhaps helped steer the police away from Joseph Scudder. Badcock had insisted that the offender was not a burglar, and because this was what Horne believed as well, he may have been able to use the profile to strengthen his hand against members of his own inquiry team who thought a burglar might be responsible. Badcock had also played a strong part in working out the 'double entry' theory, but in the end the question had become academic; until Stirk gives a frank account of events we are unlikely to know the truth about this. Similarly, Badcock was convinced that Stirk knew Yvonne in some way, and although Stirk said at his trial that he did know her and was having an affair with her, he wasn't necessarily telling the truth. The theory about the Playstation being taken to spite Joseph was mistaken, as Badcock readily accepted, although he considered that this had not damaged the inquiry in any way.

The crucial list of people selected for DNA testing was not compiled with Badcock's help – it was based on criminal records and intelligence reports by local officers. And finally, Badcock was not asked to advise on the strategy for interviewing Stirk. At the end of day, the success in finding the murderer of Yvonne Killian was due to methodical policing and advances in forensic science: offender profiling had a strictly supporting role. Perhaps the best one can say is that the profile was surprisingly accurate in many ways and helped police officers to feel confident in their lines of inquiry; but it did not contribute crucially to finding the criminal.

Horne's final remark at the Old Bailey was that he would now be moving on to the next case. For Badcock, however, it wasn't so simple. While the successful trial brought police interest in Stirk to a halt, his interest – the therapeutic interest – became if anything more intense. Perhaps the most notable thing about this interest was that it was compassionate and eager for understanding, and contrasted strongly with the growing indifference of the police and the natural vengefulness of the family towards Stirk. As the investigation drew to a close, Badcock talked on several occasions about the psychological origins of the savagely destructive sexual violence that was the hallmark of Yvonne's murder: why is it that men can end up committing such horrendous crimes? For Badcock it was not enough to dismiss them simply as the product of evil, although he does acknowledge the concept of evil and says he sometimes feels its presence very strongly in the cases he looks at. Instead he saw the crime as the end result of subtle and irresistible forces in the psyche of the offender.

He had explained before the trial that Stirk's abnormal sexual habits had their origins in a sense of anxiety and despair. Now he expanded that analysis into a moving account of how tragic crimes are set in motion long before the event, in the early experiences and life history of the offender. Stirk's feelings of anxiety and despair, he said, would have their origins in a sense of weakness from which everyone suffers: 'If you grow up in a normal family that sense of weakness, which is part of normal experience, is counteracted and overcome by the sense of being loved by your own family, by the feeling that you're not destroyed by it, and by coming over time to have confidence in your own ability to cope with these things, and a sense of trust. If those things don't happen, then the sense of weakness is something you're permanently left with, without any way of coping with it, and the way most people seem to respond to that situation is to develop relationships both with themselves and other people that are based on control. If you can't cope with the idea of being vulnerable in a normal relationship – which is intrinsic to a normal relationship – then you can try to get those needs satisfied by introducing control, either by bullying or by being covertly manipulative in other ways. To some extent these are normal patterns of behaviour, but if people can never find a way of overcoming their own weakness, it's very tempting to base their entire strategy for relationships on control.

'One of the consequences of this is that you can never actually grow as a person, and how you make your way in the world precludes you from ever becoming a rounded human being. What you can achieve instead is self-satisfaction, and most people who go down that path kid themselves that this is what they wanted all along, so they continue to exploit relationships to gain control of them. And so it goes on, and a lot of the more horrific physical and sexual behaviour comes from that, and some of it comes from going far enough down that path to realize that if you try and control people you're more likely to get what you want than if you have an open relationship. But you're still trying to kid yourself that you can have your cake and eat it, that you can have a real relationship at the same time as doing this, and then sometimes in a situation where the relationship is going wrong people can be catapulted into a sense of despair. And the despair can drive people into some pretty destructive stuff, things that they wouldn't normally think themselves capable of doing... There's a sense of rage, which is made up of anger and depression, and the depressed component is very much the sense of their own weakness.'

When this sense of weakness led people to use violence to achieve a state of mastery over their victim, Badcock said, they would experience a feeling similar to the climactic release provided by sex. The scene in the sitting room of the flat in Cricketers Close was an expression of Stirk's failed relationship with himself, where his sense of weakness had led him to do vile things that made him feel strong and powerful. The victim, he said, became little more than a thing – 'an organic bendy doll', positioned on the settee to convey a sense of mastery, contempt and omnipotence.

Karl David Stirk's appeal was turned down by the Court of Appeal in October 1999. The police have twice interviewed him since his conviction, trying to find out if he might be responsible for other unsolved sex crimes in the area. He has admitted nothing, however, and stuck coldly to the account of the events of Friday 13 March 1998 which he presented as his defence. He has become a dedicated body-builder and an expert in the provisions of the European Convention on Human Rights, which he hopes can be used to secure his early release. Badcock has not so far achieved his wish to see Stirk in prison, and it is not known if he is seeing another psychiatrist or psychologist. Asked about the prognosis for Stirk, Badcock said that it depended whether he could ever bring himself to acknowledge and feel the dread and despair that lay behind his actions.

'All one can say is that it's not impossible,' he said. 'But, my God, it's bloody difficult because his whole development has gone in the direction of trying to avoid exactly the kind of things he has to confront to become a different human being.'

If Badcock's analysis is correct, the chances of Stirk reforming and transforming himself seem very slim. The question then arises: will he ever be released? Although Stirk was sentenced to life imprisonment at the age of twenty-six, he will be able to seek his freedom once he has served his 'tariff', which has recently been set at twenty years by the Home Secretary. He would not automatically be released after that time: the final decision, under the current system, would be taken by the Home Secretary, who has the power to detain people sentenced to life imprisonment indefinitely if he sees fit. This power of the Home Secretary, however, is under challenge following the Human Rights Act which came into force in Britain in 2000, as Stirk has apparently realized: the Act applies the principles of the European Convention on Human Rights, which stipulates that the judiciary rather than the executive should dispense justice. Senior figures in the Home Office are known to accept that the current system will be ruled in breach of the new Act when a suitable test case is brought before the courts. There is every likelihood, then, that judges will in due course take the place of the Home Secretary in making the ultimate decision about how long very dangerous criminals should stay in jail.

It remains to be seen whether that will make a lot of difference in practice. Judges may not have the responsiveness to public feeling that politicians claim to have, but they do not necessarily have 'softer' views on criminal justice. When they make their decisions, they will no doubt be obliged to rely, as the Home Secretary currently does, on medical and psychiatric reports and the views of the Parole Board, which assesses a prisoner's suitability for release. In making its assessment of the risk that the prisoner will reoffend, the Board takes into account whether he has confessed to his crime and expressed remorse. But it is not unknown for criminals to hoodwink the Parole Board by going through the motions of confession, feigning remorse and pretending they have changed. That is the route by which unreformed, dangerous criminals can sometimes get back on the streets again to repeat their crimes, and it is a route that will still be available to the more cunning criminals, whether it is a politician or a judge who makes the final decision about release.

If Karl Stirk is eventually released, he may still be a relatively young man. He may also be a changed and chastened man, but a possibility remains that he could still be driven by the psychological compulsions that led to the shocking death of Yvonne Killian.

"IN LOVE WITH THE OLD FOLK"

7

'Prancing up and down the rat runs,
I think he probably gets a bit of a buzz out of that.'

Julian Boon

Jane is an eighty-seven-year-old widow who lives alone in a tidily kept house in the semi-rural southern fringes of London, where the sprawl of the metropolis breaks against the beech-clad chalk hills of the North Downs. She is tiny and frail and uses a stick to walk, but she is mentally alert, confident and articulate, with ready opinions and a keen interest in current affairs. This is her description of what happened to her on the night of 11 July 1998.

'I was lying in bed, and I have to get up several times a night, and I put up my hand to pull the switch on the side of the bed, so that I could look at the clock and see the time – first of all having put my glasses on. Well, nothing lit up. And I thought, this is very peculiar, I must have – what do you call it – a fuse gone. And so I got up to go to the door and see if I could switch the light on there. Well, nothing happened. And at this time the whole house was double locked and I couldn't understand why this had happened, you see. And then, as I walked towards the door I felt a hand over my mouth.

'And I froze, and the person doing it had a balaclava on. And then he released me, obviously realizing that there was to be no shouting and struggling. And I said to him, "I will give you the money." Because that is what I thought he wanted, and he didn't say anything. And I had the key in my handbag and I went on to the landing and unlocked something and produced the money and gave it to him. And I was still wondering how he'd managed to get in. Anyway, he took the money and instead of going he followed me back into the bedroom.

'And I wasn't aware of fear, not mentally. But my, I heard a terrible noise, and I thought, whatever is that? And it was my heart thumping – it was making a noise like thunder! Anyway, he followed me back into the bedroom, and then my legs gave way – obviously that must have been fear, and he dragged me up and plonked me on the bed and sat next to me. He then whispered one word in my ear and that was the only word he said the whole time he was here. I don't know if I should repeat that word, but he said "sex". In my ear.

'So I pushed him away and said, no. And he did not pursue it. Then he came down the stairs and wandered about the house. I couldn't understand this and I kept pushing him and saying, "Why don't you go?" He didn't answer, he walked up the stairs and I followed him, but my legs were being very awkward. And then I said to him, "You realize how old I am? I could easily have a heart attack, drop down and die." There was absolutely no reaction to this. Where did he go inside my house? The bedroom, the landing, up and down the stairs, over and over again, for some reason. I couldn't understand what he was doing, and I wanted to know what he was doing, so I followed him. He seemed quite resigned to the fact that I was following him. He was there from about midnight to about 5 a.m. And when it got light I realized he'd gone and I came down the stairs, left the stick up there in my confusion, and came into this room, noticed the curtains were blowing, and I realized he must have taken the pane out of one of the french windows there. He didn't break the glass, he cut it. And that's how he had got in, and that's how he left.

'And then, of course, I had no phone. I couldn't do anything about the police, and I was walking along outside to knock up somebody I knew. But my neighbour next door, she saw me, because it was light by this time, and asked me what I was doing. I was walking along with an umbrella 'cause I couldn't find the stick, and she sent for the police, who of course arrived and there was the usual procedure.

'Now this will probably surprise you, but I am indifferent to the man who did this. I have no feelings of revenge or bitterness or vindictiveness

*Dr Richard Badcock,
criminal psychiatrist and
offender profiler, examines
a crime scene: 'The facts
I have to build up are
psychological facts.'*

*Dr Julian Boon, academic psychologist and offender profiler:
'I want an understanding of why some people turn out to be
old ma Theresa and some turn out to be old ma Hindley...'*

*Detective Chief
Inspector Steve
Scott: 'We took what
Julian [Boon] told
us and we knocked
on the door of the
right man.'*

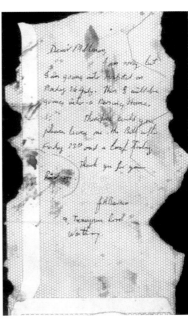

*The letter to the milkman:
when police realized it
was a forgery, the inquiry
soon gathered pace.*

*David Munley arrives
at court on the day of
the verdict. In his speech
the judge told Munley:
'You have shown not a
flicker of acceptance of
guilt or remorse.'*

*Jean Barnes (inset) lived a frugal
and reclusive life among the
possessions she had accumulated
over the years – her estate was
valued at around £500,000.*

POLICE APPEAL FOR ASSISTANCE

MURDER

During the evening of
Friday 13th March 1998
Yvonne Killian was murdered
in her flat at 51 Cricketers Close,
Erith, Kent DA81TX

Were you in the vicinity that Friday evening?

Did you see or hear anything suspicious?

Do you have any information?

Please contact the Incident room at
Shooters Hill Police Station
0181 853 1212

r name, ring Crimestoppers on
55 111

CRIMESTOPPERS
0800 555 111

*Solving the murder of
Yvonne Killian owed less
to this appeal than to police
intelligence and DNA.*

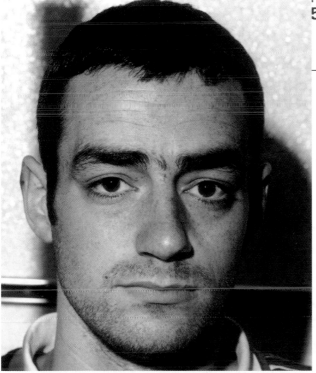

*Karl David Stirk was a burglar,
arsonist, and prowler before he
murdered Yvonne Killian.*

Detective Chief Inspector Chris Horne praises the work of his team after Stirk's conviction at the Old Bailey.

Yvonne Killian's fiancé, Joe Scudder, and mother, Audrey, try to control their grief at a police press conference.

Crimestoppers?

It is a national crime intelligence gathering and investigation scheme. It assists the police to identify and arrest criminals who are commit or have committed a crime Crimestoppers enables people to police and give information abo activity without being asked the

In London, it operates as a partn. the police, the London Crimest Directors and Crime harity). The Board romote the scheme ewards.

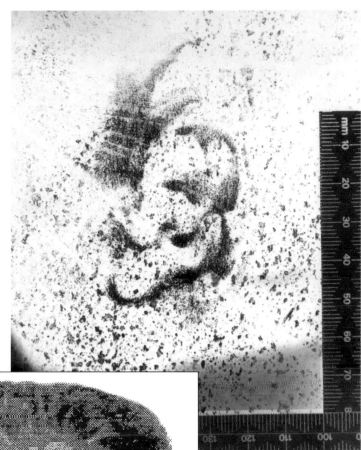

While searching Yvonne Killian's flat for fingerprints, officers instead found some thing very unusual – an earprint. A perfect match between this and a print taken from Stirk was later established.

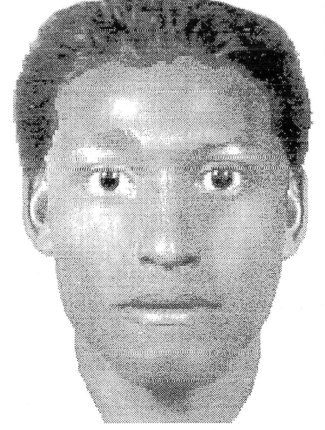

All the police had to go on was a DNA sample and an e-fit of Minstead Man compiled from sketchy descriptions from victims.

These images (1–3) of a Minstead suspect with an unusual gait were taken from moving footage that was shown on Crimewatch *but brought no new leads.*

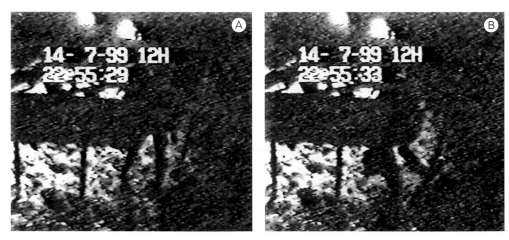

An observation camera picks up Keith Downer, the Gatwick blackmailer, walking away from his car (see photograph A) and collecting a bag (see photograph B) left by police at a pick-up point by a country road in Sussex.

③

The Farley Mount offender was masked during most of the attacks so the police artist's impression could provide little detail.

The man who preys on courting couples has driven the public away from the Hampshire beauty spot of Farley Mount.

In spite of wide appeals for information,
the police have not yet found their man.

or hatred or anything like that, I think that's counterproductive. I want him caught because of what he did to that other lady who nearly died and because I want him taken out of circulation. He's definitely not a normal individual, because it's only recently that I have discovered that he was not interested in money. His primary interest is sex, but I've only just heard that recently. So he must be a very peculiar and perverted creature, wouldn't you say? To think of him prowling round is a very nasty thought, because someone else may be in danger. That's true, isn't it?'

Jane was lucky. As she says in this interview, the same man broke into the home of another elderly woman more than a year later, on 5 August 1999, raped her brutally, and left her severely traumatized and in great pain: she was rushed to hospital and was lucky to escape with her life. He has raped two other victims, and not long after Jane's ordeal attempted to rape yet another elderly woman, who died shortly afterwards: the incident would have been classed as murder but for the fact that the post-mortem concluded she had died of natural causes. But the most astonishing thing about this criminal is that he has been active since 1992 and has committed a total of about sixty offences without being caught: he has indecently assaulted twenty-two more women in various ways, and burgled the homes of a further forty. The youngest victim was sixty-five, the oldest ninety-two. This man is probably the country's most prolific serial offender, and the nature of his crimes is particularly horrific: there is something uniquely chilling and repulsive about the sexual violation of defenceless elderly women – the infringement of a taboo that is almost as powerful as society's rejection of paedophilia. In the most twisted way, this man was, as Julian Boon was later to remark, 'in love with the old folk'.

There was something of a delayed reaction to the evident urgency of these cases by the Metropolitan Police: one reason for this was that they realized at a relatively late stage that they were dealing with a string of related crimes by one man, rather than the work of a variety of offenders. The realization came in 1998 when they re-examined a 1992 offence and advances in DNA science allowed them to link it to later offences. Another reason for the delay was that rape inquiries are nearly always given a lower priority than murder cases, and therefore tend to get somewhat pushed aside in a hard-pressed crime office with homicides coming in all the time. But internal case reviews and independent inspections of the force's work eventually focused on the fact that the crimes were indeed a series, and that sooner or later there was likely to be a fatality. The most serious of the rapes was yet to come, but the decision was taken in 1998 to assign significantly higher resources to the case and make a determined push to solve it and put the offender behind bars. The investigation was codenamed Operation Minstead – a prosaic name selected randomly off a list, with no real meaning and no specific relevance to the area or the case; but Minstead Man, as the offender has been dubbed, contains an echo of Piltdown Man, with its hint of something primitive and primeval. The tabloid press, naturally, has described him as a fiend and a monster.

The leadership of the beefed-up inquiry went to Detective Chief Inspector Duncan Wilson, a large Scotsman with an Aberdonian accent, who has spent much of his career in the uniform branch and the internal anti-corruption squad. He takes a keen interest in pistol shooting, and sailing. One of the first tasks of his new regime was a thorough review of all the crimes that could possibly be linked: Laura Richards, a civilian crime analyst with the Metropolitan Police, embarked on the long and painstaking task of looking at every offence that might have been carried out by Minstead Man, logging and comparing every available detail. One important link was DNA: the offender was generally very careful not to leave evidence behind and on one occasion took a victim's nightdress into the kitchen and carefully washed the semen off it, but there were several occasions when he hadn't been so careful and a DNA sample had been obtained. Unfortunately, as in the case of the murder of Yvonne Killian, there was no match with the relatively new database of DNA samples from convicted criminals that was established in the early 1990s.

The other main linking factor analysed by Richards was the criminal's unusually elaborate and consistent *modus operandi*. It was clear that he spent long hours observing and staking out his target houses, making sure they were occupied by single elderly women, and that his burglary skills were exceptional. Usually he cut the telephone cable before he started to gain entry. He did not break windows, but used a glass-cutter to take out a section of a window, often carefully removing wooden battens and placing them neatly nearby. He wore dark clothing, a black balaclava and gloves, and once he was inside the house he located and turned off the electricity supply. He then used a torch as he moved about, often shining it directly into the eyes of his victims to make it more difficult for them to see him. His dark clothing and taciturnity made it difficult to put together a definite description, and he had never left a fingerprint behind. 'If we had a fingerprint, we'd be up and running,' said one officer. The best the police can say is that he is black or of mixed race (one or two victims have thought he was white), that he is between twenty-five and thirty-five years old, and between 5 feet 8 inches and 6 feet 1 inch tall. Those who had heard his voice said he was softly spoken, and probably well-educated.

Richards also analysed the location and chronology of the crimes. The area where Minstead Man was committing his offences is a sickle-shaped swathe of the south-eastern rim of London – leafy suburbia, with pockets of poorer housing and council estates. It stretches from Sidcup and Bexleyheath in the east, round through Orpington, Beckenham and Croydon to Warlingham in the west, covering a total of 145 square miles.

It was 1992 when the criminal began his attacks, among them the rape of an eighty-nine-year-old woman in Warlingham. After the first spate came a gap of four years, which was unexplained, but police speculated that it might have coincided with a period in jail, in the armed services, or even at college or university. In 1996 the attacks began again, many of them burglaries combined with some form of indecency that stopped short of actual rape, and the police finally became aware that they were linked. The attacks continued at all times of year including Christmas and Bank Holidays, and included the attempted rape in 1998 in Warlingham.

In the summer of 1999, when the revamped investigation was in full swing and Richards' analysis was almost complete, there was a spate of attacks within a few days of each other, as if a kind of crescendo was approaching. 'We got to the stage,' Wilson recalled, 'when I used to wake up and wonder why my pager wasn't going off at about half past four, five o'clock in the morning.' After the rape of an eighty-two-year-old woman in Croydon in the last week of July, the police felt sure that Minstead Man would strike again soon and began to organize huge observation and surveillance operations in what were thought to be his target areas. 'There was an officer waiting up every tree,' as one observer of the case put it. The police put up a £10,000 reward for information leading to the offender's conviction. There was a sudden surge of confidence, a new expectation that Minstead Man was finally going to be caught and brought to justice for his string of peculiarly anti-social crimes.

Richard's detailed crime analysis was not the only means by which the police were trying to kick-start the Minstead inquiry. They had already commissioned some profiling work on the case from Simon Wells, one of two in-house police profilers now working at the National Crime Faculty. With Wells, Wilson and Richards devised a 'matrix' that ranked the importance to be given to certain factors like the age of the potential suspect and the kind of criminal history he is likely to have. In the search for new ideas, they also decided to seek a second profile from Julian Boon, and on 5 August 1999 DCI Wilson travelled to Leicester University with Richards and another member of his team, Detective Sergeant Steve Littler. As he waited for them, Boon was on typical cheeky-chappie form: 'And now for my next miracle... It's been one of the busiest weeks of my life and as soon as I finish here I've to get off up to Yorkshire where there's a murder case, so business is, to say the least, brisk. This is my holiday week, and I may or may not be invited back into the marital bed when I return.' Behind the flippant remark, however, lies the serious issue of the ad hoc, hit-and-miss nature of profilers' work with the police: they have to fit it in when they can between their other professional obligations, and the timing is often not ideal or convenient.

When the police team arrived, they were, by contrast, in a sombre mood. While travelling north, they had received the grim news on the telephone that Minstead Man had struck again the previous night: he had broken into an elderly woman's home, committed his most serious rape yet – the one mentioned at the start of this chapter – and once again made good his escape. His victim was in hospital in a serious condition, in danger of losing her life, and had not yet been able to give a complete statement to the police. Suddenly there was an extra urgency in the search for a new lead, a new idea, a new direction: if they didn't find this man soon, it was very likely they would have a corpse on their hands, with all the associated public concern about the failure to solve this long sequence of especially distressing offences.

Boon listened carefully as Wilson – who, coincidentally, had like him taken a psychology degree at Aberdeen University – gave a summary of the history of Operation Minstead and outlined the current investigative strategy. The principal strand in this was the possibility that whoever was selecting and targeting his elderly women victims might be a care worker of some kind who gained knowledge about them in the course of his daily life. One theory was that he might be a dial-a-ride or a meals-on-wheels driver. Wilson also mentioned two curious aspects of the case: that two of the victims had actually been men, and that the offender had shown a bizarre interest in the physical welfare of three women. 'Simon Wells, who did some initial work on this, said that was fairly unusual behaviour in his experience of thousands of rape statements,' said Wilson.

Boon thought so too, and asked for more details. Richards told him that in two of the rape cases the victims had complained of chest pains: in one of them the criminal had paused to check her condition and carried on with the assault, while in the other he had checked her condition and then decamped. In the third instance, a burglary, he had grabbed the victim and thrown her to the ground, then stopped to see that she was all right before he ran off. This incident had happened when the victim had banged her walking stick on the linen basket and shouted at him to get out of her house, and Wilson linked it to another incident where the victim had gone on the offensive: 'He'd actually exposed himself to her, she used an expression along the lines of "Now what would your mother think of the behaviour you're adopting now?" That made him put his penis away and start moving around the house.'

Boon asked if he kissed his victims ('There were a couple where kissing features'), what the houses were like ('very, very evident that a lot of elderly people live there'), and whether the victims had been receiving the same kind of social services ('Well, that's one of the lines of inquiry that we're seriously fast-tracking'). But the case where the attacker had thrown his victim to the ground made Boon particularly interested to know exactly how much violence he generally used. Richards explained that he had gripped one woman round the face and pressed a pillow on the face of another for a short time. But this wasn't the norm, she said: 'His general demeanour has been more or less respectful. Aside from the sexual assault, when they've asked to go to the toilet, he's quite happy for them to do so. He's quite happy to basically sit on the bed, and with one victim he put his head on her shoulder. There's no sort of violence or callousness towards most of them at all. One victim responded to him and was quite inquisitive about him – how did he get in, how old is he and so forth. She asked him what beer he normally drinks, just for conversation. And as he went to leave she said to him, are you going to go now? and she opened the door and said thank you for not hurting me, bye then. And he put out his hand to shake her hand as he left – and gently put her inside the door and pulled the door to and went.'

'Well, that's extremely helpful,' said Boon. There was brief discussion about the small amounts of money and trinkets that the offender usually took, then Wilson asked Boon what he called the '$64,000 dollar question' – was the level of violence likely to increase? Boon replied that it was probably not going to increase because it was clear to him that the attacker's main interest was the sex and the strong desire for the elderly victim to enjoy the sex. He said the attacker prepared his activities very thoroughly and was clearly meticulous about controlling the environment of his crime by disabling the lights and telephones. But this was not reflected in a desire to control the victim through humiliation or sadism: he was organized in his entry, but flexible in the encounter and able to master his impulses – leaving the house immediately, for example, if more than one person or the wrong type of person was in it. 'That's good news about the likelihood of an escalation of violence,' said Boon. 'So you're not going to start seeing undue bashings, cuttings and all the other charming things that certain types of offenders can move on to.' But he added that, according to the principles of 'process theory', the frequency of the offences might increase and he might even become careless enough to get caught: 'When you jump out of an aeroplane on your first parachute jump, it's a pretty hairy experience. But over time that diminishes. So you turn it into a hobby and do it as often as possible. An adrenaline rush – nothing like the same shove you got the first time, but a mild, pleasurable rush. But because that tends to plateau, you need to do it more often, vary it, take a few more risks, go into sky diving and things like that.' And he warned – as Jane had pointed out to her attacker – that the real danger for the victim might be 'the old dodgy ticker – if you're in your eighties and you're female and you're frail and you've got somebody coming in, it's enough in itself to push somebody over the edge'.

Boon appeared to be getting into an impressive stride on the basis of a quite short acquaintance with the case. His remarks about frequency seemed to tie in with events of the previous two weeks, in each of which there had been a first incident where the attacker had a frustrating experience, followed quickly by a second incident that included a rape. His principal theme now was the need of the attacker for a 'pseudo-relationship' with the victim, which drove him to try to integrate himself in her domestic scene – standing at the window and looking out, helping himself to a drink from the fridge, taking jewellery or trinkets as a souvenir, expressing concern over her physical welfare. Richards told him about the offender's bizarre habit of taking away his victims' false teeth, describing one incident where he had asked a woman to remove her top set while he was kissing her, had tried to remove the bottom set as well, but been told: 'They're my own – you won't be able to get those out, dear.' The fact that this did not lead to oral sex or other humiliating acts confirmed Boon's view that it was simply further evidence that the offender wanted 'a loving, respectful relationship, in this warped way... bloomers rather than briefs.'

The police told him they had taken steps to reassure victims and provided added protection for them because of the possibility that the attacker might return, something that Boon also considered possible. Anything visible like an alarm on the outside of the house could at the very least prevent offences, he thought, because events had shown that the criminal was cautious, and likely to move on or leave it to another night if he saw any 'target-hardening' measures. From here Boon made his first recommendation – to put known voyeurs on the list of possible suspects: 'I would be very interested in window-peerers – that is in this boy's history... he gets off on voyeurism too, he gets a thrill out of watching other people's houses on the go. And not just a thrill as in the deep interest of a cat watching a mouse, but a sexual thrill. And masturbating in the garden is a decided possibility.'

This recommendation about targeting voyeurs was to have consequences for the development of the inquiry: the police already had a potentially vast pool of suspects consisting of all the black or mixed-race burglars in south-east London, and adding people with a history of voyeurism to the list would make it larger still – and potentially unmanageable.

Boon continued his peroration on the case in full performance mode – animated, dramatic, deeply immersed in his subject and talking with great conviction. All the crime locations, he pointed out, had networks of alleyways and open spaces around them that the criminal would know like the back of his hand, moving among them 'quasi-commando-style – I mean when he goes out on the razzle dressed in his gear, I think prancing up and down the rat runs, I think he probably gets a bit of a buzz out of that, as well.' But he discounted the possibility of the man having had military training, saying he'd be too 'soft' and 'pansy'. The police were not exactly reduced to silence, but the latter half of the meeting was dominated by Boon's interpretative discourse. The session eventually closed with the police saying it would help them add new questions to the comprehensive questionnaire they were planning to give to all the victims, and asking Boon to come down to south London to look at the crime scenes. There was also a slightly nervous exchange about how Boon's initial profile bore very little similarity to the one drawn up six months previously by Simon Wells, a copy of which they promised to send him. Meanwhile they left him a package of comprehensive information running to hundreds of pages.

The Minstead case held geographical echoes for Boon because he had been brought up in West Wickham, on the edge of the criminal's areas of operation, and for eleven years had caught the train to the City of London School from Beckenham Junction: 'And Mr Ray Buckton, who was the ASLEF leader, used to regularly cause mayhem by suspending the railways in the south-east, and as a schoolboy I couldn't have loved him more.' Now, as he cleared up his office, he reflected further on what the police had told him and pronounced that it was the strongest case of gerontophilia he had ever encountered. He thought the offender would be somebody unmarried with an inability to forge normal relationships, in particular with young women; it was likely he would have been raised in a respectable family, possibly by one parent, and might have been smothered with love and spoiled. He might also have been discouraged from forming relationships with the warning that they would be too difficult or dangerous for him. The fact that some victims reported that he seemed to feel some shame about what he was doing was further evidence of that kind of background, said Boon. At the same time Minstead Man was likely to be articulate, intelligent, well-educated and quite capable of holding down a job: 'a loner, and socially isolated, but not a weirdo loner'.

'Compensatory rapist' was the term he chose to describe the offender's sexual perversion: 'I don't care for these blanket terms myself, but in this instance it's not bad because it's quite clear that the reptile concerned is compensating for something he hasn't got in his life. At least part of the thieving is recreational, it gives him a buzz, but there's also a sexual buzz, a buzz of intimacy – using the loo, going into the cellar, taking a beer, and that sort of thing. Now that is quite a well-established pattern of a particular type of offender. It really is in many ways copybook, and that was why I was able to adumbrate what the officers were about to say – you know, I was not surprised that the victims weren't stripped bare or made to do humiliating things, because that is not what that sort of offender is remotely about. That sort of offender is compensating for a need and a desire for a relationship at a psychological, mental, even romantic level. And I wouldn't be surprised if there weren't letters or expressions of concern for the victims afterwards – hope you're all right, or thank you very much, or something like that.'

The offender was also, he said, drawn to the paraphernalia of old people, such as the false teeth and walking sticks, and was likely to be keeping a collection of the pieces of jewellery and trinkets he took, rather than selling them for cash. He wasn't interested in pushing old people about or being sadistic towards them: the only way he used control was to make sure he was safe from capture and would leave no forensic traces behind, and to put him in a position to forge a relationship of some kind with the victim. In that relationship he was often flexible and far from controlling.

'And remember when he got turned off and was sent away with the words, what would your mother say about this? Can you imagine a sadistic rapist doing anything but say, you shut your mouth or I'll shut it for you? Big difference. What this boy does is lose his sexual excitement, up goes the zip, and he goes to have a look around the domesticity – unrelated to what a burglar would do, as well. No, he's doing it because he's rewarded by the sexual activity with old people. He wants to foster a relationship with them. I suspect myself that he can constantly reassure himself of his sexuality, of his sexual capability, with people he could think might almost be grateful to him for what he's done. And only when they point out that this is disgusting does he suddenly have the element of remorse or guilt. It's as if it's the nearest thing he's going to get to a successful relationship.'

While Boon was ruminating about the offender in his Leicester University office, the police party, on the way back to London, was being asked for reactions to the meeting. DCI Wilson was fairly forthright: 'Well, without being offensive to Julian, there were no major surprises. But I think the reassuring thing for us is that the ideas that we'd thrown around in an intuitive way actually have some scientific basis. When I have a conversation like that with somebody as well qualified as Julian, it gives you the opportunity to get to know the offender just that little bit better, to understand some of the things that are going on inside his head. It's quite reassuring to hear from a man who has complete understanding of human behaviour. And it helps me understand that we're actually getting a little bit closer to catching him. Julian's actually giving us some ideas about prioritization, and I think that's quite useful. I think

Julian's going to make quite a significant contribution to the investigation – one of the many investigative tools in our toolbox. And it's the complete toolbox that's going to solve the crime.'

He felt Boon had confirmed their hunch that the criminal was moving around off the roads in a 'quasi-commando' way. More importantly, perhaps, he had confirmed their concern about frequent reoffending that was becoming ever more acute. The offender had struck four times in the previous fortnight, culminating with the vicious rape of the previous night. When they got back to base, Wilson and his colleagues learned fuller details of that incident and their level of concern intensified: when the victim had refused to comply with the attacker's demands for sex, he had initially moved away, but then returned and raped her anyway, causing extensive bleeding and great pain. She was to need surgery and a long stay in hospital. This looked like a significant escalation in the level of violence, confounding Boon's view that such an escalation was unlikely, and it looked like only a matter of time before the police would be dealing with a murder.

In many ways, they were doing all they could to catch the offender: staking out the areas where he was likely to strike, using surveillance cameras, continuing with the programme of taking mouth swabs for DNA samples from men on the long and cumbersome list they had compiled. From the start, their biggest problem had been how to refine that list to manageable proportions – since it could not be restricted to known offenders only, it potentially included every adult black and mixed race male in London and the south-east. Twenty-eight officers were now working full-time on the case, with dozens more called in for special operations. People who had been attacked before were being given extra protection, and a programme of encouraging elderly people to take extra security measures was under way in conjunction with social services departments and agencies for the elderly. The glaring omission, however, was that people were not being told exactly why those extra security measures were deemed necessary. The world at large had not yet heard about the prolonged run of nasty crimes committed by Minstead Man.

Was it time to go public? There was an agonized debate in the police team about whether this would stop the criminal from offending at the very time when the dragnet was so widely spread that his next offence might well bring his capture. On the other hand, there was no certainty of this, and if another elderly woman was raped, or even killed, and it emerged afterwards that the police could have warned her and failed to do so, all hell would break loose. The question was given new urgency by the serious medical condition of the latest victim. It was an extremely difficult call, and in trying to make up his mind about it, DCI Wilson made a number of telephone calls to Julian Boon, who was giving him detailed advice on press strategy. The psychologist's view was that publicity might stop the offender in the short term, but his compulsions were clearly irresistible and he would sooner or later show his hand again. Boon, whose deep and informed interest in wine has already been noted, was later to use the metaphor of trying to hold down a champagne cork once the foil and wire had been removed.

Eventually the police became persuaded that it was more important to alert the community and potential victims to the seriousness of what was going on than it was to wait for the next offence and hope he would be caught. A decision to 'go public' was taken at a meeting between Wilson and his supervising officers, including Commander Carole Howlett, now in charge of crime investigation for the whole of south London. Clearly, the best thing would be to catch him and put him behind bars: but it wouldn't be an entirely bad thing if publicity simply put him off committing more crimes.

Asked a short time later about his decision to go public, Wilson emphasized that the police had 'a duty of care' towards the elderly and their families and had to make sure they received the best possible crime prevention advice. Telling the world about these serial crimes would encourage people to come forward with information and make the offender aware that the police knew about all his activities: 'Maybe by doing that we can exercise some form of control,' said Wilson. 'But I can only repeat myself in saying that I don't think this individual will stop.' Asked if going public might reduce the chances of catching him by scaring him off, Wilson said he thought it would actually increase the chances of catching him: he felt sure that the offender had come to the notice of the police at some stage in his criminal career and that by a process of elimination he would eventually be found. 'I think that the press strategy of making contact with the community, and being up front with the community, will actually accelerate that process.'

On Friday 13 August 1999, Wilson called a press conference at New Scotland Yard and gave some – but by no means all – of the details of the string of offences committed by Minstead Man. He revealed that the crimes had started in 1992, but limited himself to talking about the twenty offences that were either rapes, the attempted rape or the indecent assaults. For fear of alerting the offender about how much the police knew about him, he did not talk in detail about the *modus operandi*, or say that some of the offences had been linked by DNA evidence. Instead he angled the press conference towards an appeal to people who might have knowledge of the offender – prison officers, police officers and others who worked in the community. Wilson's keynote was that elderly people and those responsible for their care should be vigilant and if possible take special measures to protect their homes, and he stressed the £10,000 reward on offer. He also mentioned that a psychological profiler had been called in to help, but mercifully none of the resulting headlines used the term 'Cracker'. They did, however, use such descriptions as 'sex beast'.

The press conference had an effect like the fall of a guillotine: Minstead Man stopped in his tracks. From that day until the time of writing, sixteen months later, there is no definite indication that he has committed any further offences. The confidence of Boon and Wilson that nothing – not even publicity – was likely to stop him, has apparently been completely confounded. The possible reasons for this abrupt and protracted hiatus, and the fact that Minstead Man may still be at large, have caused almost as much anxiety and stress for the police and their advisers as they would have felt if the offences had continued. The strangeness of the attacker's motivation and the efficient conduct of his crimes have been capped by the mystery of his disappearance, for which there is no certain explanation – and which may or may not be temporary. Would Minstead Man show his hand again?

THE OFFENDER VANISHES 8

'It was like telling someone you're going to do a stake-out of Barclays before they go and do the armed robbery.'

Detective Constable Derek Reid

The decision to hold the press conference on 13 August had not been well received by some of the officers working on Operation Minstead. Many of them felt that the crimes were coming thick and fast, that the criminal seemed to be getting more careless, and that, if the police had just held their nerve for a little longer and trusted to the surveillance and stake-out operations that they had in place, they may have struck lucky. Detective Constables David Glenister and Derek Reid – known respectively as Daisy and Del – were two members of the team who hadn't been happy about the decision, but it was only nine months later, in summer 2000, that they were prepared to speak out about their feelings.

'I think the decision to go public was right in itself,' said Glenister. 'But the timing was ridiculous. I mean, this person had struck four times in two weeks, and we were in a position to go pro-active the week after. We had so many officers up there, and in my opinion we would have caught him that week, because he was busy that week. He had been out and done four, and he didn't know we were aware of it. We had up to a hundred officers for the two weeks following, manning a number of observation posts, surveillance teams, cameras. We were in a good position, had planned it all, and a few days before, they notified the press. The decision to go public was self-defeating, to be honest. It was made at a level higher than us, but everyone at the lower level said it was nonsense. If it was my decision – well, I'm not paid for those decisions, but personally I would have held off.'

Glenister's views were echoed by his colleague Reid, who called the timing of the press conference 'obscene'. He went on: 'I don't think he could have come into the cluster areas where we had observation posts and cameras and personnel, and not get caught. He only needed to show his face and we would have caught him. But the day before we went pro-active, it was splashed all over the news. Well, it was the psychological profiler who said he would carry on offending – that was what swayed it: "He cannot help himself, he will carry on."'

Glenister cut in: 'Whether you go public or not, he will still re-offend, that was the message. And in truth, he's stopped dead. Very sad.'

Reid resumed: 'Which is good from the point of view that he hasn't offended again, but not so good if he wants catching. To me it was like telling someone you're going to do a stake-out of Barclays before they go and do the armed robbery.'

Glenister and Reid were giving their views as they were driving around London on the seemingly endless task of taking DNA samples from people on a list of several thousand. They were trading on the benefits of hindsight, and it was clear that they were disgruntled and felt antagonistic about Boon's psychological profile. In contrast to what Wilson had said on the way back from the earlier meeting with Boon, they felt his profile – far from focusing the suspect list more tightly – had in fact played a part in expanding it and increasing their work load unnecessarily. In general, they were fairly dismissive about the profile: 'Well, I think he told us what we could have told him, to be honest,' said Reid. 'It's a bit similar to having a string of burglaries in a specific area where the video and the telly have been nicked, and the psychological profiler will tell you it's probably a drug addict. Well, most policemen will tell you that.' Glenister said bluntly: 'I'd liken it to a palmist.' Both officers felt Boon's work had been of less use than a geographical profile commissioned by the investigation which had used a computer programme to analyse the relationship between the crime locations and come up with an assessment of where the offender was likely to live.

The geographical profile had narrowed down the target area to about 2.3 square miles, and they felt they would stand a better chance of success if they concentrated on that area. It contained a large population of about 14,000 people, but that seemed more manageable to these two grass-roots officers than their current pursuit of DNA samples from people who lived as far afield as Hampstead in north London and Wandsworth in south-west London. They complained about the difficulties of locating people, about the task of persuading them to give a mouth swab – which they are entitled to refuse – and about the need to go back several times to some addresses if people were out. 'It's extremely labour-intensive,' said Glenister. 'And I would go so far as to say that with all the people in our system, I could certainly see out my last five years or so in the police and still not have dealt with every single one of them.' Although they felt DNA, with the growing national database, offered a good hope of catching the culprit, they actually thought a fingerprint would be more useful because the database of fingerprints had existed for much longer and was more comprehensive.

But even allowing for their disgruntlement, they appeared to make some cogent points about the timing of the press conference. Might it not have been better to delay the public announcement for several days or weeks to give the pro-active operations a real chance to seize the elusive Minstead Man? Would the risks really have outweighed the potential benefits? Like most hypothetical questions, these do not lend themselves to a definite answer, not least because there is no way of being sure that the offender would have struck again, even if the press conference had not been held. Boon and Wilson, as will become clear, began to feel that it might have been something other than publicity resulting from the press conference that stopped him in his tracks – his own sense of guilt and remorse, perhaps, or a decisive event in his life. These are questions that continue to dog this frustrating and protracted inquiry.

Nearly a year before these two officers spoke out, Boon spent much of the August holiday period of 1999 reading steadily through the thick pile of paperwork on the case and studying Laura Richards's crime analysis. She had taken more than forty cases, analysing each one from thirty different aspects, with up to ten bits of information listed under each aspect – a mountain of detail. He had also been given pictures or videos of all the victims' houses. As is so often the case with offender profilers in Britain, Boon had turned his own dining room into a makeshift incident room and was doing the work in his spare time and late at night. But it was not until 17 September, six weeks after the worst and last of the rapes and five weeks after the controversial press conference, that he was in a position to provide a preliminary report on Operation Minstead and to be interviewed about it. As he talked, he walked up and down the room in the same way that he moves around the platform in the lecture theatre at Leicester University. His analysis provided, in effect, a case study of his profiling methodology.

'The first step is always to look at salient case details,' he said. 'Now what I mean by that is details from an infinite array of potential pieces of information. It could be the shape of the house roof, it could be the colour of the wallpaper, it could be something about the victims, it could be the locality, it could be the *modus operandi* of the offender. It's very important to have a clear understanding of the nature of the crime and to try to draw out some details: whether or not there are chestnut trees in the garden or maple trees – may be important, may not be important. This case is exceptional, by anybody's standards, in that we've got in the region of forty crimes that have significant similarities amongst them in respect of the nature of the properties that are being attacked and the nature of what is being done. Now the job for me is to try to distil the commonalities and to work back from that to see what might be the salient case details.'

Boon then ran through what he considered to be the characteristics common to all the crimes, adding to and expanding aspects that had been mentioned at the preliminary meeting with the police six weeks earlier. First of all came the fact that all the homes targeted by the criminal could be easily identified as sheltered accommodation or places occupied by elderly people – some had handrails or other distinctive features, others were in areas with a high density of elderly people. And it would not take much extra observation to confirm that the occupant was a lone woman. Secondly, the criminal had impressive skills as a burglar, particularly in the silent removal of glass, including double-glazed panes that normally present greater obstacles. Other skills included cutting telephone lines and disabling the electricity supply in the house, but it was notable that he didn't use the darkness to try to scare his victims by jumping out at them or making noises. Thirdly, he often began his encounter with the victim by demanding money, as if he was just a burglar, but it quickly became clear that money was not his principal motivation.

Once he was in the house he would stay for at least half an hour and sometimes up to five hours, and would sometimes stand at the window for ten or fifteen minutes as if he wanted to be part of the victim's life – 'This is serving, in my opinion, the psychological function, which is that I don't think he'd like to think he was intruding. I think he'd like to think he was part of it – looking at the scene, being part of the scene, being part of the ongoing process.' This went hand in hand with the next point: that he tried to forge pseudo-loving relationships with the victims – the more elderly the better – wanting to kiss some of them and suggest that there was romance in the air. One notable exception to this had come when he broke into a house, using his characteristic method, and found a woman in her mid-fifties asleep in bed; this time he left without starting any of his usual activities.

Next, there was an absence of violence in his methods, which was unusual in sex crimes: 'It is very uncommon not to take control and say, you will do this or I will kill you, stab you, come back, remember I know where you live, if you do or say anything to a living soul you've had your chips – usually very nasty. What is conspicuously absent in this case is anything of the kind. At most the offender will say, don't tell anyone, and even that is uncommon, and when the victim says look, I'm old, what's in it for you, he says, it doesn't matter. He can even be bitten and not respond, he can be physically attacked and all he will do is hold back. A very large percentage of rapists gather control by saying, "Shut up and you won't get hurt." This is "Don't scream, sshh, please don't scream."'

The exception to this reluctance to use violence was, said Boon, the last of Minstead Man's attacks – the rape of 5 August, which left the victim in hospital and lucky to escape with her life. But Boon now developed in detail a theory that this had not been deliberate, but a mistake and a misunderstanding. The rape had taken place in complete darkness, and the offender may have misinterpreted the signs and failed to realize how brutal he was being. When he went to the bathroom to clean himself up, he realized how much his victim had been bleeding and that she must be in pain; at this point he became compassionate rather than aggressive, taking a towel to her before leaving the scene. So even when things got out of hand like this, there was no profanity, sadism or wilful humiliation of victims: 'There's no biting, no cutting, no hitting, gratuitous or otherwise. Even when victims have said taunting things to him, he does not react.'

Next, said Boon, there came the offender's strange interest in the victim's mouth and teeth which sometimes led him to apply considerable force until the victim yielded up her dentures or did what she was told. Then there was the sexual interest: 'This comprises, principally, basic gropings around the genital area, the breast area, and on the occasions when he ejaculates, it appears that it is a combination of masturbation and premature ejaculation, showing perhaps a lack of experience, and also the nature of what this individual finds gratifying – going into an old lady's house and interfering with her, totally against the normal sexual preference of heterosexual men in their twenties and thirties.' There also appeared to be a trade-off between money and sex, in that failure to obtain sexual gratification often increased his desire to take money or jewellery with him when he went, perhaps so that he could feel he was getting something out of it.

Finally, the criminal was very good at leaving at the right moment to make sure he didn't get caught, which indicated a large degree of control. The victims who fared best were those who indicated that they were not enjoying what was going on and wanted him to go. Because of his need to feel that he was in a relationship with them, he would sometimes comply and let them take him to the door, and there was the extraordinary case when he shook hands with his victim when he left. In one instance where his victim ran out of the house calling for help, he did not try to restrain her but made his own escape as quickly as possible. This all indicated, Boon concluded, a highly developed ability to control his impulses which was another common theme throughout the string of crimes.

His analysis of the salient case details was now complete, and Boon turned to the question of how they could be used to produce information that would be helpful to the police in investigating the crimes. He began by developing the point that the offender was that rare and complex form of deviant, a gerontophile – somebody who loves elderly people in a perverted way, who wants to be part of their world, and whose most ardent desire is to have sex with them. The perversion probably had its origins in some sort of attraction at an early stage in his life to elderly women, said Boon, and he would have been aware of it for most of his adult life: 'Gerontophilia is not something where you have a string of heterosexual relationships with people the same age and suddenly wake up on Tuesday when you're thirty-two and think, actually this isn't for me, I really fancy grannies. You know about it. You've had those urges throughout your adolescence and your twenties – it's not something that has suddenly come out of the woodwork.' Because of his long acquaintance with his own perversion, he would know in his heart of hearts that it was wrong; for part of the time he might be able to convince himself that he was doing his victims a favour by giving them sexual attention, but if he was challenged or knew things weren't working, he would often desist. After one rape, he had told his victim that he would never do anything like that again. One encouraging aspect of all this, said Boon, was that there was unlikely to be an escalation of gratuitous violence in his behaviour – the biggest risk was simply the age and frailty of his victims.

The criminal was of average or high intelligence, Boon went on: he had successfully performed at least sixty break-ins without being caught, and his methods were well thought-out and effective. (This observation about intelligence was later to prompt the police into revising their parameters about the kind of job the offender was likely to have.) It was likely that he was still living with one or both of his parents, which would be comforting to him because of his predilection for elderly people. Because of his intelligence, it was likely that he was employed, and his work – as the police had already surmised – would probably involve contact with elderly women: anything from low-level nursing to work as a home help. He would probably be perceived by others as respectable and decent: 'He is likely to be a nice boy, a caring chap. That's the way I think the outer world, which doesn't know him very well, would be likely to see him. I think they would see him not just as gentle but as respectful towards the old folk in general – in love with the old folk.'

It was likely that the criminal was not married and had only limited sexual experience, said Boon: he acted in a basic, adolescent way with his victims, fumbling clumsily and asking for 'sex, sex, sex'. If he was in a relationship with a woman, it would probably be very dysfunctional. People around him would probably subscribe to the idea that he had never found the right girl: 'Well, let me say that unless the right girl happens to be eighty-five years of age, then I have to tell you, he ain't going to find the right girl.'

The fact that the criminal sometimes produced outbursts of crude language and four-letter words with his victims suggested that he would probably have pornographic material at his home involving elderly people: much of this would be stories, but some of it would be pictures. 'Extraordinary as it may seem, magazines such as *Yours*, which caters for the elderly and shows pictures of old people sitting in their houses, perfectly innocuously, will be meat and drink to him. Bear in mind that he is into all the paraphernalia of the old folk – the false teeth, the undergarments, the drawers. And then of course there are things like Saga holiday brochures, and I wouldn't be surprised if they show elderly people in swimsuits and the like, and those pictures would, I think, be of interest to him.'

Boon felt it was unlikely that Minstead Man had a criminal history involving violence, but burglary was obviously his strength and he had probably been doing it successfully throughout his adult life. His other common activity would be 'prolific peeping', and for every crime that came to light there would probably be dozens of instances where he was revisiting former crime scenes and watching through windows as elderly people got up, went to bed or used their bathrooms in the middle of the night. He would be unlikely to be a drug user, although he had said he was to one victim who asked him if he wanted the money for drugs. The police would do well to enlist the help of people like milkmen, postmen and dustmen to look out for men who went out jogging in the early hours of the morning, said Boon. Sooner or later he would be caught, because he would not be able to stop offending until he was caught; and the only things that could be said in his favour were that he was not interested in hurting and did have a genuine capacity for remorse and conscience. Unfortunately this only came into play when something went wrong, and it was only a matter of time, in Boon's view, before someone died; and he added that if somebody was found dead of a heart attack with a broken back window, the case should be treated as murder.

Boon's final point was to caution against thinking the offender was a monster in every sense because of the gross and nasty nature of his crimes: 'The usual thing is to say that if someone's done something really dreadful in one regard, that automatically means they're in it for the full Monty of evil behaviour. Because they can do that to an old lady, they think he must therefore be into cutting, dismemberment, hurting animals, this, that and the other. No such blanket evil is necessary. Indeed, his whole demeanour with these old people is one of social competence. It's very important that eyes are open to that, and that they don't just think, ah, Stebbins down the street, he's a right weirdo, he must have done it.' Boon's conclusion was: 'It's possible to concentrate on peeping. It's possible to concentrate on burglary. It's possible to concentrate on people who have an interest – seemingly safe or other-wise – in the welfare of old people.'

It was a few days later when the police team in the incident room at Beckenham in south London received a preliminary version of Boon's written profile. DCI Wilson was interviewed about it and said that he found it helpful in several ways and repeated the recurrent and some-what hackneyed metaphor that a profile was only one 'tool in the toolbox' of investigation: 'What Julian has said has added to and confirmed some of the directions of our inquiries.'

However, he was clearly pleased about the observation that the culprit could be a care worker, because it confirmed one line of inquiry that the police were already following – a particularly difficult line because for instance there are 156 care homes and agencies in a borough like Croydon alone, all with different employment and recruiting policies, all requiring careful investigation. He also thought it useful that Boon had said the criminal would spend about 90 per cent of his time watching and peeping, and only about 10 per cent of his time actually doing things: this meant that it was likely someone had seen him watching and waiting, and therefore the existing strategy of appealing for information through the press was a good one.

He remained confident that it had been right to go to the press in the first place the previous month, that it would not stop the criminal from offending, and that it would increase rather than decrease the chances of catching him. He was also sure he would have come to the attention of the police in the past, and any details in the criminal records system might also play a part in catching him. But Wilson was more sceptical about the usefulness of Boon's observation that the culprit might be a loner and have difficulty in forming relationships: that meant it was less likely that other people knew him well or were close enough to him to appreciate that he was often away from home for long periods during the night.

Wilson was asked about the difficulties of dealing with a profiler who – like most of them – works outside the police service and has to fit his profiling activities into his day-to-day work. The frustrating thing, he replied, was that Boon was so far away geographically and a lot of their conversations had to be conducted by telephone: 'So the distance is a frustration – it would be nice if we had our profilers in-house and working with a team on a day-to-day basis, but that's not always possible. That's one of the frustrations, but I think one of the healthy benefits is that he's absolutely nothing to do with police culture and environment and provides a nicely independent perspective on some of the things we're looking at. You have to keep a very open mind as an investigating officer, you can't fixate on one line of inquiry.'

Once again the press strategy was high in Wilson's mind, because he had decided that he was going to hold another press conference at Scotland Yard a few days later. As in the case of the first press conference of 13 August, the timing of which was to prove more controversial the longer the criminal stayed quiet, this event was designed with strong input from Boon. 'He has been advising on how we actually conduct our press events and press releases, so undoubtedly before we go to press again on Friday, I'll be talking to him again,' said Wilson. He did not say exactly what Boon's advice had been, but when this new press conference took place on 24 September it was immediately clear that he was prepared to go into greater detail about the crimes.

Inquiries from the crime correspondents of a couple of national newspapers in the preceding few days indicated that they had learned about the existence of DNA evidence in the case, and he had decided he would give confirmation of this: there was suspicion and displeasure among the officers that the correspondents might have seen internal police documents. Wilson also intended to release an e-fit picture of a man he wanted to eliminate, and some still photographs and videos of a figure that could be the offender: the pictures, taken at night in one of the 'cluster' areas, were not very distinct, but there were hopes that someone would recognize his heavy, distinctive way of walking. Wilson also wanted to give out an illustration from a Sotheby's catalogue of a pocket watch with some initials engraved on its back that had been taken from a victim in 1992. But the most sensitive part of the press conference was expected to be the announcement for the first time of the true number of offences believed to have been committed by Minstead Man.

Metin Enver, a Scotland Yard press officer, prepared Wilson for the encounter by rehearsing with him the kind of hard questions he was likely to get from the assembled reporters. 'Their big news is they're going to want to know how confident we are that the forty, fifty, sixty offences are actually committed by the same man. I think that's where we've got to be cautious, in the sense that that's their scare story... although the figure of sixty does sound harsh and horrific, anything, however tenuous the similarity of the *modus operandi*, would have been included in it – we can't throw anything out until we're sure it's not a Minstead job.' The rehearsal offered a small insight into the caution, bordering on suspicion, with which the police tend to deal with the media: Wilson compared it with going into the witness box at the Old Bailey.

The rehearsal also included a remarkable passage where Wilson was grilled about the case more fiercely than any fire-eating crime reporter by one of his superior officers, Detective Chief Superintendent Andy Baker, who was in charge of crime operations for the whole south-east area of the Metropolitan Police. 'So what are you doing?' snapped Baker. 'Why haven't you caught this man?' Wilson replied: 'Well, we're following a number of lines of inquiry, er, er, in our attempt to catch this man...' Baker: 'So what have you been doing since August 13?' Wilson: 'We've been doing a number of lines of inquiry, which have been developed...' Baker: 'Do you still have the same size team, Duncan?' Wilson: 'The number varies due to extractions, but approximately twenty-five.' Baker: 'I think you said twenty-eight last time...' Baker was playing devil's advocate, trying to help Wilson prepare for anything the press might throw at him, but the exchange seemed to put the spotlight on some basic questions in the Minstead inquiry.

The first decision to go to the media more than a month earlier had been influenced by Julian Boon's advice, and when the press conference proper opened his influence was demonstrated once again. Enver's opening statement reminded everyone that police had consulted a profiler: 'One of the pieces of information given to us by the profiler is that we'd be most grateful if you'd try to prevent yourselves from labelling our suspect either as a fiend or a monster. We don't know for sure that this would generate further instances, but if you are able to help I would be most grateful.' Wilson then rattled efficiently through the main points he wanted to make, and was given an unexpectedly easy ride on the question of the number of offences, possibly because the crime writers of the main national newspapers, who are usually more persistent and hungry for sensation than their local newspaper and television news counterparts, were not at the press conference this time.

At the debriefing afterwards the officers seemed satisfied and hopeful that their pleas for 'sensible reporting' had been taken to heart. 'What we need to do,' said DCS Baker, 'is make a note of those that have been sensible and perhaps go to them first in future and the others will wither on the vine.' It is not official policy for Scotland Yard to discriminate in the way it releases information, but Baker's remark suggests that, in practice, this is what may sometimes happen.

From this point the inquiry seemed to enter a period of limbo. The press conference produced no significant new information, either about the pocket watch or the man on the video with the peculiar walk. There were no fresh offences either, and it is conceivable that the release of the information that the police had DNA evidence might have reinforced the apparent resolution of the offender not to put himself at risk of being caught, at least for the time being. Hopes soared briefly when a man was arrested in early October who seemed to fit the profile, and slumped again when nothing came of it. Information came to light that suggested that the very first offence by Minstead Man might have been four years before the date in 1992, when he was previously thought to have started, but this was of academic rather than practical value. Otherwise there was so little information coming in that the inquiry team were obliged to re-examine existing information and ideas once again.

Julian Boon at last found an opportunity to do something he ideally would have done before rather than after writing his report – visit the cluster areas where the majority of the crimes had occurred. The late timing of this visit perhaps illustrates DCI Wilson's frustration about Boon's distance from the scene and the impossibility of a day-to-day relationship: time and again when profilers are employed, there are lengthy gaps between different stages of their work which can only make it more difficult for all concerned.

Reflecting on the case before the visit, Boon developed further his ideas about the gerontophilia exhibited by the criminal at large in south-east London. 'It could just be that at a particularly hormonal moment in adolescence he was exposed to some quasi-erotic stimulus, a film or something like that, involving an old woman. And I can think of a film, *Harold and Maude*, in which a rich young man obsessively seeks a relationship with an elderly woman. Now suppose he's watching that at the age of twelve or thirteen and he gets turned on by the sex scenes. Gradually that becomes a masturbatory fantasy that then develops, and then for whatever reason he cruises down that route. It gets to him more and more. So he goes down the local old folks' home and helps out there and then has the odd feel as he says, come on, let me help you up, you know. And then gradually the whole thing gets established. Another possibility would be that he was seduced at a prepubescent age by an elderly woman and then gradually came to accept this as the norm. Or at that particularly potent time he might have been exposed to an environment where elderly ladies were around and seen more than he should have and carried it forward.'

It was a windy, golden autumn day when the police took Boon on a journey round several of the 'cluster areas'. The excursion reminded Boon of his childhood in the locality and took him, coincidentally, past the home of one of his former teachers. The police drove him to suburban streets with romantic, sylvan names where semi-detached bungalows with large picture windows are surrounded by hedges, open spaces, walkways and footpaths. 'Paradise for him, paradise,' commented Boon. 'He'll know these ratruns round the back of the houses like the back of his hand... These railings for the staircase in front just indicate elderly people so clearly, I mean, it's almost like a beacon for him, isn't it? You see, we're standing here and that man hasn't even seen us. Now he's making his cup of tea... There's a sort of menu board as his eyes would see it. It would be like a magnet to him. He is, to vary a modern term used in discos and the like, sharking. For those my age and older it really means going out looking for totty or crumpet. He's doing much the same thing in his terms, going out looking for vulnerable victims who can satisfy his needs.'

They stopped in the sunshine to stroke local cats and speak to the relatives of victims, and looked at the route the offender had actually taken to break into houses. They also walked between the houses, getting a feel of how a prowler could easily spend hours in the area, unseen himself, but observing people through their windows: it remained Boon's view that the offender spent about 90 per cent of his time doing just that. 'I'll bet you he's done this,' he said, 'simply sitting in the back garden at night, watching the lights go on and off, what time does she go to bed, hoping she's going to leave the curtains open so he can see her going through in her nightdress. I think that's how he's identifying his victims.'

Again he predicted that the offender would not be able to stop himself from offending again, and that the police would find him because they were going about the task in the most intelligent way possible, homing in on geographical and behavioural details.

During the tour a conversation began on the subject which was to be possibly the most crucial aspect of the case from now on: the suspect list. One of the officers told Boon that if you consulted criminal records in, say, the London borough of Croydon for reported incidents involving peeping toms, you obtained a 25,000-strong list. Boon suggested that doing it in a more concentrated area and focusing on incidents in the early hours of the morning might more than halve the figure. DCI Wilson said that the team were working hard trying to get the suspect list down from 5,000: 'We have actually tasked local police divisions to give us as much intelligence as they can on anyone peeping, theft of washing from lines and that sort of thing. We've trawled just about every database that we have to get our suspect list.' He also said he was trying to obtain the staff and patient list of a mental hospital, near to the main cluster of offences: Boon's view, based on the principle that it was misguided to think that weird crimes must necessarily be committed by people with obvious mental health problems, was that it was a mistake to concentrate too much on people associated with the hospital.

In the autumn a routine police internal review said the team working on the Minstead inquiry could be larger. As Christmas approached the police decided to increase surveillance once again over the holiday period, partly because it was a time of year when the offender had struck before, and partly because of Boon's advice that he would be out there observing and prospecting even if he was not actually committing crimes. The results proved disappointing: the offender did not show up, and several officers went down with influenza after overnight vigils in bitter sub-zero temperatures. The Millennium came and went, and still there was no breakthrough and no further crime by Minstead Man. In March 2000 DCI Wilson revealed that he now had 3,500 people on his suspect list and that 1,000 of them had been eliminated after giving DNA samples. His major incident team had thirty-three officers, of whom only five or six were working on the Minstead case because of the pressure of other inquiries, and the previous week only five new DNA swabs had been taken. He conceded that there had been a dip in morale, and explained that he was calling in Neil Trainor from the National Crime Faculty to use a computer programme to analyse the fifty-eight crime sites and try to reduce his 'hunting area'. Trainor eventually produced the analysis mentioned earlier that narrowed down the area where the suspect might live from 145 square miles to just 2.3 square miles.

Meanwhile Boon continued to reflect on the case, mulling over the question of how long the offender could keep his impulses under control before returning perhaps to burglary, but then being tempted into indecent assault and rape once again. For the first time he raised the possibility, explored more fully later in the year, that the offender had committed suicide, either out of regret over the rape of 5 August 1999, or out of general self-disgust: many people did kill themselves, asserted Boon, when they become weary of struggling by themselves with socially unacceptable sexual desires. But he dwelt longer on the question of the offender's sense of shame and remorse, especially over the episode when he had probably thought the victim was enjoying it, then got 'the shock of his life' when he realized she was not. Now, for the first time, Boon began to speculate on the question of whether it might be possible to play on the offender's sense of remorse and issue an appeal for him to turn himself in.

By May the police had succeeded in persuading *Crimewatch UK* to screen an item on the case, including a clip of film reconstructing the offender breaking in and assaulting one of his victims. DCI Wilson phoned Boon to ask his advice about how to pitch the appearance on the programme, and Boon began by repeating that it would not be helpful to cast the criminal as a fiend. He told Wilson the offender should be described as intelligent, calm and methodical, but also as probably unable to hold down a normal relationship. If it was suggested he was ill and needed help, there was a possibility the offender would come forward, Boon said. He also raised the point about appealing to the man's conscience: 'I think he may well be willing to listen if someone was to point out that these are old ladies, and if someone just appears in their house in the middle of the night they may well just conk out – and you and I know that it's going to happen some day. But he has the capacity to feel remorse, repentance, the things to do with emotion. Perhaps he can be reached in that capacity.'

A TV crew from *Crimewatch* used a bungalow in one of the cluster areas to re-enact the attack on Jane, including a sequence where the criminal tells the victim not to scream, refuses to take the money and go and instead puts his head close to hers and asks for sex. There was constant concern among the film makers that they might be making the clip 'too spooky', and the director asserted that they didn't want to scare anybody watching the programme. Meanwhile Wilson explained that he had asked for the programme to be done in order to release more information about the case and appeal once again for people to come forward. The new information was that the offender spent a long time waiting outside and watching his victims, and that the geographical profile had suggested a tighter area where he might live.

Wilson confirmed that he would be following Boon's advice about not labelling the culprit as a monster in the interview he would be giving to the *Crimewatch* presenter after the reconstruction had been screened. On the other hand, he said, he would not be following his advice about appealing to the criminal's conscience and suggesting he should give himself up. This kind of appeal was something which, in his experience, did not work particularly well and would not be appropriate in this case: 'It can become a bit of a personal challenge to the offender, and he may accept the challenge to go on offending. That's not the purpose of the exercise – the purpose of *Crimewatch* is to raise awareness, to actually get people to come forward and help me identify who this individual is.' Using the programme, he said, was a balance between the risk of triggering new offences and eliciting useful information from the public.

Wilson had accepted Boon's advice about going to the press in the first place, and about many aspects of media strategy such as how much information to release, how to present it, and how to characterize the criminal. With hindsight, it was debatable whether it had been the best idea to go public on 13 August 1999, just as the major surveillance operation was moving into gear. Now, however, Wilson was deciding not to act on Boon's advice about issuing an appeal, demonstrating the principle that both men had always adhered to – that the final decision was always up to the senior investigating officer. If such decisions to ignore a piece of advice are proved by events to be correct, well and good; but if the decisions yield no tangible results, there is bound to be speculation as to whether they were correct. The question is likely to linger whether an appeal for the criminal to turn himself in might just have borne fruit.

Wilson was also asked at the time of the programme about the size of the team still working on the inquiry, and it was clear that Minstead was not being given the highest priority any more. The size of the suspect list generated by the various sources of information meant that there was an enormous and time-consuming amount of work to be done, he said. However, he was responsible for investigating other major crimes in his area, and police practice sometimes dictated that new murders took precedence over the Minstead inquiry, thus reducing the rate of progress. 'Solving Minstead is a high priority,' said Wilson. 'But there are other investigations I have to deal with as well, so it's a question of balancing priorities.'

Crimewatch produced calls that led police to several people who turned out to have no connections with the offences, and the scent soon went cold again. Spring turned to summer, and still Operation Minstead refused obstinately to move forward. There was no breakthrough, there was no new offence to give potential new leads, and a variably sized team of detectives continued to drive around the cluster areas seeking DNA swabs from a list of potential suspects that had still not been refined and reduced to what those at grassroots level considered to be a manageable size.

DCs Dave Glenister and Derek Reid, quoted earlier in this chapter on the question of the timing of the crucial press conference the previous August, had strong feelings about this subject too. Although DCI Wilson had been talking in March about a suspect list of 3,500, this pair were under the impression in the month of June 2000 that the list actually ran to more like 10,000 names: all the black and mixed-race men in southeast London with a history of burglary and voyeurism. And there was, they pointed out, no guarantee that the suspect was on that list at all. There was probably more work waiting to be done than on the inquiry into the murder of the TV presenter Jill Dando, said Glenister – but that inquiry had forty-six people working on it, with backup staff working on the computer system. 'The number of people who are on our suspect list makes it unworkable with the small number of officers that are employed on it,' he said. 'That's my own personal opinion.'

Asked why the list was so long, Glenister's views were quite clear: 'It's because the profile that we've been given doesn't necessarily exclude anyone.' Reid echoed him: 'A lot of the responsibility for the length of the list is down to the psychological profile. But they give you advice and you ignore it at your peril. If his name was on one of the lists and we chose to ignore it, you can imagine the criticism that would then be shoved our way. Common sense tells you that a lot of those people could be taken off that list, but then you are taking a gamble. So what happens is, you try to do everything.'

The gamble may have been necessary if the inquiry was to be focused and to come down to a manageable size, but that gamble was, it seems, never taken. The next development came in early September 2000 when a review of caseloads in south-east London led to Wilson's investigative team being transferred wholesale on to Operation Trident, a concerted attempt to solve some of the murders within the black community in south London. There was resistance to this plan, as some members of the existing team wanted a chance to reap the fruits of the long hours they had put in. But the higher command insisted on a change and, as the time came to hand the inquiry over, Wilson admitted that murder inquiries had sometimes pushed Minstead down the agenda. 'If the new team is in a better position than mine, it's only fair to welcome that,' he said. 'It's only fair to the victims.' Asked what advice he would give his successor at the head of the operation, he replied: 'I suppose the one message I'd give him is to see if you can cut down that list of thousands of suspects a bit – maybe depend a bit on the evidence from the geographic profiler and identify potential suspects that are location-specific.'

The frustration was, he said, that a dedicated team created more than two years earlier to work on Minstead had been eroded over the previous six months as officers were taken off it to deal with murders, which was simply a result of the way the Metropolitan Police operated over major crimes. Asked if it was right that murder should take priority over rapes, he replied: 'If the murder happens now, then the murder has to be investigated now, and other inquiries are put slightly further down the agenda. I would have to say that's not a very satisfactory state of affairs, but unless you increase the staffing levels by 50 per cent overnight, you're going to run out of people... The one worrying aspect is that, whether by natural causes or his own hand, he may be dead, which is frustrating, because if he is we've got no facility to check the DNA. So ultimately we might never know.'

A truckload of documents was duly sent to the new head of the Operation Minstead team, Detective Chief Inspector David Zinzan, a tall and enthusiastic young officer with a background in the Metropolitan Police anti-terrorist branch and a commendation from the Assistant Commissioner. On the day of the formal handover, he stood in a room with Wilson, visibly shocked as he stared at the dozens of thick files that awaited him. 'When you first see all the documentation in one room you realize just how big the inquiry is,' he said. 'And you actually look at how many people there are in the system, in excess of 7,000 potential suspects, and at best there's one person in there that's the right person, and at worst there's no one in there that's the right person. It's quite a daunting task, really. I've got to prioritize it, there are too many people there and it's not realistic for me to swab several thousand people.' Nevertheless, it was primarily through swabbing for DNA that he hoped to succeed in finding the culprit among the 10 million people in the London area: 'Unless he's got a twin, there's only one person with that set of DNA, and once we've found him we'll be in a position to charge him. But it's going out and getting the DNA – selecting the most likely first and then swabbing them, and making sure that police stations in London are taking DNA when people are charged, because this offender could be arrested for shoplifting or some minor offence – nothing to do with this at all, not even suspected of it, but the DNA would be compared and might be identical with the scenes of crime here. It's very powerful, DNA, and it's probably the best way forward here, using people like Julian Boon to guide us in the right people to be looking at, and then swabbing them. You've got an offender who is going to repeat. There's no doubt in my mind that he will strike again, and whether it's a year break or two-year break, he will come back.'

Zinzan immediately set about using eight new staff allocated to the inquiry to impose priorities on the suspect list and reduce the numbers from whom DNA swabs would be sought, using the 'matrix' devised more than a year earlier. The main guideline was to bring to the top of the list all black men born between 1964 and 1972 who had a background in burglary or dishonesty and a link to the cluster areas. Whenever he could, Zinzan borrowed and seconded officers from specialist police squads in south London to work on the case. He was so determined not to put up with the fluctuations in manpower which had bedevilled Wilson's time on the case that he soon decided to go right to the top. He visited Scotland Yard, made a presentation to Assistant Commissioner William Griffiths, head of the serious crime group, and asked for the inquiry to be 'ring-fenced'. Griffiths was persuaded of the seriousness and urgency of the case, and since then Zinzan's team has been given no 'whodunnits' – difficult or long-running murder inquiries which would drain staff from Minstead. It hasn't made Zinzan very popular with his overworked colleagues, but he is unapologetic: 'You can't do a task like this without resources,' he said. 'Mass screening comes down to lots of cops knocking on doors. And sometimes you've got to get the top man on your side – your boss's boss.'

The result was that by the end of January 2001, another 400 people had been swabbed and the suspect list was down to 1,400. Local papers were being regularly briefed, and a video on the case was being circulated to police stations in Surrey, Sussex and Kent as well as London so that all police officers would start to 'think Minstead' in their day-to-day work. An independent advisory group was also set up to help in about twenty cases where young black men had declined to give DNA swabs because of a lack of trust in the police. It was clear that Zinzan was thinking laterally, working on all fronts, and taking a no-nonsense approach: one aspect of this was glimpsed when the dissenting remarks made the previous summer by Detective Constables Glenister and Reid came under discussion. 'Personally, I'd have taken them out and hung them,' he joked.

As the new team made progress, Boon also returned to his theme that if Minstead Man was still alive he was bound to reoffend: 'He has tasted the nectars at a very deep level of the thing which has meant a great deal to him over the years, and it is inconceivable that the desire to do it will have gone away. How great is his resolve not to reoffend after the debacle of his most recent attack – saying I'm not doing this, I'm out of there, this is it – I just don't know.' Asked finally whether going public in August 1999 had been a serious mistake, Boon said that the halt in the attacks may have been caused as much by the offender's thoughts and decisions as by the press conference: 'What I think stopped him was the way the last major offence unfolded... when he realized what was happening he would have felt self-disgust, loathing, this is not what I want, this is not right, this is terrible. And I think that is what is under-pinning the hiatus... The upside, if we're looking for one, is that there has been a cut in what was becoming a torrent of offences.'

For good measure, he emphasized that all the decisions had quite rightly been made by the police: 'I make it abundantly clear that the psychological tail must not wag the investigative dog – first point. Secondly, I ain't God, I ain't got the super powers or anything...'

And so the painstaking work goes on. Although he did not succeed in catching the offender, Wilson maintains that his stewardship of the inquiry was both productive and successful in the sense that the criminal stopped offending and good mechanisms were put in place to catch him. It remains to be seen whether Zinzan's focused and purpose-ful approach will yield dividends, given the clever and elusive nature of the criminal. Another element in this story is the role of the psycholog-ical profiler: was he a help or a hindrance? Boon provided a detailed and masterly portrait of the formation and activities of a deeply deviant criminal, but it did not lead to a crucial breakthrough or turning point.

Perhaps DC Dave Glenister, one of a group who profess themselves happier since their transferral from Operation Minstead to Operation Trident, should have the last word: 'Profiling, obviously, has its limita-tions – it has led to increased numbers of people being placed on the system – people who may have been involved with old people, burglars, sex offenders, to name but a few – and the numbers generated have not been easy with only a few people working on it at any time. I honestly believe it will get solved, but I think it will be solved by a routine stop or arrest when he comes back on the DNA database... It's just too big, it's not controllable, and that's the problem with that particular inquiry.'

'A FULLY PAID-
UP SADIST' 9

*'If you put a number of policemen
together they would probably have come
up with a similar profile to Dr Boon's.'*

Detective Constable John Ashbey

The police station at Gatwick Airport, an uninviting building by the
perimeter fence, about five minutes' walk from the terminals, is rather
different from Britain's average 'cop shop'. About 200 officers are based
there, some of them involved in the constant armed patrolling required
at Britain's second largest international airport, which handles more
than 31 million passengers a year. Others deal with more mundane
matters such as baggage theft, the occasional bout of air rage, and the
common-or-garden offences that arise from the everyday life of a 28,000-
strong working community. Towards the end of November 1997,
however, something quite out of the ordinary cropped up.

A blonde woman in her thirties arrived in a state of great distress to
be interviewed by the CID after she had telephoned them earlier in the
day. She was one of the cabin staff for one of the many airlines that
operate from this busy airport, and was clutching a letter she had
received at work which had shaken and frightened her deeply. The officers who saw her glanced at it and instantly realized why – it was a blackmail letter of the nastiest and most pornographic kind. 'Dear X,' it read
in capital letters. 'You don't know me but I know you quite well. I'm
unemployed, but make a little delivering things in my van. I've not had a
girlfriend for five years, I have decided I am having you. You must do the

following. Go to a professional photographic studio, dressed in your full uniform, including gloves, handbag, stockings, suspenders and high heels – brown. I want 40 pictures in gloss colour, 10 by 8, so I can see your tits, with your skirt on but pulled up – no knickers, clear views between your legs. See diagrams. If you don't comply, next year at some stage when it is safe for me, I will throw concentrated sulphuric acid in your face. I will not stay around to watch your flesh melt off. I will get you, no question. No more chances, no more warnings. You can't hide, and if the pictures aren't there by December 12, that's it. If I can't see you, no one else would ever want to once I've done my job next year. Do yours and you won't need to look over your shoulder all year. By the way, you will probably be blinded too, unless you are lucky.'

This horrifying message, complete with hand-drawn sketches of the poses the woman was required to adopt in the photographs, was followed by detailed instructions about leaving the pictures, wrapped three times in black bin bags, in a ditch by a sign on a minor road not far from the airport. The detectives asked the woman for as much information as possible so that they could start the search for the man responsible for writing this sick and cowardly letter. She was given advice about measures she could take to reduce the risk to her safety, and senior managers at her company were told about the situation. The preliminary view of the police was that the writer was probably employed at the airport in some way, although the letter had been posted at Kingston upon Thames in Surrey, more than 20 miles away. Discreet inquiries were made about some of the male colleagues who would have come into contact with her. The letter was taken away for detailed forensic examination, but none of the fingerprints found on it matched any of the prints held in the national archive of prints of convicted offenders. The woman did not comply with the demands in the letter, and the deadline it gave passed without incident. To her increasing distress, however, there was no early arrest: the police waited for the offender's next move, hoping it would provide crucial clues about him.

The next development came on 12 February 1998, when the same woman received a second letter in the same handwriting, all in capital letters once again. This had been posted at Gatwick and read simply: 'You have nothing to fear now, nothing will happen.' The police speculated that the offender might have got wind of the police inquiry and decided to back off, and the woman was able to relax to some extent, although the letter was no guarantee that the man had completely lost interest in his foul proposals. For nearly a year there were no further developments, and then, just after Christmas, another frightened woman came into the police station with another letter, posted in Kingston upon Thames like the very first one. This victim worked on the ticket reservation staff of a different airline, and like the first victim was a blonde woman in her thirties. The handwriting of the letter was the same, but the writer had now switched to talking about himself in the plural, as if suffering from delusions of grandeur: 'We need your uniform for a film. If you don't supply it we will take it. We will find out a bit about you, and then when the time is right and you are off guard, we will take it. Even if you are wearing it. We will also take one of your fingers for making things difficult for us.' There followed detailed directions to the same drop-off point, and a nasty and gratuitous insult to round things off: 'Don't be a cunt, X, make life easy for all of us. You know everything can be forgot.'

Again, the woman was given advice and protection, and did not comply with the demands. The earlier police inquiry was rekindled, but again there was no arrest. In this case there was no follow-up letter, and things went quiet again until the spring. The third victim, another blonde woman in her thirties and a colleague of the first victim, received a letter in April 1000, which was evidently from the same man, saying he had drawn up a list of 'forfeits' for her. The first of these was that she should put her complete uniform in a plastic bag and take it by 10 May to the same drop-off point he had specified in his letters to the other women: he would contact her again, he said, to tell her which additional forfeit he had chosen by a throw of the dice. The follow-up letter came a month later, posted at Gatwick like the previous one, and warned her if she didn't deliver the uniform he would place an obscene picture of her on the Internet. This woman, like the second victim, had been photographed for her airline's published promotional literature, and the letter writer threatened to graft her picture on to a pornographic image of a woman with a wine bottle in her vagina. He would then put it on a website with a message for people to telephone her airline, ask for the 'cabin crew performance manager' and detail which degrading activities they wanted her to perform.

The final victim also worked for the airline that employed the first and third victims, but had brown hair and was only twenty-two years old. It was worrying that this woman was so much younger and therefore more vulnerable, but the principal concern of the police was the date of the letter: it was posted in Dartford, Kent, on 19 May 1999 – only one day after the second letter to the previous victim. This meant the man was stepping up his attacks and sending letters to two women at once, becoming bolder and therefore potentially more likely to act on some of his unpleasant threats.

Once again this letter talked of forfeits, but used a different approach: 'I was on your flight once and I managed to find out who you were. I waited for days outside the car parks to get a few pictures of you. I thought you saw me – did you? I think about you all the time, as I don't have too long to live. I've sold my house, given up my job and decided to go out, fulfilling every fantasy I've had and doing whatever I want. All in all I'm your worst nightmare... Before I die I will throw acid over you. It's so strong nobody will ever recognize you again... Here is task one. Write me a letter. Describe your breasts and how you masturbate.' This letter again carried the threat to post a picture of her on the Internet grafted on to an image of a woman with a frog in her vagina, accompanied by an invitation to phone a number, asking for private shows of the victim with all types of objects squeezed into her vagina and rectum.

The effect of such repulsive material on a woman who was much younger than the others was extremely traumatic: even though the police were confident that the offender did not know her home address, she was so disturbed that she moved out of the area in order to feel less accessible to him. The other women did not react so drastically, but police officers who spoke to them could tell they were badly affected by the letters, especially by the anonymity: was the offender the man who worked alongside them? Was he watching her house?

Meanwhile the police had used a specialist crime analyst, Samantha Thompson, to study the cases in detail and draw out all the similarities and points of difference. When she suggested contacting an offender profiler, the man in charge of the inquiry, Detective Inspector Steve Johns, decided, as he put it later, that they had 'nothing to lose' by doing so. He contacted the National Crime Faculty, and on 23 June 1999 – two weeks after the latest letter – he travelled up to Leicester University with Thompson and another colleague, Detective Constable John Ashbey. Julian Boon, busy marking examination papers and handing out information to prospective students for the following academic year, took them into his room to hear their description of the cases and the contents of the blackmail letters.

One of Boon's first reactions was not so much that of an offender profiler as that of a man with considerable experience of criminal cases and a good memory. Before the police passed him copies of the letters to read, he had been asking detailed questions about the colour of the victims' hair and uniforms and about the promotional leaflets in which their photographs had been used. But as soon as he had read out half of the first letter to the first victim, he called a halt with a typical Boon-ism: 'Oh! Well, ringy ding ding! Because – I'm almost sure of it – I've seen this offender before. It will take me a while to find it, but I have to tell you, Steve, that I have definitely seen this chap before. Finding it, of course, is another matter, in my excellent filing system.'

It was about a year previously, he recalled, that he had dealt with a case in Sutton in south London, where a seventeen-year-old girl who worked in a shop had received a threatening letter telling her to dress up as an air stewardess and have pornographic pictures taken of herself. The details that had rung a bell in Boon's mind as he looked at the letter had also been present in the Sutton case – drawings illustrating how the photographs should be posed, and the requirement that forty copies should be printed. As the session continued, Boon rummaged in his filing cabinet and found the name and telephone number of the police officer who had worked on the earlier case. At the time this connection with the previous case looked like no more than a happy coincidence: events were to show that it was more significant than that.

In between the phone calls and visits to the filing cabinet, Boon continued to go through the letters, wasting little time in beginning his analysis of the unpleasant psychopathology of the person who had written them. When he read the phrase about the sulphuric acid melting the flesh of the first victim, he seemed completely confident about the territory they were now entering: 'Ooh! We are moving heavily into what in the jargon is known as "anal sadism". Very, very pure form. To someone like me it's an extremely educational articulation of this particular type of personality. He is thinking about her having this humiliating drive to take these dirty pictures to the drop-off point, and he would look on them as dirty, filthy pictures, because that's what gets him going. And the idea above all else is for her to feel humiliated, and powerless and degraded. He can't achieve anything himself. He can't be positive. He hasn't got any useful things to contribute, so he has to reduce somebody else to that level. Secondly, he'll be wired into – for want of a better word – wankery and all sorts of pornography, particularly related to air hostesses. That is his particular bent. It's my opinion that it's a huge excitement for him to draw these diagrams, which have detailed anal content. No surprise to me that he will be getting off on constructing that letter, trying to make her feel frightened, powerless, degraded, and allying that with an interest in anal sex.'

Boon agreed with the police that the offender worked at the airport or had done so in the past – 'He's an airport-phile as well as a kinky chap… if he's this wired-in to air hostesses and so on, I can't help but feel that he would want to be at that airport at all costs – even if it's just to be a cleaner, so that he can sort of watch them coming and going, which would just be a total turn-on.' He also thought that the offender's home would be stuffed with hard and soft pornography involving air stewardesses – 'It's his life, and a very, very sad one.' More worryingly, Boon also considered it likely that he had written many other letters of this kind that had never come to light, and that if girls in their teens received such material it could potentially drive them to suicide.

What impelled such offenders to write letters like this was the need for control, he said: 'These people are so weak in their own ego that they are unable to control events for themselves. They are fundamentally frightened individuals. So the more they can exert control over somebody else, the more they feel they can gain power for themselves, the more they feel they can predict events – because if I have someone in complete control, then clearly I can predict the outcome. And then, if we ally that to what is patently this man's life obsession with fetishism, then we are not really looking for someone who is a happily married man with four children. We're looking for someone who ain't got a life, basically. And I always like to use nice pedestrian language, because I'm always suspicious of jargon.'

Another aspect of such people, he went on, was that they craved excitement, which was a natural trait in all humans and animals, but were unable to find it through positive or creative means: 'I mean, you won't find this guy in the front row of *Twelfth Night*!... All he gets is this low level stimulation, expressed negatively with various individuals. And once he gets bored with one or it's not having the desired effect, well, let's go on to the next one and maybe he'll strike lucky and get hold of some lovely woman's underwear or whatever – gives you the collywobbles.' Boon thought it was the chronic boredom and need for stimulation that had led the man to talk about forfeits in his letters and say specifically they were designed to make 'the game' more exciting and titillating. He also noted that the offender had contacted three of the victims twice, in two cases using the gambit of the forfeits to give him the excuse for writing the second letter to tell her the result of his casting of the dice.

All this made him think that the man obtained his biggest thrills simply from writing the letters: 'So on balance, that leads me to conclude that he is not a doer, he is a writer. There are people who would be cheerfully capable of doing this, but mercifully they are rather rare, and they wouldn't bother with all the writing. They would just abduct. I mean, we've had famous criminals who've done that. But this is all in the writing – cowardly, sensation-seeking. This is as far as he gets – I hope. So he's giving himself a chance to come back and write another letter and get excited while writing it.' This description of the man as a writer rather than a doer led the police to ask if that meant he was unlikely to actually visit the drop-off point specified in the letter, but Boon's feeling was that he would find it 'absolutely irresistible' to go there: he saw a clear distinction between action of that kind, and the kind of action involved in carrying out the violent threats. This point was to feature strongly in future police decisions.

The mention of using a computer to alter photographs of the last two victims led Boon to recall that the kind of anal sadist he was talking about was, typically, very interested in machinery: 'They've got lonely, sad lives for one thing, but a machine is what they like because machines are predictable – they don't let you down. There's no risk involved. You are not going to get rejected. If they break down they can be fixed or replaced – easy. No suggestion that you're at fault, the machine is at fault. But people can let you down. So he's weak, ineffectual, unsuccessful, both in terms of relationships and professional life, I think – I always add the words "I think", so then I can retract it!' Reflecting on the threat to throw acid at the victims, Boon also thought the man might have a facial disfigurement or be 'under-endowed in other departments, I'll say no more than that'. This would give him an extreme feeling of inferiority, leading him to try to take away from somebody else the looks or potency that he didn't have himself. 'So he will be an ugly bastard, as well as everything else,' concluded Boon.

As the meeting neared the end, he drew together some of his conclusions about the probable characteristics of the offender. It was likely he was in a low-level fringe job at the airport – the police agreed with this, and said they had already investigated several people who did cleaning jobs in places where they would easily be able to observe air stewardesses coming and going and take note of their names. Boon also thought it possible the offender was indeed a van driver, as he had said in his letter to the first victim, and that his delivery routes took him down the road where he wanted the women to drop off their uniforms and the pictures he had demanded. The man would be in an older age group, he speculated, because in the Sutton case he had wanted the victim to have herself photographed in the kind of round 'pot' hat that stewardesses used to wear in the 1950s. The likelihood that he was in a low-level job did not mean he was unintelligent, however: 'People like this have plenty of mental capacity to be able to conjure up fifty-eight different varieties of sending someone to hell and back.'

Boon added: 'There is just one other thing I would say about his type of offender – he won't be in a flourishing, productive, self-actualized relationship. I stand by that and nothing is going to get me off it. However, the other side of sado is masochism. So if you can find somebody who is into being moderately humiliated, tied up, whipped, chained and all the rest of it – find a female who is maso and prepared to put on this kind of gear, then to that extent he could be in a relationship – and from their eyes a successful one, but not from yours and mine.'

DC Ashbey said several people had thought the writing in the letters was very feminine, but Boon remained convinced the man was writing them himself rather than getting a female accomplice to do it for him: 'I think he's writing them himself, simply because he's getting so much pleasure from writing them. Every line is causing him to drip mentally with sexual elation. It's just too precious to him to do this, and frankly he wouldn't want to share it. And just one other thing while I'm on it – videos. It ain't going to be *Bambi*! And if there's a film where acid gets chucked over a face, I'll bet you he's got it. Or some sort of charming video nasty where there's smouldering flesh under acid, something like that. He'd love to play that time and time again.'

At the end of the meeting a phone call came through from DC Dan Wright of the Metropolitan Police in Sutton, the man who had dealt with the case Boon had remembered when reading the first letter. While the Sussex officers made arrangements to meet Wright the following week, Boon found copies of the letters written by the Sutton offender and shared some of the details with them when they came off the phone. 'Now the thing is, he's so much more intimate in what he wants to do with this particular victim, who was only seventeen years old. It's similar stuff, only much more vicious and intimidating, all about damaging her over a period of time. But he's not what we call a necrophile, in that he doesn't want her to die. Death isn't in it for him. He must have her alive, because having her alive and tainted, humiliated, is a constant reminder to him of his power. Whereas dead – that's going too far. He's shot his fox, if you see what I mean, it's the chase and the writing – absolutely topnotch control, sadism, humiliation. I mean this one goes into such charming things as crushing nipples, removing teeth, one by one, day by day – no point, really in going on. But it's your bloke with knobs on, and it's one of the clearest cases of the anal, sadistic sexual offender that I have ever come across.'

It was a confident, virtuoso performance by Boon, and the Sussex officers set off for home visibly encouraged by what they had heard. In particular they were impressed by Boon's statement that the man responsible for the letters would not be able to resist going to the drop-off point at some stage to see if any of his demands had been complied with. Boon's views on this were boosted when the Sussex team met Wright and other Metropolitan Police officers who had run the Sutton case and heard about their experience with surveillance of a different drop-off point. They had apparently staked out the location for two days around one of the dates given by the offender, but nobody had turned up; when the operation had ended, however, the officers had left an empty bag and envelope at the scene to see what would happen, and shortly afterwards the victim had received another letter asking her if she was trying to trick him with empty bags. It was therefore clear that the offender had visited the scene, even though the surveillance operation had missed him. Before their visit to Leicester, the only surveillance carried out by the Sussex officers was when they had staked out the scene on one of the specified days, taking the victim with them in case she recognized any passing cars or people. In the light of Boon's opinion and the information from Sutton, however, they now felt a protracted surveillance operation would be a good idea, and worth the considerable expense.

DI Johns organized a round-the-clock operation in mid-July 1999 for up to two weeks at the place on the country lane that the letter writer had specified several times. A concealed video camera was installed to observe the location, and two teams of two officers lay in wait a little way on either side of the spot.

The surveillance operation began on a Monday morning, and for nearly three days the officers sat there, bored and uncomfortable, with nothing happening. But when the summer light faded into night for the third time, their luck changed dramatically. Later in the summer DC Ashbey described the magic moment of getting a result and the laughable excuses from the offender that followed: 'We had a camera overlooking the site, a bag of clothing was deposited and we kept watch on it, and about half past ten on the Wednesday evening the bag was collected: the camera sees a vehicle or shows a vehicle's headlights illuminate the scene, and the silhouette of a person gets out of the vehicle, goes straight to the bag and then returns to the vehicle. It's not clear enough to see the bag in the person's hand, but you can see the person go back to the car. He was stopped a very short distance away from the drop-off point with the bag on the front seat of the car. So he was arrested, and brought into custody at Gatwick, where he was interviewed with a solicitor and gave his explanation for being there. His explanation was that he'd been working on his house all day long and decided to go for a walk some time after ten o'clock that evening. He parked his car nearby in a country lane, walked across a couple of fields and then stumbled across this bag which he believed was rubbish or possibly a dead animal, because he'd found a dead badger stuffed in a black bag like that once before. So, because he liked the countryside and didn't want to see rubbish lying about, he returned to his car, drove back to the scene, put the supposed bag of rubbish on the front seat so he could dispose of it at his home address. So after the interview it was decided that he should be bailed, but he did allow us to take his fingerprints before he left the station, and a few days afterwards we were able to get a match on outstanding fingerprints on two of the letters. So it was all down to the man that was arrested at the scene.'

The man in question was Keith Downer, aged forty, a senior British Airways engineer who lived near Redhill in Surrey and worked at Gatwick Airport. He was a clean-shaven man of average height and build with dark brown hair and reasonably good looks who had been married, but was now divorced and had a regular girlfriend. She was utterly shocked, according to the police, when she heard about the offences, as were Downer's friends, family and work colleagues: to all appearances he was a perfectly normal, hard-working person, and he had never been in trouble with the police before. When the fingerprint evidence was put to him he exercised his right to say nothing to the police about it, but when the case came before Chichester Crown Court in December 1999 he pleaded guilty to eight offences of blackmail, including the one in Sutton, and was sentenced to eight years in prison. It was said in mitigation that Downer had never intended to carry out any of his threats, and when the case went before the Court of Appeal in autumn 2000 his sentence was halved to four years. This was, according to the police, a decision that his victims have found extremely upsetting.

Boon was delighted to hear about the arrest. 'My view was that if they led him along just a little bit with some of the paraphernalia he was wanting, he would turn up to a drop spot. I always believe in being extremely modest about any apparent successes because we must remember the investigating officers do the other bit. But it does seem an instance where investigative experience coupled with a psychological perspective has worked – a two-point fix on the same thing. And from a research point of view, I have never come across a more graphic articulation of a sexual anal sadistic personality. A lot of what was going on there, if you read it you just think, oh, there's a sad old perv. But there's so much more. And it couldn't be a better and more useful articulation of that particular personality type.'

The police were also generous in their appreciation of Boon's contribution. DI Johns said that it gave them three important leads: the link with the case in Sutton, the intelligence that the offender had gone to the drop-off point in that case, and the prediction that he would find it impossible not to go to the location in the Gatwick cases as well. 'Julian gave me the confidence, if you like, to carry out a lengthy surveillance operation rather than just perhaps twenty-four hours at the drop-off point,' said Johns. He was also complimentary about the aspects of the profile that had been proved right – the fact that the offender was older rather than younger, and that he worked at the airport and had a penchant for airline uniforms and air hostesses.

'Other things were slightly less accurate,' he said. 'He has a very good job and he doesn't work in the lower grade menial type of employment that Julian had suggested. He also suggested the man could well live alone or with parents, and as it transpired our offender lives alone but had a girlfriend. Julian also said that there'd be uniforms, underwear, paraphernalia at the home address. None of it – we suspect it's somewhere else and it's an address we don't know about.' Boon had also said the offender was likely to be ugly or disfigured, and this was not the case.

DC Ashbey also had mixed views about the contribution of the profile: 'It was worthwhile going to see Dr Boon, just for the fact that we found out about these other letters that had been sent to a girl who was being investigated by the Metropolitan Police. And it was useful to get some sort of confirmation about who we're looking for, although I think if you put a number of policemen together they would probably have come up with a similar profile to Dr Boon's.' Despite this dismissive remark, Ashbey admitted that Boon had changed his thinking about the question of whether the offender would ever have carried out his threats. His own view had been that if someone made a threat they would probably carry it out, but after dealing with the offender he had come round to Boon's view that the man was more interested in writing about his unpleasant fantasies than actually putting them into practice.

Apart from the halving of Downer's sentence at the Court of Appeal, the Gatwick blackmail case looked like a success for all concerned. Critics might point out, however, that a persistent surveillance operation at an earlier stage might have produced a similar result much earlier and spared some of the victims their ordeal. It was clear that the police derived benefits from their dealings with Julian Boon, including the confidence-boosting effect of receiving independent advice that chimed with some of their own thinking. DI Johns said afterwards that seeking the profile had been the right thing to do and he would not be against doing it again in future cases. But he also produced what was probably the best summary of the importance of his visit to Julian Boon's office at Leicester University: 'Well, it was useful, but probably not for the right reasons.'

When it was put to Julian Boon that his profile had been wrong on three key points – Downer's work status, appearance, and current relationship with a woman – he admitted he had made a mistake. The difficulty had been, he thought, that Downer had been 'staging' – deliberately presenting himself as something other than what he really was. This was a ploy that was familiar to profilers in cases where the staging was designed to deceive the police about the offender's identity – a clever embezzler pretending to be illiterate, for example. But what had deceived him in this case was that the staging had been designed not to obscure the offender's identity but to increase the feeling of terror for the women: 'It was done because it stoked up the impact – stoked it up because the letter writer comes across as particularly revolting, particularly un-good looking. So therefore you're not only having it done to you, you're having it done to you by somebody who presents as Quasimodo, as it were... But I wouldn't miss it again, and it has to be emphasized that psychological profiling is like all scientific endeavour, constantly evolving, emerging and going forward.'

But Boon remained confident that he was right about Downer's sexual make-up 'whether he's the Pope or brother Tiddly Push'. And – unusually for him as an academic rather than a clinician – he said he would very much like the chance to talk to the offender and find out more about his sex life and the origins of his sadistic tendency to derive a sexual thrill from the powerlessness of others. Boon thought that his fantasies might have been acted out to a limited extent with former wives and girlfriends, 'but with the real McCoy reserved for an immensely private world'. He also wanted to know whether Downer had been raised in a stable, consistent environment: 'I would love to know the degree to which that environment had loving relationships, genuinely held, and I would like to know about siblings and birth order. I'd like to know how he got on with cats when he was twelve – or didn't get on with cats. Or dogs or other animals, anything that could be made helpless. We know that sadistic offenders have an elevated level of pet abuse in their childhood – that is, sticking knives into animals, pulling claws out, cutting whiskers off and all the rest of it.

'This sadism has to come from somewhere, and there are different views and explanations, but my preferred understanding is they have lacked genuine empathy in upbringing. They have lacked consistency in the way people have related to them, so they don't come to trust relationships. Hence they like the predictable, and in extreme form they need the predictable – not the awful world where people let you down and that sort of thing. Now most of us can cope at least to a degree with that, but these people can't. So the way round that is to control others, and then you have a certainty of outcome which you haven't had in your upbringing. It then becomes allied by simple conditioning to sexual experience. You feel empowered and at the hormonal stage of fourteen this gets allied to and backed up by the sexual buzz. And gradually through various enactment of fantasies it builds up and builds up.'

In the case of Karl Stirk's murder of Yvonne Killian, Richard Badcock had also emphasized the sense of powerlessness and the need for control that he thought had played a part in the psychological build-up to the crime. The big difference between Stirk and Downer, however, was that Downer appears to be, in Boon's assessment, 'a writer rather than a doer'. If he is correct, the chances of Downer inflicting serious physical harm on anyone seem slim. But Boon was also convinced that Downer's proclivities will never change; the important question, therefore, will be whether he will be able to keep them under control when he comes out of prison shortly, or whether they will again spill out in the form of threatening letters and inflict terrifying experiences on more innocent women.

'A WELL BROUGHT-UP PSYCHOPATH' 10

'I have to say that I haven't heard a lot today that
suggests a particular strategy which I can now follow.'
Detective Superintendent Steve Watts

There were not many drinkers at the Rack and Manger in the village of
Crawley, near Winchester: it was a Monday night, rarely a busy one for
public houses, and the landlord was preparing to call time. Suddenly,
without warning, the door burst open and a teenage girl staggered into
the pub, shaking and screaming hysterically. The customers rallied
round and calmed her down and comforted her, and she managed to
tell them that she had been kidnapped by a masked man who had
assaulted her and threatened to rape her. 'The look on her face will stay
with me for ever,' recalled Lorraine Pinner, the daughter of the landlord. 'She told me the man had bundled her into his car and tied her up
with sticky tape, round her hands and all round her face and eyes.'

The police were at the pub within minutes and gradually, over the
ensuing days, the sixteen-year-old told them the full story. She and her
boyfriend had gone for a walk at a nearby beauty spot called Farley
Mount and had been sitting in the back seat of their car in a car park
called Hawthorn's Post: it was a dry evening in April 1996. The pair
were kissing and cuddling when a figure suddenly loomed up in the
darkness, the driver's door was pulled open, and they were confronted
by a man in a black balaclava pointing a handgun at them. It was a
moment of sheer shock and terror, a brutal invasion of privacy and intimacy. But at least the attacker wasn't violent: instead he was calm and

forceful, making them turn and kneel on their seats, facing the back-rests, and tying their wrists with plastic ties – the kind used for bundling cables together or, in larger sizes, tying plants to stakes. He next took off the boyfriend's belt and used it to tie his wrists before cutting off and removing the plastic ties, as if he was eager to leave behind nothing he had brought with him. Then he asked for money, rifled the girl's handbag and pushed it roughly over her boyfriend's head, so it acted as a blindfold.

He then pulled the girl out of the car, reached into a grey-blue holdall, brought out a roll of silver-coloured sticky tape and wrapped it round and round her head, leaving a gap under her nostrils so she could breathe. Fortunately the tape settled in such a way that there was also a small gap below her eyes that allowed her to see a little. The attacker then pulled the car keys out of the ignition, tossed them away into the darkness, seized the girl by her coat and dragged her away to his own car. When the boyfriend shouted and pleaded for him not to hurt her, he said that he was only 'taking her for a walk' and that he would soon let her go. She struggled and kicked out as she was pushed into the back of the man's car, which she thought might be a red Vauxhall Cavalier.

There now began a nightmarish ride round the darkened lanes of the quiet countryside to the west of Winchester. The girl, later described by the police as brave and spirited, was consistently unco-operative, refusing to lie down on the back seat and be quiet, trying to observe details of the car from underneath the tape, and telling her abductor to let her go. He told her he was taking her to a house not far away, and she tried from her local knowledge to work out which roads they were following, even though he seemed to be changing direction and doubling back in order to confuse her.

Eventually he pulled into a lay-by, and rummaged round the car, cursing that he had lost his mask and giving her the chance to see his short dark brown hair and green rugby jersey. Then he pulled her out of the car and started touching her body. Her statement to the police read: 'He asked me my name. I did not reply. I could just see that he had put his hand down towards the belt on his dark trousers, and he said:

"You know you want it." I said "no", and pushed him away forcefully. I said, "You can just let me go with this thing on my head and you can just drive off. I'll just walk away." He walked me round to the other side of the car, and ripped the tape off my head, pulling my hair painfully. I was in front of him and he handed my coat round and said something like "keep walking". I put my coat on and walked. I heard him get into his car and drive off. I half ran and half walked to the main road and turned left towards the Rack and Manger pub.'

Four years earlier in November 1992, a twenty-year-old woman had been less lucky. She and her boyfriend had been to a village pub and then driven to Farley Mount, where they'd parked in one of the several car parks. They both noticed a car with an array of bright headlights driving into the car park and then reversing out again, and shortly afterwards they climbed into the back seat to make love. 'I was lying on the seat and my boyfriend was on top of me,' she later told the police. 'My trousers and knickers were halfway down my legs. Suddenly the driver's door was opened and a man shone a torch at us. We both looked round and the man said, "All I want is the money, if you stay calm you won't get hurt." He then said, "Get on your knees and face the back of the car." My boyfriend and I did this as the man was holding a gun at us. It was a black handgun, 8 to 10 inches long, and single-barrelled.'

There then followed virtually the same routine as was used in the attack on the teenager and the three other attacks that police believe have been committed by the same man: the binding of the hands with plastic cable ties, the taping of the woman's head, the taking of the car keys that were then thrown away into the darkness. In this case, though, the attacker forced the boyfriend into the boot of the car before carry-ing the woman away over his shoulder, half-naked, joking that it was a good thing he used to be a fireman. She was dumped in the back of a pick-up, a piece of canvas was pulled over her, and the pick-up took off on a half-hour drive, sometimes stopping and reversing before setting off again. When the vehicle eventually halted she was carried inside a house and upstairs to a bedroom, where he told her he was going to wear a condom and would find her some 'pretty clothes' to put on.

'When he came back into the room he put more tape over my eyes,' she later told the police. 'It felt like three strips. I then felt him cut the ties off my hands and feet. He told me to sit up, which I did, and he lifted my arms up and took my jumper and bra off so I was naked. He then put a dress on me which was woollen and loose. He didn't say anything to me. He was sitting on the bed which was a single bed, quite low down. Then he laid me down and went out of the room for a minute and came back. He opened my legs and got on top of me. He pushed the dress up and was touching my breasts...' The victim then described the intimate details of the rape, including the way the attacker, in a casual manner, asked her to change positions. She concluded: 'He then told me to take the dress off and put my clothes back on. He then tied my hands and feet up again with string. I managed to mumble, "I want to go home."'

The attacker asked her where she lived, brought her a coat when she complained about being cold, and then apologized for what he'd done, saying he had been a widower for six years, deprived of sex. Then he put her in the pick-up again, drove around for what seemed to her like an hour, and set her down on a grass verge. He cut her arms and legs free, removed the tape from her face, which had been covered throughout the rape, and shone his torch on it, saying he wanted a good look at her. Finally he told her to look away and drove off, leaving her to run down a hill, find a house and ring the doorbell for help. Meanwhile, back at the car park, her boyfriend had managed to free himself from the boot of the car and was desperately but vainly searching the country park for his companion.

The three other Farley Mount attacks were in 1991, 1994 and 1998. In the first, the attacker followed the same routine with a student and her boyfriend who went to Beech Cliff car park on a January evening. They saw another car come in and reverse out, and a few minutes later were confronted by a masked man with a handgun, who bound their wrists with plastic ties and demanded money. He then used rope from the car boot and cut away one of the seat belts to tie their hands, removed the plastic bindings, and put nylon bags over their heads. One of the most noteworthy things about the incident was that while he was doing this the attacker asked the pair, almost chattily, if they were nervous. The girl later told police, 'My boyfriend said, "Yes, I'm nervous," and I said, "Yes, I'm nervous." And the man said, "Not as nervous as me," and I said, "Do you wanna bet?"' The girl was forced to turn over and the attacker started to touch her private parts, but when he realized she was having a period he changed his mind and left her alone. The car keys were taken and thrown away, and the masked man disappeared into the night.

Then there was a lucky escape on a November evening in 1994 for a twenty-two-year-old woman and her boyfriend, a serviceman. They were kissing and cuddling in Forest View car park at Farley Mount when they realized a dark figure in a mask was standing by the door pointing a gun at them. The doors were locked, and when the man demanded money the boyfriend wound the window down a fraction and passed two five pound notes through the gap. He was told this wasn't enough, and agreed to open the door. But this time the attacker, perhaps realizing the boyfriend was strongly built and likely to resist, made no attempt to tie them up and instead just demanded the car keys and retreated in a dark-coloured saloon. The couple soon recovered the keys and drove rapidly back to their homes nearby.

The fifth attack, in May 1998, was also a lucky escape. A nineteen-year-old woman and her boyfriend were in Forest View car park, listening to the radio and cuddling with the doors locked. They noticed another car come into the car park, drive around and leave. 'We started making love with my boyfriend kneeling in the footwell, but effectively on top of me,' said her statement to the police. 'Our seats were reclined fully. Whilst making love I recall the car suspension was creaking and the windows were misted on the inside. Suddenly my boyfriend and I froze almost simultaneously. Someone was at my side of the car and was trying to pull open the locked door with his hand. As I froze I looked up and out through the misty window. I could see the outline of a male person standing there. He said nothing but just looked at us. He was from my estimation between 5 feet 6 inches and 6 feet in height. He said nothing, he did nothing, he just held on to the door handle. My boyfriend appeared to panic, he sat up and almost jumped over into the driver's seat in one movement. I sat up but was too terrified to look at the man any further. My boyfriend started up the engine and drove off out of the car park at speed without switching his lights on.'

This string of particularly nasty attacks at Farley Mount illustrates how difficult life can be for the police when they are pitted against an intelligent criminal who plans his moves carefully, thinks on his feet, and is obsessively careful about leaving behind anything that could be used to identify him. Crucially, he has never left any DNA or other forensic evidence such as fingerprints or fibres. Since the rape in 1992, Hampshire Police have devoted enormous resources to trying to catch the offender, putting up warning posters, increasing patrols and conducting observations and stake-outs. They have followed up tips from the public, leads from their own intelligence officers, and lines of inquiry suggested by criminal records. They have repeatedly put out appeals for more people to come forward in confidence, because they feel there may have been other attacks by the same man that have gone unreported – the victims may have been conducting secret affairs and assignations about which they did not want the rest of the world to know. (One other victim did come forward to describe an incident that might be related, when a couple saw a masked man standing in front of their car with a shotgun, just looking at them.) There have been a number of developments in the inquiry and a number of arrests, but police have never got as far as charging anyone for the crimes.

It was not, however, until 1998, after the latest of this series of unpleasant attacks, that they decided it was time to see if a psychological profile of the offender might help them. Unusually, the police asked for two profilers – one from the academic world and one with a clinical background – to work on the case together, as if to be sure they were getting a fix on it from all possible angles. Accordingly, a meeting was arranged with Julian Boon and Richard Badcock.

In July one of the main officers on the case, Detective Sergeant John Gunner, arrived in Leicester with his colleague Jackie Foster, a civilian crime analyst with Hampshire Police who had made a detailed analysis of the five incidents. Boon and Badcock listened to Gunner and Foster reading out the detailed statements from the victims and their boyfriends, and studied the maps of Farley Mount country park, a 1,300-acre area of downs and woodland with a large war memorial and a dozen car parks. They were told that the park is frequented during the day by walkers and people exercising their dogs, and at night mainly by courting couples and by voyeurs – some of whom have been interviewed by police about the attacks – who come to spy on the couples. The two profilers were astonished to learn that a yew tree in one of the car parks is often used as a perch by voyeurs, and Badcock was later to put his life in danger by climbing into the tree during a site visit as part of his quest for complete familiarity with the crime. Even before hearing the detailed statements from the victims, Badcock came to the preliminary conclusion about the offender that 'before he graduated to molestation he was a voyeur, and still is'.

As in other cases, the profilers soon set about focusing on the details of the crimes that they found significant and deducing what they could about the offender. After hearing details of the 1991 incident, Badcock observed that the criminal's preparation and choice of timing and location were 'high level'. He had enough self-control not to overplay his hand and to back off when difficulties arose, and he clearly had 'a well-functioning psyche'. He contrived a smooth and chatty interaction with his victims, using false chumminess to allay their fears, 'as if they were all part of a ripping wheeze or adventure'.

Boon also agreed that the offender was 'worryingly accomplished' and had clearly committed similar crimes before, even though the one in 1991 was the first to come to light. His methods and clothing suggested that he saw his activities as a 'one-man military operation', where he got a thrill out of interrupting courting couples and incapacitating the male in order to emphasize his own macho superiority. At the same time he was restrained and avoided risk, showed no sign of sadism, and if he was a betting man he would be sophisticated rather than compulsive: 'He's clearly high in intelligence, socially skilled, and he might even have a job where exercising social skills and manipulating people is part of it… It wouldn't surprise me if he's been in what they call the weekend army, the Territorials.'

The 1992 case, in which the victim was taken to a house and raped, offered the two profilers richer, if more confusing, material. Badcock said the criminal's insistence that the victim should wear a woollen dress during the rape was 'tantalizing', and he was intrigued by the way he had looked at her face with a torch afterwards as if trying to commit it to memory. He thought the offender was lying when he told the victim he hadn't had sex for six years, and that he was probably the kind of man who had frequent liaisons and one-night stands.

Badcock fixed on an incident described in the boyfriend's statement, when the criminal was having difficulty removing sticky tape from his head as he forced him into the boot, and made a casual and jokey comment about the kind of tape made these days. 'It looks as if what we're seeing is the emergence of a psychopathic character, someone who's able to be casually and plausibly reassuring to the victim. I think it requires a particular mental attitude to the whole thing, and in particular an absence of certain kinds of sensitivity to other people, so here's a man who knows how to exploit people. He knows the social tricks of the trade, as it were, in the way that a salesman might – you know, the archetypal kind of glib, shady salesman, the guy with good verbal skills but no sincerity, likeable but not to be trusted. So, the dear boy's a voyeuristic psycho. Moral development would not be his forte – or rather, he is likely to have quite an acute sense of moral judgement, but it's going to be in highly restricted areas, so he'll be acutely aware of people's judgements of himself, but he won't apply the same values to his judgement of other people. He'll recognize them as people, but they'll be things that you can use and manipulate. Back to the psychopathy, yeah.'

The conclusion that the offender was a psychopath – and therefore among the most difficult and dangerous type of criminal to catch – clearly had an important impact on the police officers, as if they had not considered the possibility before. Gunner's face fell when the word was first mentioned by Badcock, and Boon immediately and emphatically agreed with the interpretation: 'Absolutely – I simply couldn't agree with that more.' Boon pointed out another detail that indicated the offender's ability to keep control and think on his feet: the car alarm had gone off when he was taking the ignition keys in the case of the woman who was raped, and instead of panicking he had dealt with the situation calmly and found out from the boyfriend how to switch the noise off. He also seized on the fact that the criminal had carried the victim up the stairs of the house 'as if he was carrying prey or something like that – you've bagged your tiger, as it were'. At the same time, there was no sign of any desire to hurt. He agreed that the man had the social skills of a manipulative salesman – he would see his crimes as naughty rather than wrong: 'I'm a bit of a lad for doing this sort of thing – that would be his hallmark.'

On to the third offence in 1994, when the young woman and her burly boyfriend were disturbed in a Farley Mount car park. Boon's main observation was that the offender was anything but a man of impulse, because he negotiated with his victims and backed off when he sensed that the boyfriend might offer resistance if he was told to turn on his stomach and submit to being trussed up with cable ties. Badcock took up the theme: 'He uses his natural social skills to play the victim like a fish on a line – willing to let victims go if they're not suitable or the times aren't opportune. So if an unexpected threat like a large and well-built man comes along, then he's not fazed by it, shows no signs of fear, negotiates in a way that seems unnecessary, and simply walks away. There aren't many sex offenders, I think, who are capable of showing this kind of prudence and control. Just thinking about this swift facility to negotiate and be calm makes me think that as well as being a voyeur he might have been a fraudster. Maybe he's a car salesman!'

Or an estate agent, suggested Boon – he did, after all, have access to a house for the rape. Or a politician, or a member of the Cabinet, responded Badcock, warming to the joke – 'because it's not just the ability to tell the lie, it's where the person you tell the lie to has the willingness to be deceived, to accept – so car salesman, estate agents and politicians spring to mind'.

'To think you were going to be Lord Badcock of Wakefield!' cut in Boon.

'Not now!' said Badcock.

The B&B double act, put on here for the benefit of the younger and somewhat bemused DS Gunner, went on hold for discussion of the fourth offence – the abduction in 1996 of the teenager whose ordeal was described at the beginning of this chapter. Badcock felt that the fact that she behaved in a 'bolshie' way probably saved her from greater harm, prompting Boon to remark that although the offender was a psychopath, he was at least 'a well brought-up psychopath'. It was notable, Boon continued, that he wanted an element of co-operation from his victims and when he got it he acted as if everything was normal – for instance, at the point where he had chattily asked his victim to change positions during the course of the rape. In the present case, he said, the teenager wouldn't co-operate, and instead of turning ugly he had let her go – 'a sort of annoyed withdrawal, a bit like a kid who might take a girl for dinner and then takes her home and she won't kiss him'. Badcock also pointed out that while he was carrying out the bizarre and frightening act of taping up his victim's head, he talked about it in an ordinary, conversational way: 'He's probably anti-violence. He's not a pervert. He's got a definite moral system, it's just that it's different to a normal one. But it does contain a working intimacy with conventional social manners.'

Of the 1998 offence, when the surprised couple managed to start their car and make their escape, there was little more to say. Instead the two profilers discussed a rape in the 1980s in a car park in the area of another police force, which some officers thought might have been committed by the same man because the *modus operandi* was similar. Their eventual conclusion coincided with the latest police thinking about this crime – that the differences were greater than the similarities, especially in the psychological aspects. One important contrast was that the attacker in the additional case was comparatively impulsive and careless, leaving body fluids behind that have been used to produce a DNA sample.

It was at this point that the first signs began to emerge that the two sides in this discussion – the police on the one hand, and the profilers on the other – might not be speaking quite the same language. In the case of the murder of Yvonne Killian and in Operation Minstead, the police signalled the importance they attached to the decision to use profilers by sending officers of the rank of chief inspector to the crucial initial discussions. In this case it was notable that the police officer who came to the introductory meeting was a sergeant – two steps down the hierarchy of rank. Although Detective Sergeant Gunner was obviously an acute and intelligent officer, he admitted openly that he'd never dealt with profilers before, and the long and complex discussion of the cases by Badcock and Boon ended on an uneasy note: there was a pause, and Gunner then asked: 'So, in effect, then, what can you do for us?' Badcock, amid embarrassed laughter, replied: 'We've done it.'

Gunner said on the way home from the meeting that Boon's and Badcock's thoughts about the offender's previous crimes and the type of job he may have would help police to focus their inquiries more tightly. But some of Gunner's remarks about the pair also struck a guarded and sceptical note: 'Very intelligent,' he said. 'Very nice gentlemen, not at all the sort of eccentric boffin one would expect, to be honest. But I'm not going to say this is the be-all and end-all, I'm not going to say that what they've given us will definitely identify this chap.' This episode highlights once again that profilers are generally still some way off winning the hearts and minds of the average constable and sergeant: in the Killian and Jean Barnes cases, this became clear at the somewhat uncomfortable meetings between the profiler and the full investigative teams, and in Operation Minstead it emerged when DCs Glenister and Reid (aka Daisy and Del) were invited to give free rein to their opinion of psychological profiling.

It was not until some months later, in November 1998, that Boon and Badcock travelled south to look around the various sites on Farley Mount where the attacks had taken place. They were met and shown around by the man in charge of the inquiry, Detective Superintendent Steve Watts, a tall, authoritative, rugby-playing type of policeman: he is shrewd and well-educated, and his qualifications include a master's degree in investigative psychology from Surrey University. There, he was a student of one of Britain's pioneers of profiling, Professor David Canter, whose achievements and statistically based methods were described in Chapter 2. (Canter's approach is not shared by Boon and Badcock, who both employ a clinically based methodology that emphasizes the uniqueness of each case.) On his way to Farley Mount to meet the profilers, Watts made it crystal clear what he saw their role to be: 'This investigation is my investigation. I have the sole responsibility for making sure that it's progressed effectively and efficiently. I'm in control. I will listen to what psychologists have got to tell me and deal with it in the appropriate way, but I will make the decisions.' This was a position neither Badcock nor Boon would disagree with, but the robustness of its expression was unmistakable.

Watts met up with the two men a short distance from their destination and they drove the last few miles together. Although Farley Mount is only five miles from Winchester and is well used by dog walkers, families and courting couples, it has a remote and inaccessible feel to it, with rolling downs and woodland – some sparse, some dense – crisscrossed by paths and a few narrow roads. Watts apologized for missing the earlier meeting, and was fairly straightforward about why he was now bringing profilers into the investigation: it had already been going on for seven years, had explored every conceivable line of inquiry, but was getting nowhere and was suffering from a crippling lack of forensic evidence. He was realistic enough, he said, to know that they wouldn't tell him 'the name and address of the offender and the colour of his hair and the fact that he lives with his mother and drives a rusty vehicle'. But he hoped they could help him decide how to use resources to best effect – whether to concentrate inquiries round Winchester, for example, or to look further afield. In particular, he was hoping for advice on whether the man responsible was likely to commit further offences, and if so how soon.

When they arrived at the main car park at Farley Mount, however, there was something of a shock for Boon and Badcock: the place was bristling with the media. There was a TV team from *Britain's Most Wanted*, the ITV answer to *Crimewatch UK*, and a crew from the local BBC TV station. Neither of the profilers had been consulted or forewarned about this. Both were visibly upset, and Watts explained that he had invited them along in order to give them the material they needed 'all in one hit'. Boon and Badcock clearly felt they wouldn't be able to discuss matters freely during the tour of the site if there were microphones under their noses the whole time; they also felt very strongly that no publicity should be released in the short term, for fear of scaring off the offender from returning to his haunts and perhaps getting caught at a time of year when he had offended previously. Watts pointed out that if publicity prevented crime it was no bad thing, but arranged for the BBC team to leave and reassured Badcock and Boon that none of the material shot by the ITV team would be used until the new year.

It was a tense start to the afternoon, and the tour of Farley Mount went ahead in a media scrum, with cameras and cables and sound booms getting in the way. The atmosphere was relieved somewhat when Badcock, in the interests of scientific thoroughness, climbed into the yew tree used by voyeurs at one of the car parks, and nearly fell out of it: 'The psychology of sitting up here is different to the psychology of being in complete control,' he declared. 'Good God, you've only got a limited view, haven't you?'

As the sun set on a cold afternoon, they visited the different car parks and discussed where the criminal would have parked his car, how he would have approached his victims and abducted the women. The ambience was subdued and irritable, with occasional outbursts of joking and larking about. Then everyone climbed into cars and drove along the routes thought to have been used by the offender when he took the rape victim to the house and dropped off the teenager near the Rack and Manger in 1996. As they went they discussed the latter case – the most intriguing to the profilers because it was the only one where the offender had had 'a bad hair day', as Boon called it. He had taken off his mask while driving around the countryside, and had then become rattled and started swearing when he had trouble finding it again, shortly before he had released his unco-operative victim. The unusual thing here, said Boon, was that he had backed off at a point where many offenders would have turned violent in an attempt to get their way: it was another illustration of his highly developed sense of discipline.

Now that they had seen at first hand how rough and inhospitable the terrain was at the very time of year some of the offences had been committed, the profilers became more definite about their feeling that the culprit had the skills and planning ability that were likely to come from current membership of a disciplined organization such as the army,

RAF or police. At one point it was asked if the attacks had all happened when the local beat officer responsible for the area had been off duty – the joking implication being that a policeman with local knowledge could be a prime candidate. The offender used the terrain, Badcock said, like an experienced piano player using the full range of the keys: 'You're looking at officer status, probably not high rank, but officer material… He can do the *Telegraph* crossword as well.' Asked what such a man would think of the voyeurs up the trees, Boon replied: 'He's a Rolls Royce intell-ectual, an intelligent man who's out on his big-game hunt, while they are a sad bunch who have nothing in their lives. This bloke would have a life as well as this night-time recreation.' Boon clearly thought the offender had graduated well beyond simple voyeurism, while Badcock had earlier considered he might still be a voyeur – a small but interesting difference of emphasis between the two profilers about the stage the offender had reached in his criminal career.

All through the conversation there was a certain sense of animosity and opposition between the profilers and police, partly because of the unexpected media presence. Watts wanted to know if the profilers thought the man would kill one of his future victims if he felt they might be able to identify him, and was sceptical when they replied that they thought this wasn't the man's style. He was also sceptical when they told him they thought he would live locally rather than some distance away – a question that would play an important role at a later stage in the inves-tigation. Altogether, it was a slightly unsatisfactory day out, and the impression was intensified that Watts did not have a very high opinion of what the profilers could offer him. But at least the outing closed with a joke, which came from Boon as the moon rose above the ancient downs and copses of Farley Mount: 'You don't want to go up that tree at night, do you, Richard, by any chance? You may find you've got friends if you go up there now.'

Watts told Boon and Badcock during the Farley Mount tour that he hoped their next meeting would be a kind of 'summit' about the case. When the time for that meeting came, two months later in January 1999, the unease that both of them already felt about the media strategy over

Farley Mount had been compounded by the item about the case shown a few weeks earlier on ITV's crime programme *Britain's Most Wanted*. It had used footage taken during the Farley Mount visit, including shots of Badcock struggling to get down from a yew tree. This was not the reason they took issue with the programme, however: their objections were that the programme had gone out before Christmas, contrary to their understanding that it would not be until the new year, and that they thought that the programme had made prurient and sensational use of the material. At the same time, they recognized that all they could do was advise, and that the final decision on press strategy, as on other aspects of the inquiry, lay with the police – and it was clear to them by now that Watts, as he had said to them at Farley Mount, considered publicity to be 'the oxygen of the inquiry'.

There was also some tension in advance of the meeting because Adam Gregory, from the behavioural science section of Surrey Police, was going to be there to explain his analysis of the case: this had been started the previous August, just after Boon's and Badcock's initial involvement, drawing on a computer database of more than 900 sexual crimes. Gregory had used the method of multi-variate statistical analysis, developed by Professor David Canter, in co-operation with the local police, in his time at Surrey University in the early 1990s, and outlined in Chapter 2. The difference between this approach and the clinical methods of Boon and Badcock gave rise to some uneasy jokes. 'We'll offer to show him ours after he's shown us his,' said Badcock. 'It'll be a genuine battle.' Boon demurred: 'Ha, ha, certainly not. It will be a synergistic exercise, or whatever these Americans call it. The idea is that we put it all on the table and see if we can't come to common ground from different perspectives. I think they just want a final resolution to the contribution of the offender profilers and to give an element of closure to our contribution.'

The meeting began with Boon running through a lengthy profile of the offender, developing and adding to the points he had made the previous July: the offender was probably between thirty and forty, with a normal appearance, able to function adequately in society, sexually competent but probably not involved in a well-functioning relationship, physically fit, and possibly employed in a manipulative occupation like selling. He was intelligent, flexible, forensically aware, knew how to control himself, and liked to get his victims' compliance; at the same time he was a psychopath in the sense that he was impervious to the feelings of others. He probably lived close to Farley Mount, was very likely to reoffend, but very unlikely to escalate his activities or kill anyone. Badcock added his analysis, emphasizing the criminal's self-restraint, the probability that he had at one time been in work with a disciplinary code such as the army or police, his local geographical knowledge, and the satisfaction he would derive from 'outwitting PC Plod'.

Gregory was evidently nervous as he offered his analysis in the presence of the two other highly qualified men, especially as he disagreed with them on some details. His view was that the man did have adequate social skills, but was probably living by himself in a relatively poor area. More importantly, he thought that the rape in the area of another police force in the late 1980s was committed by the same man, and that the pause in offences since 1998 meant that he was now in prison. The discussion soon lost its way in polite but tense wrangling over the details of that additional case, and eventually Superintendent Watts moved in to summarize the situation: what all the profilers agreed on, he said, was that the offender was a control freak, had good local geographical knowledge and adequate social skills, that he liked 'survivalist' or weapons-related activities, and was very likely to reoffend.

Watts then articulated a common problem for police officers when working with profilers, which had also arisen in the Minstead case: the information they come up with may be fascinating, but it doesn't always help in a practical way. 'Our difficulty in interacting with people like yourselves,' he said, 'is that the information we get is not easily searchable on police or other available public sector databases. And that's sometimes very difficult, although once the person is identified a lot of what you're saying will be very useful in developing interview strategies and so on. But in terms of leading us down the road, giving us an avenue of inquiry that will eventually lead us to identifying him and obtaining sufficient evidence to arrest him and put him before a court, I have to say that I haven't heard a lot today that suggests a particular strategy which I can now follow.'

When Boon and Badcock pointed out they had suggested checking people who had been involved in deception and fraud as well as sex offenders, Watts returned to his theme, his underlying impatience with the case becoming ever more clear: 'The problem is if you start searching on these sorts of broad parameters – show me all the acquisitive offenders in Hampshire, show me all the fraudsmen in Hampshire – you can start to chop away using some of the other parameters that you've produced, but you're still left with a vast pool of people to research.' As if spurred on by Watts's negative reactions, all three profilers now made fresh attempts to suggest new ways of trapping the offender and refining the search parameters – putting decoy couples in the Farley Mount car parks, quietly changing the rota of the constable who patrolled the area, checking mail order clients of firms selling balaclavas and army camouflage jackets, looking into people with a history of both sex offences and acquisitive offences not involving violence.

But Watts was not to be mollified, and embarked on a litany of the huge amount of work that had already been expended fruitlessly on the case: everybody at a local agricultural college had been checked out, the comings and goings of various units at local military bases had been followed up, police forces had been asked if they employed anyone who might be a candidate, range wardens for Farley Mount Country Park had been looked at, wide-ranging inquiries had been made about the make of car and pick-up the offender might have been driving, and a full review had been carried out of all the possible forensic evidence, including scrapings from car seats and fibres from clothing. There had been a lot of media appeals, and a fresh story was about to be published in a local paper featuring 'the beast of Farley Mount'; none had so far brought in the necessary information.

A number of houses had also been identified as the possible rape location, but the difficulty there was that the victim was still too upset to visit them to see if any matched her memory. Nearly 500 people had been interviewed, but the lack of evidence made it possible that the offender was among them and hadn't been picked up. 'Once you get to them,' said Watts, 'unless you're going to tear everyone's house and vehicle apart, which isn't acceptable in the society we live in, and you haven't got any other evidence, what do you talk to them about? It's the most frustrating thing. You can ask them what they were doing on the date of the offences, let's have a look at your vehicle, do you have access to cable ties, that sort of thing. But you get to a stage where you hit a brick wall, you can't ask any more.'

Watts concluded a long and frustrating meeting by saying he preferred the 'more empirical' statistical profiling method used by Adam Gregory and delivering a sideswipe to the method of Boon and Badcock: 'In terms of its utility to me as an investigator, its usefulness to me in finding the person who's committed those offences, it's really very limited, to be quite frank. We've still got a number of lines of inquiry to follow, and they will be followed until we're happy that we've done what we can. But there has got to come a time when we say we've done all we possibly can. As much as anything, I'm the manager of resources and finances as well as an investigator, and there comes a time when it's not possible to continue an inquiry against the background of other issues that are occurring. Now it may well be that the criminal is thinking that he's won. If he does think that, then I hope he doesn't do it again. If he does do it again then I'm absolutely sure that I and the Hampshire Constabulary will put in the same sort of resources again to see if we can identify him.'

The message was unmistakable: the senior investigating officer felt he had done everything that was humanly possible, had left no stone unturned, and had already covered the suggestions the profilers had made earlier in the meeting. He had tried every tool in the toolbox, as it were, and used not one but three schools of offender profiling. Now it was time to conserve resources and call it a day, at least for the time being. The Farley Mount investigation, it seemed, was about to go into mothballs.

THE GREAT TEMPTATION

*'Profiling is not about identifying individuals.
It's about identifying characteristics of
offenders from the offences.'*

Richard Badcock

Two months later, in March 1999, Detective Superintendent Watts and
several members of his team were sitting in a room at the Winchester
headquarters of the Hampshire Constabulary, looking at their watches
and tutting impatiently. They were anxious to get on with a meeting to
wrap up Operation Kayak, the codename given to the Farley Mount
inquiry, and two key officers were late – Detective Sergeant John Gunner
and Detective Constable Louise Fuszard. When they finally walked in, the
sarcastic remarks that greeted them failed to wipe the confident smiles
off their faces. They already knew that the files they had under their arms
were likely to change the course of the inquiry and bring it to life again.

Watts thanked everyone for their hard work over the past months,
but said the offender had not been brought to justice and all viable
inquiries had come to an end. All that remained to do was tie up a few
loose ends, such as ensuring that the Forensic Science Services had
looked at all the samples sent to them, and making an agreement to
contact the police force covering the area where a similar attack had
taken place if there was a new attack either there or on Farley Mount.
There were a few more checks to be made about the owners of vehicles
that had been observed repeatedly visiting Farley Mount during a recent
'frequency analysis', including one man who claimed to have been in

the SAS; and there were plans to be made for patrols at Farley Mount during the upcoming April anniversary of one of the offences.

Finally, there was some curiosity about a man calling himself Red Devil Master, who had come to the attention of the police through a trawl of the Internet. The Master ran a website subscribed to by twenty-six women who were 'willing participants in bondage and sado-masochistic activities', according to DS Gunner. He pointed out that interests of this kind didn't chime with the Boon and Badcock profile, and there was no suggestion that Red Devil Master was tying up women without their consent; but Watts wasn't entirely happy about dropping the Master as a potential suspect.

Watts said: 'I think the biggest thing for me out of our day up at Leicester with Julian Boon and Richard Badcock and Adam Gregory was really when I asked them the 64 billion [sic] dollar question, "What else do I need to do to catch this person?" and they weren't able to come up with very much more than we'd already done. One thing they talked about was re-interviewing the rape victim from 1992, and I've given that a lot of thought and my view is she is still very traumatized by the events. She was properly cognitively interviewed on two occasions, and I'm not prepared to have them go and put her through it again.' Once more, Watts made it clear that he preferred the kind of statistical profiling done by Adam Gregory – the kind he himself had studied at Surrey University – and agreed with Gregory's contention that the Farley Mount offences and the one in another police force area had probably been committed by the same man. He had one further complaint about Boon and Badcock: they still hadn't delivered their written report, despite repeated requests to do so.

Now it was over to Gunner and Fuszard to introduce what looked like a breakthrough. It had its origins in the item about Farley Mount in the pre-Christmas TV broadcast of *Britain's Most Wanted*, the filming of which had so upset and inhibited Boon and Badcock during their site visit. More than 250 people, including a spiritual medium, had tele-phoned the police after the broadcast, and although much of what they had to offer proved worthless, some leads were followed up. Fuszard now described the one that had caught their attention: 'We had a phone call from a lady who'd met a man called Mr X [his real name cannot be used for legal reasons] on a course in midsummer last year. And the only reason why she phoned up was that he came across as if he thought he was God's gift to women, but gave her the creeps, basically. During the course he produced a knife from his pocket, and on other occasions he had some shotgun shells in his pocket – he was bragging about being a hunter, shooter and fisher, and had four-wheel-drive vehicles. She really didn't like the way he came across. When we first looked at him he didn't appear particularly interesting. But we've done quite a bit of research on him since that time and he's got more and more interesting as a result of it.'

Gunner said they would now give X's history, 'basing it on the profile which Boon and Badcock have given us, and you'll notice why we're particularly interested in him'. Watts was quick to intervene: 'Well, you're not basing his history on the profile, are you?' Gunner replied: 'Not at all – comparing.' Watts: 'You said "basing".' Gunner: 'Did I?' Watts: 'Freudian slip.' The significance of this exchange was that it touched on a confusion that was to run through much of the rest of the case about the legitimate use of a profile. Boon and Badcock, when they heard about Mr X, began to fear that he had become a suspect not because there was any reasonable suspicion or evidence against him, but simply because he matched significant parts of the profile. It is an article of faith for them and most police officers that profiles cannot be used as evidence, at the stage either of investigation or prosecution. The question was to arise in the coming weeks whether all the officers on the Farley Mount team were always fully alert to the temptation of giving the profile too much weight.

Mr X, said Fuszard, was born in 1947, making him fifty-one at the time she was speaking (this was one detail significantly out of kilter with the profile, which gave his maximum age as about forty). He joined the armed forces in 1963, then joined one police force in southern England before a brief period in another and then a third, where he became a detective. In 1979 he was sacked after being convicted of a serious offence of dishonesty. While he was in prison his first wife divorced him, and after he came out he worked for a computer company before moving to Hampshire in 1983 and becoming a driver for a year. Then he joined a company whose activities involved selling, moving to a second such company in 1995, working as a roving representative: the fact that he was involved in selling had reminded the police officers that the Badcock and Boon profile had suggested he could be in that kind of job. From 1989 he had lived not far from Farley Mount, and since 1993 had lived on the South coast with his family. His latest home was more than 60 miles away, but Gunner pointed out that it was not far from the main road to Winchester, at the side of which the abduction victim of 1996 had been dropped.

Preliminary inquiries had shown that Mr X had failed to declare his criminal conviction when applying for employment, claiming instead that during the years he had been in prison he had been a security consultant, a job he'd left when his contract had ended ('So he's got a bit of a sense of humour!' said Fuszard). This falsehood on an application for employment meant that the police had the option to bring a prosecution against him for it any time they chose. A check through Hampshire's own criminal records also turned up an incident from 1990, which DS Gunner described in a typically straightforward fashion: 'A woman breaks down outside the back of his house, she's got the bonnet up and is looking under it. He was standing there, hot sunny day, in his swimming trunks. She became aware of him with his plonker in his hand, masturbating – quite obviously towards her. She didn't like this so she obviously scarpered and made a complaint. I've got a statement from the policeman who actually went to see him. When he got there the bloke had his shorts on by then and says, oh yeah, I'm expecting you, come and talk about it. Very embarrassed about it, didn't try to deny it at all. And he says the only reason I did it was my wife's pregnant and I haven't had sex for a long time. I saw her, it was an urge. The policeman said, you know, get yourself a magazine and do it indoors.'

The excuse about his wife being pregnant was of course comparable to the one produced by the Farley Mount offender, who had told his rape victim he was starved of sex because his wife had died. The indecency incident when the woman's car broke down was also compounded by a more recent event at Mr X's workplace, where a woman colleague had complained that he had touched her breasts. No formal action had been taken because Mr X said the touching was an accident and a witness cited by the woman had declined to give evidence. All the same, Mr X had left the company under a cloud, launched a claim for compensation at an industrial tribunal, and set himself up as an independent consultant. Gunner floated the idea of interviewing the complainant at his company: 'She might tell us some other things, what he used to do in the cupboard with her, that sort of thing.' Meanwhile there were other aspects of his life that interested the police: he had owned at various times the kinds of vehicles that might, according to the partial descriptions given by victims, have been used in attacks at Farley Mount. He was also fit, liked the outdoors, one of his hobbies was clay pigeon shooting, and he was a member of the British Association for Shooting and Conservation, and the World Wildlife Fund. 'All profile fits,' said Gunner.

He outlined plans for further inquiries, including a trip to have a look at X's house, and Watts had little hesitation in giving the go-ahead. 'I mean, he's got to be worth looking at,' he said. It might eventually be a good idea to carry out some systematic observations of Mr X's activities, he added. There was a new sense of excitement in the room now, as if Operation Kayak was emerging from a long period of dormancy; but before the meeting ended there was a further exchange that touched on the role that the profile was now playing in the inquiry. 'I mean, he's only obviously interesting because he fits the profile, that's the only reason,' said DS Gunner. Watts picked him up on this again: 'Well, it's not just fitting the profile, it's the location he's in as well. It's not just that he fits what Julian and Richard are telling us – there are other issues which make him interesting.' Either way, it was clear that there was suddenly a new impetus to the inquiry and that the Boon and Badcock profile, treated somewhat dismissively earlier on, was to some extent the engine of that impetus.

April 26 1999 was a big day for DS Gunner and DC Fuszard: it was six weeks after the wrap-up meeting had turned into a relaunch, and this day was devoted entirely to the Farley Mount inquiry. First there was a journey to look at Mr X's house, using the route he would have used if he were indeed the offender, to familiarize themselves with the local geography and allow them to plan effectively for an eventual arrest. And in the evening they were due to take part in a regular night-time visit to one of the car parks where one of the offences had happened at precisely this time of year. They had been doing more research on their man since the meeting, turning up more details that seemed to implicate him. During the one-and-a-half-hour drive from one county to another they were talking so enthusiastically about what Gunner called 'our last major line of inquiry' that they managed briefly to drive the wrong way up the A3.

The profile was again high in their minds, even though the written version of it had still not been delivered. Gunner said he had told Boon about the new suspect and hoped he would devise an interview strategy for the police and even come down to Hampshire to monitor the interview: it sounded almost as if the arrest and interrogation of the new suspect was a foregone conclusion. In general, however, Gunner's remarks about the role of the profile were more circumspect: 'Prior to talking to Boon and Badcock, it was always felt that this offender would have a good knowledge of guns and forensics. So when we got to look at this chap we said yes, he's got both, and connections to the area. So he's got everything. It's just nice that he does appear to fit the profile, but that isn't – don't misunderstand us – why we're thinking of arresting him. Because that's not evidential.' Fuszard also pointed out that the phone call after the TV programme would have prompted them to look at this man even if no profile had been done. In fact, she revealed, he was the last to be looked at from the list of possibilities that the programme had produced – so the profile had not even had the effect of bringing him higher up the list.

Otherwise the journey was remarkable only for the banter, which gave brief and intriguing glimpses of the common currency of police life: desultory chat about the price of lunch in pubs they were passing, discussions about how much overtime they might clock up by the end of the night, their dislike of Earl Grey tea, unguarded speculation about how they would search the new suspect's house after 'kicking the door in' at the crack of dawn. When they reached their target's house, they found that one of the cars they were interested in was parked outside, but not the other. 'It's a big house, so it's gonna take a lot of people to search it,' was Fuszard's initial response. 'Quite a lot of time to get through it all.' They took a careful look at the street layout, and talked about getting plans of the house from an estate agent or even taking an aerial photograph – 'That'd be good at the briefing,' said Gunner. Then they headed back to Hampshire, talking in astonished tones on the phone to colleagues about the just-breaking news of the murder in London that day of the television presenter Jill Dando.

The plan for the night visit to Farley Mount was that Gunner and Fuszard would sit in a car in one of the car parks, acting as decoys and hoping that the offender would be out and about and prepared to take greater risks than he had previously – as Boon and Badcock had said he one day might. They would be connected by radio microphones and earpieces to a backup car containing two other officers, and to the local beat policeman, PC Chris Mussellwhite, who would be on foot nearby, ready to warn his colleagues about any cars approaching from the Winchester direction. There would be no armed officers on the scene because the rule was that the firearms unit could not be deployed unless there was specific information – not just an outside possibility – that an armed man would be at large. If a man who looked like the offender then did his characteristic initial sweep of the car park, Gunner and Fuszard, wearing body armour and fluorescent jackets, would get out of the car and disappear into the bushes while their support car would disable the suspect's car with a portable 'stinger' they had borrowed from a Winchester police station – a spiked metal device that can be swung in front of a car to puncture the tyres. Then they would contact the tactical firearms unit and otherwise play it by ear. If any genuine courting couples arrived and parked up, they would be advised to move on.

Owls were calling across the deserted countryside as the decoys settled into place and ten o'clock approached. The minutes ticked past slowly, and the combination of boredom and tension produced strange, disconnected conversations about curry, the sexual habits of Gunner's pet ducks, and the terrible deaths of some of the five rabbits he had got from a rabbit rescue centre – two by an unexplained illness, one by an airgun pellet in the head. 'So vigilante groups are now out looking for the bunny killers,' he declared. PC Mussellwhite also contributed an anecdote to pass the time: 'We get peepers up here as well, people who go around peeping on courting couples, and some of those have been beaten up quite badly, although none have ever complained to the police about it. There's one man who's been peeping for many years and he's had his car trashed twice. He's been beaten up at least three times – even followed to his home and beaten up – but he still comes up here peeping.'

Suddenly the banter was interrupted by a warning that a car was approaching: it came into the car park, and a figure got out and began walking around. Tension mounted in the car containing Gunner and Fuszard. 'He's coming on foot,' gasped Fuszard. 'Oh shit, he's having a pee. He's having a pee, he's having a *pee*.' The hot news went out across the radio link, and eventually the weak-bladdered visitor climbed back into his car and drove away into the night. Mussellwhite, who was meant to follow the car to the car park, arrived too late. 'They didn't even have a shag,' complained Gunner. 'Frightened the life out of me, that did,' said Fuszard.

It was the only incident of the night: once again the attacker of Farley Mount had stayed away, remaining one step ahead of the police force that had racked its brains trying to catch him. The most poignant moments of the episode came as PC Mussellwhite, standing in a field with his dog at his side and his cigarette glowing in the dark, talked sadly about how one man's predatory obsessions had stopped local people making free use of one of the county's best-loved beauty spots: 'I've lived and worked in this area for many years, I used to bring my children up here to play, and it's just upsetting for the general public to be deprived of this lovely area for fear of such a serious offender. This place is very quiet compared to what it used to be a few years ago. It's a great shame, it's a beautiful country park and a lovely place to be.

'As for the offender, he's intelligent, he's calm, I doubt whether anybody in the outside world knows he commits this kind of offence. I think he's too much in control of himself, and that's the worrying part about it. He's not a freak or brain dead or anything, he's a guy who thinks, who calculates, tries to remove any risk to himself, which makes it far more worrying. He's doing it intelligently, not through some psychotic illness, I don't think he's got anything wrong mentally with him at all. Self-gratification, that's the only thing I can put it down to. It's how he enjoys himself – no other reason that I can think of. I spend a lot of time up here at night if I'm on lates. I'll spend a couple of hours up here because there's substance abuse as well as courting couples. So I just try to move the couples on because they're too vulnerable at the moment. And I take note of vehicles, people, anything I can find, really.'

The summer came and went, with no new offences reported and no decision taken to arrest the favourite suspect, and when Superintendent Watts met Gunner and Fuszard about Farley Mount at the beginning of September 1999 he asked for a complete update. Gunner began by referring again to the informant who had telephoned after the *Britain's Most Wanted* programme, inadvertently touching yet again on the ambiguous role the Boon and Badcock profile had played right at the start. 'She said, "I know him from a course and various things about his behaviour and his personality lead me to believe that he may fit your profile as described on TV." And on *Britain's Most Wanted* we had Badcock and Boon giving a bit of a profile.' If the original informant was treating the profile almost as if it was evidence, no wonder it was difficult for the police to avoid the same pitfall.

Gunner had been busy in the interim, filling in gaps in the knowledge about Mr X. His first wife had been interviewed and revealed that he used to have a handgun; he had also obtained a shotgun certificate. The woman who alleged he had touched her breasts at work had also been interviewed, but had been unable to cast new light on him. He might have worked on a route going past Farley Mount when he was a driver, and at the time of the 1994 attack he had owned the kind of car described by one of the victims. On the other hand, he hadn't acquired one of the other cars in question until two months after the attack in which such a car had been mentioned. The big question was still: should he be arrested?

Two of the companies where he had worked had been seen by the police and were prepared to lay complaints against him for securing employment without declaring his criminal conviction. This meant that the police could arrest him, take a body sample for DNA testing and compare it against the DNA trace left by the rapist in a different police force area (who was still considered likely by some officers, if not the profilers, to be the same man as the Farley Mount attacker). But Watts was highly sensitive to the fact that it would not be appropriate to arrest him for one kind of offence and then conduct interviews and searches in relation to an entirely different offence. 'I don't want a suggestion at a later stage that we've used this as a back door to get him into custody,' he said. 'As you say, we're going to have to pull the house apart to look for the material, the bag, the gun, the mask, the tape and everything else. If we nick him for the dishonesty offences, and he gets charged, he's not going to be in custody very long – straight up and down jobs. But then he's going to be out within a few hours, which won't give us time to do the things we want to do. And we're not even going to be empowered to do the things we want to do, because we haven't been upfront about which job we're nicking him for.'

There then followed a notable section of the meeting in which all three officers ran through what they knew about the suspect and appeared to assess some of the points as justifications for arrest by reference to the profile. 'We've got the evidence of the females about his confidence, the ladies' man issue,' said Watts, 'which again ties in from my recollection to the profile.' Gunner added, 'And we've got his lawful access to knives, being in a fishing club. And our profiler said if he was stopped and found with a knife, he would have a reason to say, well, I'm a fisherman, there's my fishing gear in the boot.' Fuszard joined in: 'The type of employment he's taken as well, the profile said about him being a salesman and in this kind of selling job, and he's a salesman.' Was this perhaps coming close to what Boon had several times referred to in discussion about different cases as 'the profiling tail wagging the investigative dog'?

Watts felt that more preparatory work should be done before an arrest, including investigation of Mr X's finances and observations designed to get an idea of his movements: he might lead them to a place where he kept his equipment, 'and then you might be lucky and get him going up to Farley Mount and sitting there and having a walk and so on'. But it was clear Watts felt that once the time was right they should no longer hesitate: 'It seems to me we've got to grab the bull by the horns with this bloke. We're only going to get one chance with him. So we need to work out an arrest plan for when we go in and take him, a search plan for the premises, scenes of crime plan, forensic strategy... and then we can look at an arrest subsequent to November, can't we?' Plans were even laid to ask the forensic laboratory to do a fast-track, seventy-two-hour DNA profile with a sample obtained from the suspect.

After the meeting Watts was asked what had convinced him to go ahead and plan the arrest. He replied that it was a combination of the profile and other pieces of information. 'The profile has been useful,' he said. 'But I'm not going to rely solely on that. I'm going to look at it based on my experience as an SIO in similar sorts of jobs. The advice the profilers give us is based on their background as scientists, they are dealing with people who commit serious sexual offences. It's not evidence, though, and I can't rely on something which isn't evidence. I can use it as a guide. I can use it as a way of directing my inquiries and as an aid to making decisions in relation to where I put my resources. I've got to consider the facts that we have against the speculative information we have in the form of the offender profile. And I've got to make a decision based on all those parameters.'

November came and went, and the police observations of Mr X over two anniversary dates of crimes on Farley Mount yielded nothing more interesting than his participation in a drinking session at a working men's club. And still the police did not move against him. Their interest continued, however, and in February 2000 Watts brought in Neil Trainor, the geographical profiler from the National Crime Faculty who had earlier examined the Minstead case, and took him on a tour of Farley Mount. Watts admitted at the outset that he had limited expectations, because it was well known that the computer programme used by Trainor was effective only with a minimum of five well-separated sites: here the sites of the offences were virtually the same in each case. But Watts denied that he was getting desperate: 'It's just so that, at the end of the day, I can demon-

strate that I've followed every viable line of inquiry. And this is one.'
He confirmed that the observations of Mr X three months earlier had
produced 'bugger all', and he related an anecdote about the frustrations
of police life. 'Once, years ago, we followed around a professional
snooker player who would be well known to you,' he added, 'and do you
know what he spent most of his time doing?'

'What?' asked the interviewer.

'Playing snooker.'

'What?'

'Playing snooker. Ha ha. Every day. From one snooker hall to
another.'

'And what were you interested in him for?'

'Cocaine.'

As for the Boon and Badcock profile, Watts repeated his earlier line:
'I'm not going to do anything in terms of interviewing or arresting just
on the basis of similarities to a profile.'

How was this long-drawn-out minuet with Mr X going down with the
profilers themselves? Boon and Badcock were kept aware of the situation
either by phone calls or through the grapevine of the small world of profilers and their senior police contacts. Boon took a back seat on the case
from this point onwards. Badcock, who was due to write the report on
behalf of both of them, was finally interviewed about the case again in
April 2000, nearly two years after he and Boon had first become involved
in it, and more than a year since the police had fixed on Mr X as their hot
prospect. In the interim Badcock had moved from his job in Wakefield to
be a consultant forensic psychiatrist at Rampton Special Hospital, among
the oilseed rape fields near Retford in Nottinghamshire. Sitting in his
office, he admitted he was being very slow in delivering the report, and
said the obvious and rational explanation was pressure of work.

'But my experience is that when I fail to meet deadlines there's
usually some other issue as well going along in the background, and I
think in this case it's a sense of unease about what the report may be
used for. I'm happy that I've given the analysis my best shot, and I've
given an adequate verbal feedback, as it were, but I've just got a tiny bit

worried that perhaps the police were trying to get something out of the written report which it simply isn't intended to convey, and I do wonder whether they're perhaps relying on the written report to somehow grab the identity of the actual offender, and that isn't what profiling is for.

'I don't think they want me to say, yes, it's Joe Bloggs, he lives at number 13 or whatever, but they do want the profile to be so specific that there can only be one person it fits. That makes me think, firstly, that they're anxious to match a particular person to the profile, and secondly that the supporting evidence in the investigation may not be as strong as they would like, or not as complete as they would like. I think they're probably feeling a bit stuck and hope the profile will help out in some way – which it won't. And so I'm not delaying it because I don't want to be helpful, I'm delaying it because I want to make sure I know in my own mind what's really going on, and also that I don't go beyond the bounds of what I should do in the written report.'

He talked about the importance of the relationship between the profiler and the investigating team, and suggested it had not been as good in this case as it had in some others. The absence of rapport was not a new problem, but this case highlighted it more than most. However he was not concerned enough about the situation to take it up directly with the police, or to refrain altogether from writing his report. Instead he intended to make sure that the conclusions he put forward would be 'both firm and broad'. His report would make it clear that it was not identifying a specific individual, because that was the task of detection; instead it was identifying a particular personality type. And how would the Hampshire squad react when they received it, Badcock was asked? 'They'll probably ignore it,' he joked. 'No, they'll probably give me a ring and ask me whether there's anything more individual, more identifying, that can be done.'

Three weeks later DS Gunner, like his boss three months earlier, was having a frustrating time with Neil Trainor, the geographical profiler on loan from the National Crime Faculty. Having toured the crime locations on his previous visit, Trainor was now reviewing the maps and statements and offering his unfortunately limited conclusions. 'What you try to do is give the police what you can with the information that's there,' said Trainor. 'You can't sort of make it appear if it's not there, you know.'

At the end of the session with Trainor, Gunner could at least feel that another avenue had been thoroughly explored, even if the only new idea it yielded was that the village of Leckford should be re-examined to see if it might contain a property that fitted the rudimentary description of the house where the rape victim was taken. Asked what the score was now with Boon and Badcock, Gunner said he was impatient to get the written report so he could use it for preparing his rationale for interviewing Mr X. Did it irritate him that the profilers had been so slow? 'Yes it does,' he replied, 'because I've been looking at this man X for more than a year, and before I can really approach him, I need the report in writing as a base for my rationale. At the moment I'm just going on conversations that I had with them, and rough notes, and I need to highlight everything they're saying – contacts in the sales world, indecency offences, and then I'd say look at our man, this, this and this. But at the moment I've got nothing to compare it with. I would have liked to have spoken to him by now, eliminated him or implicated him.'

Gunner revealed that he had been given a month to work exclusively on Mr X, and then he would have either to arrest him or 'put it to bed', even though he recognized that there would be an outcry if the public found out the investigation was being wound up. He admitted that if he arrested Mr X immediately and conducted a search of his house, he might be vulnerable to accusations of wrongful arrest: 'That's why I need this Boon and Badcock document, so we have our rationale for arresting. So if anyone says why did you arrest this man, we can say, here you go, that's why – if you read that, Your Lordship, don't you think it's reasonable to suspect this man might be involved?'

Gunner's words appeared to confirm the profilers' worst fears about the use to which their profile might be put. But when Badcock was next interviewed about the case in July 2000 – virtually on the second anniversary of his first visit to Hampshire – he was able to announce that he had completed and delivered his written report. He knew the police had a particular suspect in mind, he said, so he had prefaced it with a section in bold type saying that a profile could not be evidence of identity. 'The inferences of the report don't prove the identity of the offender, but they are true things about him, I think. They don't tell you who it is – that's a task for detectives, not for middle-aged forensic psychiatrists.

'There will be a temptation to misuse the report, because if they've got somebody in mind and the only evidence they've got is circumstantial, then they'll try and beef it up any way they can – who wouldn't? But I'm equally clear that that's not what reports are for. If it helps to focus thinking so you can get evidence, that's right and proper. But if it's used as evidence itself, that isn't. The only thing about the report that I'd be happy about being used in evidence is the understanding of the motive.'

He was asked: 'So if they do use it as an arrest justification, what would you say?'

'Don't do it!' replied Badcock. 'If they say, well, Joe Bloggs fits this profile exactly, surely that means he's it. I say, no it doesn't, because you don't know whether Fred Smith two doors down the road isn't exactly the same – and totally innocent as well. Profiling is not about identifying individuals. It's about identifying characteristics of offenders from the offences. If you've got a list of suspects, then the profile is quite useful in prioritizing the investigation. There is one area in which I hope the report may be helpful, and that's in terms of thinking about interview strategies.'

The warning could not be clearer – but would the police take heed of it? Or would they stray into what profilers, speaking in private, call 'Paul Britton territory'? In October 2000 DC John Gunner was out and about with a local beat officer, PC Sian Newland, following up an idea gleaned from the geographical profile offered by Neil Trainor. They were driving through the village of Leckford, trying once again to match local properties to the rudimentary description given by the rape victim of the house to which she had been taken – a place where there was some kind of generator or electrical equipment in operation nearby, where it was possible to drive up to the back door, and where the staircase was so low it was easy to bang your head. It was a small irony, given the profile's suggestion that the criminal could be a salesman, that many of the houses in Leckford are holiday homes owned by the John Lewis Partnership, whose every other employee is probably a salesperson.

As they passed an apple farm and a mushroom farm, speculating about the offender's route with his captive eight years earlier, Gunner talked about Mr X and whether they might ever find a better suspect. Asked about the report from Badcock, he said: 'Well, now I've finally got it, it's a bit brief, I'll have to say, when you compare it to the several conferences we've had with both doctors. I would have liked a bit more detail, but it encompasses exactly what we're looking for... the report gives the rationale, yes, because you can see that Mr X fits certain aspects of that profile. As I said, I'd like to speak to Dr Boon about an interview strategy.'

In this respect, Gunner was due to be disappointed. When Boon and Badcock met towards the end of 2000 to consider the request for such a strategy, the answer – after much havering and deliberation – was 'no'.

'I'd be absolutely against anything that could even be considered to be making somebody fit a profile,' said Badcock. His view was that the police request for advice on interviews meant that the health warning on the written profile – 'not to be taken as proof of identity', printed in bold type – had either not been appreciated or had been ignored: 'It would be wrong from our point of view and a mistake from their point of view, wouldn't it?' Boon suggested, and Badcock agreed, that the police should be advised to interview Mr X in the normal way, and bring in another profiler if they felt he was a genuine suspect and should be investigated further. The new profiler should not be given their profile, so his or her views could not be 'tainted' by it.

At the same time, the two men could not resist looking at the information provided by the police about Mr X and assessing whether he might be the right man. In doing so, they inevitably compared him to their own profile, which was what they were warning the police about. Their view was that more information was needed about the reliability and motivation of the two women who had complained about Mr X, and that his flashy behaviour – bragging about his outdoor activities, showing off a knife and cartridge cases – was not consistent with the offender's cool and controlled style. 'Mmm, doesn't ring it for me,' said

Badcock. 'We're not allowed to let things ring,' said Boon, reminding him that they were, in effect, doing what they were counselling others to avoid. 'Yes, I know,' said Badcock. 'But I agree with you entirely,' said Boon. The fact that the two men allowed themselves to be tempted into the territory of comparing the suspect with the profile in the absence of real evidence makes it all the more understandable that the police might do the same thing.

When Watts and Gunner met to discuss the next step, Gunner explained that the profilers had told him it would be difficult for them to provide an interview strategy 'because it might be seen that they might try and make their profile fit the offender, if you like, so I tend to agree with that'. But he had nevertheless asked the profilers to share with him their misgivings about Mr X: 'The most important difference as far as they're concerned is that our offender appears to be very subtle in his approach to his victims, and this is a bit of a macho man, robust, a bit over the top, and not subtle at all.' Once again, the officers faced the question of whether to arrest Mr X, and their conversation indicated they were indeed aware of the pitfalls foreseen by Boon and Badcock. Gunner said that the man had become of interest primarily because of the profile rather than because of evidence. 'Yeah, that's what concerns me,' replied Watts. 'We've got no evidence to put before a magistrate to say this is why we suspect this person may be engaged in this activity, and this is what we seek to find.'

Because of the doubt that a magistrate would grant a search warrant, the two men agreed that they would talk to Mr X informally rather than arrest him and search his house. This would entail the risk, if Mr X was indeed the offender, that he would immediately get rid of any incriminating objects in his house, but the detectives felt that such a clever criminal would be more likely to keep such objects at a different location anyway.

Interviewed later about his decision not to arrest Mr X, Watts said frankly: 'You have to look at what the evidence is, and to be honest the evidence is very thin – it amounts to his similarity to the profile that Julian and Richard have prepared, which is important information, but certainly not evidential.' These were words that could easily have been spoken by Boon and Badcock, and after some doubts at earlier stages of the case it seemed that at the end of the day police and profilers were talking the same language. Watts recorded his irritation about the delay in delivering the profile – 'We find that often with professional people of that ilk' – repeated his earlier view that it had been 'not that helpful', and said he was disappointed by the refusal of an interview strategy.

The rest was anticlimax. DS Gunner and DC Fuszard visited Mr X in December 2000, and almost as soon as he opened his mouth they knew he wasn't their man: he spoke with a noticeable north-eastern accent, which none of the victims had mentioned. After two hours, the officers emerged to say that Mr X had been pleasant and co-operative and had voluntarily supplied them with a mouth swab for a DNA sample that could be compared with the DNA from the rape in the different police force area that some thought might be related to the Farley Mount offences. But the sample was sent to be processed over the normal five-week period instead of being put on the fast track, and it was clear the officers had few expectations. Quietly and methodically, the Farley Mount inquiry was now, in police jargon, being 'put to bed'.

Watts said he felt there was nothing else to be done: he had 'pushed and pushed and pushed', he said, and there had been considerable internal police force resistance to keeping the inquiry open: now there was nowhere else to go. But he would be very surprised if there wasn't another offence in the future, he said: his own experience and the advice from Badcock and Boon suggested that if mature people got into committing crimes like this, they would find it harder to stop than younger people. 'I don't think it's the sort of thing you can draw a line under. I think it's the sort of behaviour where having got away with it so many times, and having got whatever the buzz is which he gets out of it, I think he's going to go for that buzz again.'

'A GROUP OF ANARCHISTS' 12

'There has been an approach of enterprising amateurism in the practice of profiling, and what we desperately need is to impose a discipline on that.'
Tom Williamson, Deputy Chief Constable of Nottinghamshire

Three men behind bars – a psychopath, a sadist, and an individual whose psycho-sexual disturbance is so profound that even the compass-ionate Dr Badcock fears he is beyond treatment. Two men still at large – one with a bizarre compulsion to seek sex with elderly women, and another whose cleverness and cunning have led many who know the details to fear that he will never be caught. The balance sheet of the cases in this book is likely to bring only moderate comfort to a public that wants to be reassured that the most dangerous criminals will be caught quickly and incarcerated for long periods.

Here, however, the main question is: was the effort to solve these cases helped – or even hindered – by the involvement of offender profilers and, if so, in what way? The attempt to find an answer comes against the background of a simmering debate about whether profiling is worthwhile and how it should be organized and developed in the future. The debate has been given a new urgency by the debacle of the Rachel Nickell case and the disciplinary hearing against Paul Britton, which has damaged the image of profiling but failed to impede its overall progress. There are many pressing questions about the advan-tages and disadvantages of profiling, how it should be practised, the ways it can be used, and how it should be controlled. Many of these questions are illuminated by the five cases that have been examined.

In Operation School – the case of the murder of Jean Barnes in Worthing – there was a good relationship between the profiler, Julian Boon, and the senior police officers. It was noticeable that they liked and respected each other and seemed to speak a common language. The profile helped police to prioritize the man who was prosecuted and found guilty, and Boon's advice on how to interview him was successfully adopted by the police. It was also evident from the way the culprit, David Munley, behaved during his interrogation that many of Boon's observations about the offender were accurate. A more precise comparison of the profile and the culprit – somewhat academic from the police point of view, but valuable feedback for the profiler – is likely to come only from detailed clinical interviews with Munley in prison, which will not necessarily happen. Operation School, though difficult, long and complicated, brought what the police might call a good result all round.

In the case of the murder of Yvonne Killian in Erith, there was a reasonably good relationship between DCI Chris Horne, the senior investigating officer, and the profiler, Richard Badcock. The discussions between the two men clearly helped to focus and develop the thinking about the baffling events in the flat where the killing took place. In the end, however, the breakthrough that resulted in a life sentence for Karl Stirk was achieved by a combination of police intelligence and DNA profiling. If no profile had been done, the crime would have been solved in the same way, and just as quickly. As in Operation School, it was clear from the way Stirk behaved during his interviews with police that many of the profiler's general observations of the offender's character were accurate; but once again, Badcock's insights into the criminal's psychopathology have yet to be checked in detail through clinical interviews with him in prison.

The Gatwick blackmail case was a peculiarity, where Julian Boon, as well as giving profiling advice, was able to offer the intelligence that there had been a very similar case in the Metropolitan Police area. One interesting question for the Sussex Police was whether they should have taken steps earlier than their meeting with Boon to discover for themselves whether neighbouring forces had experienced any comparable blackmail cases. Meanwhile, it would be possible to speculate that if Boon had not supplied the link to the related case, his profiling advice would still have helped the police to get their man.

Until they consulted Boon, the police had held back from mounting a full-scale surveillance operation at the drop-off point – partly, no doubt, because of the cost, and partly because they were not convinced that the offender was necessarily going to go there. Several of his deadlines had passed, after all, without any retaliation by him to the fact that none of the things he wanted had been left there. One factor that prompted the police to change their mind and commit themselves to the surveillance operation was the information they gained from the link with the Metropolitan Police case. But the other was Boon's opinion that the offender would not be able to stop himself from going to the drop-off point at some stage: even without the link to the other case, then, Boon's advice might well have precipitated the move that trapped the offender. In that context, the fact that some aspects of his profile were wide of the mark seems to matter little. It was also noticeable that, in their comparatively brief contacts, Boon and the police officers struck up a good relationship in which each understood the role of the other.

The other two cases were more problematic, partly because they remain unsolved. Operation Minstead – the search for the gerontophile rapist – again involved a reasonably good relationship between the Senior Investigating Officer, DCI Duncan Wilson, and the profiler, Julian Boon. The profile he supplied was long and detailed, the discussions and consultations were extensive. The SIO decided to fall in with the profiler's advice about the timing and likely effect of press conferences, which caused consternation among at least some members of the investigating team. Other media advice by the profiler, notably the suggestion that an appeal should be made to the offender's better nature in a *Crimewatch* broadcast, was not acted upon because of Wilson's belief it could serve as a challenge to the offender to strike again. There was also a perception by some officers that the profile failed to provide information that could narrow the focus of the hunt for the offender, and instead had the effect of widening it to unmanageable proportions.

Eventually the investigation was passed to a new team whose leader immediately announced that the urgent priority was to narrow the focus of the search and concentrate on taking DNA swabs from a smaller suspect list. The Minstead profile, therefore, hardly looks like a triumph: but any such perceptions about the profile must be linked with the general difficulties of the investigation. Perhaps the most obvious problem was the fluctuation in the manpower devoted to the case, notably when officers were diverted to murder inquiries.

Finally, there was the case of Farley Mount. There was always a sense that the profilers had been called in so that the investigators, apparently preparing to pull the plug on an expensive and fruitless inquiry, could at least be sure that they had left no stone unturned. The profilers quickly became wary about the agenda, and their relationship with the investigating team was sometimes tense and hesitant. Things took a turn for the worse when they arrived to examine the crime scene and found themselves, without warning, surrounded by reporters and cameramen. But when a fresh suspect came on the scene as a result of a tip from someone who had met him, the police appeared to take greater interest in a profile about which they had earlier been fairly dismissive. The anxieties of the profilers changed in turn: now they were worried that their work was going to be used as evidence of identity, something that they insist it can never be. There were anxieties – not, in the end, borne out – that similar mistakes might be made to those that had bedevilled the Rachel Nickell case. Farley Mount, with its delays, conflicts and grey areas, was sometimes an uneasy and unsatisfactory episode.

It was also the case that brought into focus the crucial question of the legal status of offender profiling. As was seen in Chapter 2, the Rachel Nickell case never got to the stage where the court might have been asked to address the question of whether the similarities of the accused man to the offender profile amounted to evidence against him. The very idea that a profile should be presented as evidence in this way horrifies both Boon and Badcock, who are always anxious to define the limitations of the work they do. Paul Britton has also said he is against using profiles as evidence. If a man is accused of a stabbing, evidence that he habitually carries a knife would be excluded by the criminal courts as 'evidence of propensity', as would the fact that he had a previous conviction for a stabbing. Criminal lawyers say an offender profile would fall into the same category and be likewise excluded, and that this state of affairs is unlikely to change.

There was no suggestion in the Farley Mount case that the profile could or should be presented to a court in this way, but it seemed at one point – to the dismay of the profilers – that it was in danger of being used in a quasi-evidential fashion at an earlier stage of the criminal justice process. Police are obliged by law to have 'reasonable suspicion' to arrest someone, and if they cannot demonstrate such suspicion they are vulnerable to being sued for wrongful arrest. Would a suspect's similarity to an offender profile amount to 'reasonable suspicion'? Such a case has not yet been tested before the courts. Some senior police officers think that a profile would not do by itself, but a profile in conjunction with a modicum of other evidence would suffice for the test of 'reasonable suspicion'.

In the United States, where the rules of evidence are different, it is common for profilers to give evidence in court if their specialized knowledge is deemed to be helpful to the court in understanding evidence or determining facts. In Britain there have been very few occasions when profilers have been called to give evidence. In one case, where a police operation was devised partly on the advice of the profiler, he was called to the witness box to explain why officers happened to be in a certain place at a certain time, watching for a certain kind of behaviour, when the accused man was arrested. There has been a tendency in British law in recent years to expand the categories of expert evidence admitted by the courts, and Richard Badcock believes the time will come when profilers are called to give evidence for similar reasons as in the USA. Julian Boon, however, believes that the usefulness of all expert evidence is undermined by the adversarial system of justice in the British courts, which he says has the effect of allowing the jury to hear a partial account only. He hankers for an inquisitorial system as found in some European countries, where an expert would be permitted to present his findings in his own way rather than in response to barristers' questioning.

These grey areas in the Farley Mount case about the nature and limitations of profiling also figure in some of the other cases described in this book. The meetings that Badcock and Boon had with the full investigative teams in the cases of the murders of Jean Barnes and Yvonne Killian were nervy, uncomfortable affairs, where many of the officers exuded a sense of both scepticism and limited comprehension. In the case of Operation Minstead, Detective Constables Glenister and Reid found it difficult to stop themselves being very forthright about the profiling work of Julian Boon, possibly because they had started with exaggerated expectations and were therefore disappointed when it failed to deliver a dramatic breakthrough.

SIOs who attend National Crime Faculty courses on running major inquiries come away with few doubts about what profiling can and cannot offer them – a case in point was DCI Horne in the Killian case, who was both hard-headed and open-minded about it. There would appear to be a case to offer better training and information to more junior detectives about offender profiling and its uses. The somewhat undefined nature of profiling, discussed later in this chapter, means that would not necessarily be an easy task, but on the evidence of the cases in this book there is a definite need for improved mutual understanding between the general run of police officers and profilers.

What else, then, do the cases in this book have in common? One of the most notable things was that none of them had a timetable, a defined procedure, or a formalized system of payment. As ever, the profilers had to juggle the work with their full-time jobs, and were rarely available to meet the police at short notice, especially since they both live and work a long way from the locations of these five crimes. Telephone consultation was rather easier, but was regarded by all concerned as less satisfactory. The process of producing a full written profile, which is what most police officers want in the end, was therefore very lengthy, and in the special circumstances of Farley Mount – where the profilers feared misuse of their work and the delay was to some extent deliberate – it took two years. In all five cases the police were unhappy about the length of time it took to get the written report in their hands, although it would be difficult to argue that these delays had seriously hampered the investigation. Payment is also somewhat erratic, and not necessarily at a prescribed rate. In this formal and administrative sense, it often looked as if there was no system or framework at all.

On a more positive note, it was clear in all five cases that the profile played a role at the heart of the investigation, stimulating thought, discussion and ideas. The role may not have been crucial or decisive to the outcome in all cases, but it was always dynamic in terms of how the investigation was run. There was also, to a varying extent, a sense of satisfaction on the part of the senior investigating officers with the involvement of the profiler. DCI Steve Scott became a friend of Julian Boon in the course of the inquiry into the murder of Jean Barnes, and declared himself a convert to the use of offender profilers. 'It gives us reassurance,' he said. Boon is now helping him again in a difficult serial rape case. DCI Chris Horne was also complimentary about the contribution of Richard Badcock to the Killian case, even though he was, quite justifiably, careful to avoid giving him direct credit for the solution of the crime. DCI Duncan Wilson pronounced himself satisfied with Julian Boon in Operation Minstead, even though the contribution of the profile to the progress of the inquiry was debatable. His view was that profilers from within the police service would not be able to provide the vital external perspective from which he thought police officers benefit. In the Gatwick blackmail case, DI Johns said that the advice of the profiler gave him confidence. Even in the Farley Mount case, Detective Superintendent Watts, the most sceptical of the SIOs, appeared to appreciate the opportunity to discuss the case with intelligent, well-informed professionals from an organization other than the police. He said that dealing with them was 'a support, really, for my decision process'.

It seems unlikely that these SIOs were merely parroting some current orthodoxy in favour of profiling, and what they say appears to confirm one of the main conclusions of a report on offender profiling called *Coals to Newcastle*, published in 1995 by the Home Office. It was written by Superintendent Gary Copson, a Metropolitan Police officer who conducted a research project asking SIOs what they thought of both statistical and clinical profiling advice they had received in 184 different cases. Only in five cases (2.7 per cent) did officers believe that the profile had led to the identification of the offender. But in 112 cases (60.9 per cent) they said that the profile had furthered their under-standing of the case or the offender, and in ninety-five cases (51.6 per cent) they felt that the expert opinion of the profiler had reassured them in their own judgements. Sixty-eight per cent of the officers who returned Copson's questionnaire said they would seek profiling advice again, and half of them said they would use the same profiler again.

The question in the survey on whether the profiles had furthered the investigators' understanding led to the production of an anony-mous 'league table' of nine profilers who advised in six or more cases: the 'yes' responses for each individual ranged from 87.5 per cent of their cases to 44.4 per cent, and it is understood that Badcock and Boon were in the top few. A second phase of Copson's research, now awaiting publication, assessed the accuracy of profilers' predictions by comparing them with the actual characteristics of people arrested and prosecuted: the aggregate accuracy ratio was found to be 2.2:1 – that is, 2.2 points correct to each one incorrect. For clinical profilers like Badcock and Boon the ratio was higher, at 2.9:1, while for statistical profilers it fell to 1.8:1. Among individual profilers it ranged from 6.8:1 to 1.5:1, which suggests a large variation in skills in the profiling community. The greatest accuracy, according to the new research, was delivered by clinical profilers, who were correct 79 per cent of the time. On the basis of those figures, perhaps investigating officers should bear in mind that, on average, a fifth of the advice from the best profilers is likely to be misleading.

So it would appear that SIOs like, above all, to have someone from the outside world with whom they can compare notes and ideas when they are conducting difficult and multi-faceted cases. This apparently matters as much to them in the end as any 'hard' results that might make a definable contribution to solving the case. One prominent senior officer has said some SIOs use profilers as 'a comfort cloth' or 'a sounding board'. This aspect of the role of the profiler prompted Superintendent Copson to declare in a recent interview that the most important part of the practice of profiling was the relationship between the profiler and the SIO. 'It's the spark that exists between you and the person advising you which can generate new ideas,' he said. 'That's why it's important for you as an SIO to speak to the person who's right for you, rather than having someone allocated to you in an impersonal, bureaucratic way.'

In all the cases in this book, the profiler was allocated to the case through the bureaucratic channels of the National Crime Faculty; but in four of them the crucial relationship between the SIO and the profilers was good or very good, which suggests the method of introduction may be less vital than Copson believes. The less happy relationships in the Farley Mount case were, arguably, a consequence of elements other than the fact that Boon and Badcock had been allocated to the case by the NCF rather than chosen by the SIO.

One of the men who has played an influential part in the development of offender profiling in the UK thinks it is vital that SIOs should not be allowed to choose the profiler they work with. Don Dovaston, former Assistant Chief Constable of Derbyshire and now an adviser to the National Forensic Science Service, says there should be no flexibility about this: 'Let's face it, an SIO could have been kidded soft by the chap he wants to go back to. It's been proven time after time that a cosy relationship can be a great folly. There are now sufficient people on the accredited list of profilers for the right person to be allocated to deal with all the aspects of a case that a SIO is concerned about.' Allocation of cases is now being more rigorously controlled by the NCF than at the time when most cases in this book got under way, he says, and a contractual framework is now in place to ensure that police and profilers always have a clear understanding of the task to be performed. Richard Badcock, however, says that half of his cases are still coming directly from officers he has worked with before, which suggests that control by the NCF is not as comprehensive as Dovaston believes.

The new arrangements have been agreed by the Association of Chief Police Officers, the umbrella group for the forty-three chief constables in England and Wales, so there is less scope for individual forces to go their own way any longer. In each case there is now a requirement that a written profile will be produced within a specified time and payment made at a set rate that depends on the complexity of the case and the time the profiler spends on it. The new arrangements also require profilers to commit themselves to a confidentiality clause, which is regarded as particularly important by Dovaston because of cases in the past where he says profilers have inappropriately disclosed details of cases to the media or people outside the investigation. 'These various protocols have been in place for about two years now and are well founded and supported,' says Dovaston. 'We now have an agreed practice that is supported by the authority of ACPO, and the whole system is mandatory and more rigorous than it used to be.'

Meanwhile the debate continues about the relative merits of in-house profilers, of whom there are so far only two on the NCF approved list, and part-time outsiders. The in-house practitioners are police officers who have taken degrees in psychology and gone on courses such as the one in Dundee attended by Badcock and Boon; they are more likely to be available to SIOs at short notice and to be able to deliver reports on time. On the other hand, they do not have the broadening and leavening effect of experience in other work, whether academic or clinical, and may be vulnerable to the depressing and debilitating effects of over-exposure to the details of the country's worst crimes. Some people also feel that individuals who are first and foremost police officers make less good profilers because their training is to find hard evidence rather than examining and interpreting all the circumstances, both physical and psychological.

Outside profilers, as mentioned earlier, are preferred by some SIOs because they provide a different perspective, but it is hard to see a way around their comparative unavailability and the length of time it may take them to produce reports. One related development is the increasing employment by police forces of specialist civilian crime analysts such as Samantha Thompson in Sussex and Laura Richards in the Metropolitan Police: their contributions were praised by Julian Boon in the Gatwick blackmail case and Operation Minstead.

Tom Williamson, Deputy Chief Constable of Nottinghamshire, made it clear at a recent conference of profilers at the National Crime Faculty that the new dispensation of greater police control of profiling, including a better system of quality assurance, was born of 'a number of causes célèbres', in particular the Rachel Nickell case. 'The concerns can be summed up, I think, by saying that there has been an element of enterprising amateurism in the approach to profiling, and what we desperately need as a service is to impose a discipline on that.' Detective Chief Superintendent Doug Smith, director of the National Crime Faculty at the time of the conference, talked of the need to present profiling reports in a standard form, though without inhibiting individuality. He wanted to see quality assurance, ethical standards, and effective sanctions in cases where profiling reports could be demonstrated to have fallen short of the required standards.

There was no substantial opposition at the conference to the proposals for greater control and standardization, most of which still remain to be worked out and implemented. No doubt there are a few people who will regret the passing of an informal system where there was extensive local autonomy and flexibility, and dealings between the police and profilers owed something to the old pals' act. Richard Badcock says he can see why the police want greater control: 'They've had their fingers badly burned by high profile cases that have led to adverse publicity, or by very expensive but useless advice. There is advice that is over-definite or over-interpreted, where the limits of confidence in the contents of the profile aren't set out and the police are given a picture of a case that is presented as truth rather than educated guesswork, where the basic assumptions and reasoning are not set out.'

But Badcock also believes there are wider and more important issues about profiling that remain to be addressed. The desire of the police for proper accreditation of profilers and control over the process of employing them does not confront the vital question of how to establish good practice and get proper research and development under way, he says: the process of control is objectionable to some profilers because it doesn't contribute to the essential task of producing better profiles. 'The idea of being regimented while nothing else is happening is something my soul revolts against. If regulation is all there is, what are you regulating? If you don't develop the subject, it will diminish or become idiosyncratic. If there is not a drive to develop profiling that is at least commensurate with a regulatory system, you will be regulating an empty vessel. The way the subject develops will be down to how the individual develops it.

'At the moment profilers come together rather like a group of anarchists. A lot of it is about working out a common language, because we don't all use the same concepts and we don't have the same ideas or the same professional pressures. The only thing that pulls us together is an interest in doing this kind of work and its outcome. But the range of agendas is huge, none of it is settled, half of it is not even declared in the open, and we're still trying to think it through.'

Julian Boon concedes that the police need an accredited list so they can be sure the profilers they use are not charlatans or well-meaning amateurs – 'They need to be able to tell margarine from butter.' But he also expresses concerns similar to those of Badcock about the need for measures to bring practitioners together: 'We have such diverse backgrounds and techniques, and inevitably there will be fragmentation. Some work is put under the banner of psychological profiling, some under statistical and so on – you have that breadth. Hopefully we can all learn from each other, but we'll have to see.' What neither man is willing to say in so many words is that there is a lot of bitchiness, backbiting and rivalry, both within and between the two main camps of statistical and clinical profiling.

Eighteen months after the conference, there was little progress on the key question raised by both men: what exactly is it that is being controlled? It is still routinely stated that there is no real agreement about what profiling actually is and how it should be done. A variety of formal definitions have been produced, all couched in general terms and all tending to say that proper analysis of crime scene evidence can indicate the personality type of the individual who committed the offence. Badcock's favourite formulation is that profiling is 'the application of the principles of science and psychology to find what is unknown and required about the offender from what is known about the case'. Beyond that, it is clear that profiling is an offshoot of other disciplines rather than a discipline in itself, and that there are almost as many approaches to profiling as there are practitioners. Profilers who are psychiatrists and psychologists are subject to the standards and sanctions of their professional regulatory bodies, but there is no regulatory body and no generally accepted code of practice for the specific activity of profiling. It is more a corpus of experience than a science, and there is not always much common ground between the people who do it. There is a distinct impression of a number of mutually suspicious armed camps sending the occasional emissary back and forth, but never really getting down to constructive dialogue.

Badcock is also worried about the strain put on individuals as a result of the fragmentation of this small professional world: 'The activity itself can leave you rather exposed because you don't have the support of colleagues. You're living by your wits, every case is hard work if you do it properly, and it's quite a strain. That's all much easier to accept if you feel part of a greater overall endeavour. If not, all you get is irate calls saying haven't you finished that profile yet, we want it this week.' He is also concerned that many of his colleagues in psychiatry do not accept that profiling is part of their province: 'The ones I actually talk to and the ones I go through cases with can see very clearly that it has relevance for forensic psychiatry. But there's still a lot of work to do to build up the concept of profiling and show other psychiatrists why they should be spending time doing it.'

The way forward, he now believes, is to establish some kind of academic or clinical framework to foster the integration and development of profiling and give it more intellectual ballast, and some influential senior police officers have no objection to that, providing the police service is not involved in running or paying for it. 'You could develop that vital body of knowledge in an institution,' said Badcock. 'If it's left to individual practitioners it will take years to build up to the stage where you can make good generalizations about the practice of profiling. Individual wisdom can't generate the same kind of information as an established body of knowledge.' One way of translating individual wisdom into established knowledge might be some kind of systematic recording of information from cases where there has been an opportunity for a practitioner to compare a profile with reality through post-conviction interviews with offenders.

Badcock summarizes his views by saying that profilers can no longer manage with ad hoc arrangements and urgently need to 'get their collective act together'. But at the moment it is hard to see how that is going to happen: there is certainly no clear prospect of the establishment of the kind of wide-ranging institution Badcock has in mind, either in a university or a health authority. The best that can be expected, it seems, is that there will be piecemeal developments: improvements in police training about profiling, improvements in accreditation and quality control by the NCF, conferences and symposia that bring practitioners together and produce new collaboration and cross-fertilization. One specific worthwhile target might be to bring down the barriers between clinical and statistical profilers and work towards a hybrid process that makes the most of both approaches. Badcock, meanwhile, intends to contribute by publishing articles and books, taking part in media discussion, and generally trying to raise the profile of profiling.

The one option that seems to be definitely closed is that of turning back the clock: most informed people agree that offender profilers, for all their occasional idiosyncrasy and fallibility, are now permanent figures in the landscape of crime investigation. The real *Cracker* is here to stay.

INDEX